SHAKESPEARE'S MONEY

SHAKESPEARE'S MONEY

HOW MUCH DID HE MAKE AND WHAT DID THIS MEAN?

ROBERT BEARMAN

OXFORD
UNIVERSITY PRESS

OXFORD
UNIVERSITY PRESS

Great Clarendon Street, Oxford, OX2 6DP,
United Kingdom

Oxford University Press is a department of the University of Oxford.
It furthers the University's objective of excellence in research, scholarship,
and education by publishing worldwide. Oxford is a registered trade mark of
Oxford University Press in the UK and in certain other countries

First Edition published in 2016

Impression: 2

Published in the United States of America by Oxford University Press
198 Madison Avenue, New York, NY 10016, United States of America

British Library Cataloguing in Publication Data

Data available

Library of Congress Control Number: 2015949827

ISBN 978–0–19–875924–9

Printed in Great Britain by
Clays Ltd, St Ives plc

Foreword

Much of my working life has been spent in the cataloguing and arrangement of archive material and in its interpretation as evidence of past events. In the process I have inevitably come to feel that, if the documentary evidence is not there, then there is little point in speculating about what might have happened. Even the evidence we do have is not always reliable or sufficiently definitive, but at least something survives on which to base an argument as opposed to a hypothesis dependent on the discovery of new data. As it happens, and as is repeatedly pointed out, the evidence for a study of Shakespeare's life is very limited, but I have chosen not to lament this shortage of material or to give vent to customary expressions of frustration; rather to take a positive attitude towards what evidence we do have to interpret one particular aspect of his life which is not often discussed, namely to what degree did Shakespeare prosper financially and what place in society did he thereby come to occupy. After all, to his contemporaries this would have been the most immediate measure of his success; and indeed, is the best-documented aspect of his career.

Several people have read drafts of what follows and I am very grateful for their comments, particularly from David Ellis, Mairi Macdonald, James Shapiro, and Martin Wiggins. Stanley Wells has also been generous with his time and advice. The staff at the Shakespeare Birthplace Trust's Library and Archive, where the bulk of the original documentation I have used is safely lodged, have been very helpful, as have those at The National Archives, the Folger Shakespeare Library and the College of Arms, particularly in their prompt and efficient supply of images. I have also benefited from the frequent use of the facilities offered by the Shakespeare Institute (University of Birmingham) Library. David Kathman has generously supplied me with copies of unpublished material and John Taplin's encyclopaedic knowledge of the genealogy of Shakespeare's local contemporaries has been invaluable. But it would be remiss not to include posthumous tributes to those earlier scholars who over the years have provided transcripts and facsimiles of all the key documents on which we depend, most notably J.O. Halliwell-Phillips, E.K. Chambers, B. Roland Lewis and S. Schoenbaum, whose frequent appearances in the footnotes bear witness to the enduring value of their work. Lastly, I must thank my wife, Jan Bunyan, my sternest critic when it comes to matters of grammar and infelicities of expression but whose superior computer skills also came into play when, in the twelfth hour, I was driven to the use of updated (and unfamiliar) operating systems and programmes.

Robert Bearman

June 2015

Contents

List of illustrations

Abbreviations

BL   British Library, London
CSPD   *Calendar of State Papers Domestic*
HMC   Historical Manuscripts Commission
ODNB   *Oxford Dictionary of National Biography*
SCLA   Shakespeare Centre Library and Archive, Stratford-upon-Avon
TNA   The National Archives, London
WCRO   Warwickshire County Record Office

I

Introduction

It is not possible to write a biography of William Shakespeare within the normally accepted meaning of the word. One would hardly think so in view of the number of attempts which have been made, but the basic requirement for such an exercise simply does not exist—namely, a body of evidence allowing insight into the subject's feelings and views backed up with details of his or her day-to-day life and of the opinions of others on the subject's shortcomings, achievements, and appearance. Even in the most fully documented of lives, there will be gaps, but, provided other, and longer, episodes of the subject's life can be explored through the survival of letters, diaries, and a wide range of other documents in which he or she may feature, a full enough picture will emerge. But for Shakespeare, such material is almost entirely lacking: in fact, Shakespeare is mentioned by name in handwritten documents drawn up during his lifetime on fewer than a hundred occasions. None of these is in his hand (though four are signed by him) and only two or three can be said to establish his own feelings in a direct manner—his attitude, for example, towards the attempt to enclose some open field area at Welcombe, just outside Stratford, in which he had a vested interest, and some of the clauses contained in his will. A similar number may reflect views which his contemporaries had towards him—Richard Quiney's letter, for instance, asking him for help in negotiating a loan of £30. We also have Ben Jonson's appraisal of Shakespeare's abilities and character, which, because it may never have been intended for publication, has the air of a genuine assessment, even if by a person with his own agenda and written some years after Shakespeare's death.[1] But on the one occasion that Shakespeare was

---

1. It was not published until 1641 from notes made after 1623 (Chambers, *William Shakespeare*, ii, p. 210). Henry Chettle's apology to one of the three 'play-makers' (not

asked to provide evidence concerning an episode in his own life—during the so-called Bellott/Mountjoy case of 1612 when he was asked to give evidence on a matter in dispute between the protagonists, and when his version of events would have been carefully recorded—he claimed, almost inevitably, it now seems, not to have been able to recall any helpful details. Although in reaching some sort of assessment of his personality we may be tempted to include posthumous tributes, these tell us little beyond what we already know, that he was an influential and much admired poet and playwright. By and large, he was also law-abiding—or at least, there is no record of his ever having seriously run foul of the law. In contrast to Christopher Marlowe, whose life can be more satisfactorily reconstructed through his eventually fatal involvement in the murky world of espionage, Shakespeare is only twice recorded, in 1597 and 1598, as personally at odds with the authorities, in his case as the result of his failure to pay his taxes; and even then the most obvious explanation is mundane—that he had moved house. True, it was also at about this time that a writ was issued requiring that Shakespeare, having apparently moved to Southwark, be bound over to keep the peace as a result of his involvement in a quarrel between two local men, William Wayte and Francis Langley, but even here it seems he was drawn into a dispute not of his own making and in which he played a very minor role.[2] In the face of such meagre resources, we might normally expect a biographer to abandon hope. A scattering of references to the potential subject might perhaps be used for a skeletal reconstruction of his or her life, but such a study would not be the stuff of biography as it is normally understood. A man who rarely emerges from the shadows—and whose sporadic appearances then pose as many questions as they answer—would under normal circumstances be thought too challenging, if not impossible, a subject.

There is, of course, nothing 'suspicious' about this poor harvest. The survival of documentary evidence from this period depended overwhelmingly on whether or not it remained in the hands of either an institution or a great landed family with the resources to provide a safe haven over a period of time. Governmental records, at parish, county, and national level, and those of educational, ecclesiastical, and other

---

specified) addressed in Robert Greene's *Groats-worth of Wit* (Chambers, *William Shakespeare*, ii, pp. 188–9) is sometimes thought to be Shakespeare, but this is by no means clear (below, pp. 28–9).

2. Below, pp. 63–4.

official institutions, therefore form the bulk of what has survived, buttressed by the archives of land-owning families who managed to maintain their status over several generations. This is far from saying that the
archives falling into such categories have survived in anything like
their entirety. Here huge tranches have been lost too, but at least there
was a framework of sorts to catch some of them. Alongside these, the
most common survival are bundles of title deeds for the simple reason
that the owners of freehold property from all social levels took zealous
care to preserve them as proof of title and to pass them on when properties changed hands. Beyond this, the chances of survival of any personal or business papers, once they had served the immediate purpose
for which they had been created, were very slim indeed. It follows that
biographical data for particular individuals, especially at this early
period, depend largely on whether or not they came within the orbit
of record-keeping agencies. If he or she (usually he) operated from
within one, of course, data are comparatively plentiful—for example,
we know more about the daily life of Shakespeare's father John,
because of his involvement in the affairs of the Stratford Corporation
and whose records have survived in some abundance, than we do
about Shakespeare himself. If he or she was frequently involved in legal
disputes, either as plaintiff or defendant, then further revealing data can
often be unearthed from the records of central and local courts. For
members of the country's landed elite, and those who worked for
them, data can normally be retrieved both from family papers and
the records of the institutions in whose affairs they became involved.
Shakespeare, however, attended a school whose records are lost, did not
go to university, was hardly ever involved in legal proceedings, and
worked for most of his life, not within a government institution or for
a great landed family, but for a theatrical company whose records
no longer survive. We do have his title deeds for the very practical
reason that his successors in title took care to preserve them, but
otherwise, for him as for countless thousands of his contemporaries,
we largely depend on the number of times his activities were recorded
in the files of those organizations whose archives have come down
to us. Thus our knowledge of Shakespeare's involvement in the
Welcombe enclosure comes not from his papers but from those of
Thomas Greene, which he left behind him in the Corporation
archives—he was the town's steward—when he sold up and left
Stratford in 1617. Similarly, the precious bundle of Richard Quiney's

correspondence, including the famous letter to Shakespeare and its other references to him, has survived simply because it was subsumed into the Corporation archives as the result of Bailiff Quiney's death in office in 1602. On other occasions, Shakespeare and his family are recorded in parish registers, wills, surveys, and tax records on a disappointingly meagre number of occasions, but entirely typical of many other men and women who lived and worked outside the official establishment or the households of the great. There are important exceptions to this, of course, often the result of the chance survival of rare or atypical archive material. The 'diary' of Philip Henslowe, for instance, the manager of the Rose Theatre, crucial for our understanding of the Elizabethan theatre, only survived because it passed into the hands of his son-in-law, Edward Alleyn, and thence into the care of the college he founded at Dulwich. Records for Shakespeare's company—the Chamberlain's, later the King's Men—which must also once have existed, unluckily, though typically, have not come down to us.

In contrast to this almost total absence of material on which to base an intimate biography, there stands, in Shakespeare's case, the First Folio, a near-comprehensive record of Shakespeare's unique contribution to the development of the English theatre.[3] We also have additional evidence of his poetic output in the separately published *Venus and Adonis*, *The Rape of Lucrece*, and the Sonnet sequence, likewise regarded as of fundamental importance in reflecting his outstanding literary talents. It is no wonder, then, that the life of the author of this formidable output should be a subject of absorbing interest. However, no biographical record of any substance has been unearthed since the discovery in 1910 of Shakespeare's involvement in the Bellott/Mountjoy case referred to at the start of this chapter, and nearly all biographies subsequently published, from sheer lack of new evidence, veer quickly into other areas. Studies of the world in which Shakespeare lived are still a profitable line of enquiry despite the lack of material evidence on how Shakespeare viewed the issues confronted by his contemporaries. Less helpfully, many writers then move on to a discussion of the plays as if, though we know little, if anything, about how Shakespeare lived from day to day, his literary output can nevertheless inform us as to what sort of man he was. At worst, of course, we are

---

3. *Pericles* (for which no satisfactory text apparently existed) and *The Two Noble Kinsmen* (collaboratively written with John Fletcher) were excluded from the First Folio.

treated to idle speculations which, through sheer lack of evidence, can be neither proved nor disproved but which evolve into unhistorical hypotheses quickly taking on lives of their own. David Ellis has recently and entertainingly drawn our attention to the limited value of much of this so-called biographical work.[4] No one emerges totally unscathed from his survey: indeed, the cumulative effect is a sobering one even for those who regard themselves as sceptical observers of current developments in Shakespeare biography.

However, although on the face of it, Shakespeare's life might not seem a fitting subject for conventional biography, there may still be room for a different approach. The surviving evidence for the reconstruction of Shakespeare's career may be sparse and often dismissed by his literary admirers as made up largely of unexciting and fragmentary records of his business dealings, but this very evidence does at least reflect what was, to most of his contemporaries, his most obvious achievement, namely the establishment of his family as minor gentry, significant in itself, given its lowly status in the early sixteenth century but particularly so in the light of his father John Shakespeare's business failure in the 1580s. At a time when the family unit provided the only reliable protection from misfortune and its coherence the surest way of maintaining status, when the head of this unit had clear duties towards his dependents, and when his success could move the family into the higher reaches of society (or his failure have the opposite result), an immediate concern for his and his family's predicament is as likely to have been Shakespeare's priority concern as any idea that he was playing a leading role in the inauguration of the English theatrical tradition. Rather than indulge in fruitless speculation as to his daily life, or about possible influences on him at any one time, perhaps a more mundane, if necessarily brief, investigation into how Shakespeare set about making a living, and to what degree, in monetary rather than artistic terms, he was successful might help us see him as a man unable, in his daily concerns, to escape from the preoccupations of those around him. This should not, of course, do anything to hide the fact that this very success reveals a remarkable ability, almost unique amongst his immediate contemporaries, of transforming the hitherto humble craft of playwriting into a means of making a very comfortable living, although even here, as is argued below (pp. 146–53), it was from his involvement as a sharer in the profits of his acting company that he

4. Ellis, *The Truth About William Shakespeare*.

derived the major portion of his income. But for the purpose of this present exercise, let us simply do for Shakespeare what we have to do for the majority of men and women of his time who have left us with very little personal data to go on—endeavour to track the rise and fall in his financial fortunes and to ask what this tells us, not about his achievements as a poet and playwright but about his position in society at different points in his career, in the eyes of his contemporaries the most readily apparent measure of his worldly success.

In the course of what follows there will be an inevitable emphasis on what might be called 'local' or 'Stratford' records, inevitable because it is these, and almost exclusively these, that provide material evidence on the question of how Shakespeare managed his business affairs. Even his will, due to his determination to build up a local property portfolio, presents him primarily as a man of Stratford. By way of contrast, although we can reasonably assume that Shakespeare was in receipt of an income as a sharer in the Chamberlain's (later the King's) Men and in the Globe Theatre, an almost total lack of material evidence requires us simply to hazard estimates as to what this might have been. Similarly, his income as a writer, either of plays or in a 'freelance' capacity, remains undefined. Indeed, virtually the only record of Shakespeare earning any money for a specified task is the payment to him in 1613 for devising a motto for the *impresa* for the earl of Rutland. His purchase of the Blackfriars Gatehouse, also in 1613, does provide 'non-Stratford' material evidence concerning Shakespeare's business affairs (even though it has been interpreted in various ways), but the evidence for similar investments in Stratford, and the effect that this had on the conduct of his affairs (the row over the proposed Welcombe enclosure being the best example) is so much more abundant that it is in this area that we are obliged to focus attention. This does not mean that no attempt will be made to gauge Shakespeare's income over the course of his career, but it will inevitably remain the case, especially as Shakespeare's family remained based in Stratford, that it will be in the context of a medium-sized market town that we can more easily assess his family's changing status as the result of his endeavours as an actor/playwright; and although this will not preclude comparison with his theatrical colleagues to establish whether, within his profession, he was more (or less) financially successful, in the eyes of his Stratford contemporaries, and in the wider community, it would have been the changing social status of the family which would have been the obvious measure.

2

Early life

Family background

William Shakespeare's grandparents were well-established country dwellers. Richard Shakespeare, his paternal grandfather, was less well-off than Robert Arden, his mother's father, but neither claimed to be, nor was ever described as, of higher rank than that of husbandman, the lowest of the three bands (after gentry and yeomen) into which the managers of the land were roughly divided.[1] Richard Shakespeare held land in Snitterfield, a few miles north-east of Stratford, but not as a freeholder. On one of Snitterfield's two manors, held from 1546 by the Hales family, he had copyhold interests,[2] but he is better documented as the tenant of a nearby farm held of Robert Arden, forming part of a second manor which belonged, until the Dissolution, to the College of St Mary, Warwick.[3] Robert Arden was a freeholder not only of this property in Snitterfield but of another in the same village, the two together comprising over a hundred acres. Robert Arden's father, Thomas, had acquired the first of these holdings in 1504, and Robert himself the other, in two stages, in 1519 and 1529.[4] Robert's membership of Stratford's Guild of the Holy Cross in Stratford and of the Guild of Knowle, both of which he joined in 1517/18, confirms his

1. The identification of Richard as the father of John Shakespeare (and thus William's grandfather) is a reasonable deduction, though it could be questioned (Chambers, *William Shakespeare*, ii, p. 26).
2. For notices of him on the court rolls for this manor, now held at the Shakespeare Centre Library and Archive (SCLA), see Halliwell, *Outlines*, ii, pp. 207–8; Chambers, *William Shakespeare*, ii, p. 27; Eccles, *Shakespeare in Warwickshire*, p. 8.
3. Chambers, *William Shakespeare*, ii, p. 27; Eccles, *Shakespeare in Warwickshire*, pp. 7–8. Richard's tenancy is best treated in Page, 'The location of Richard Shakespeare's farm in Snitterfield'.
4. SCLA, BRU 15/2/4, 9; ER 1/1/23; Chambers, *William Shakespeare*, ii, p. 39; Page, 'Location of Richard Shakespeare's farm', p. 95.

status.[5] Robert also held lands in Wilmcote (in Aston Cantlow), a mile or so to the north of Stratford, where his family had been settled since at least 1501, comprising a copyhold estate, which after his death in 1556 passed to his wife (subject to the life interest of his daughter Alice in a half part) and land called Asbyes, which he bequeathed to his daughter Mary (Shakespeare's mother).[6] The marked difference in the social standing of the two men is reflected in the valuations of their goods taken on their deaths, Richard Shakespeare's being put at £38 17s. 0d. in 1561 and Robert Arden's at £77 11s. 10d. in 1556.[7] These figures should also be seen in a wider context. Of the sixteen inventory valuations of the goods of men described as husbandmen, drawn up in Stratford between 1568 and 1607, only three exceeded Robert Arden's. On the other hand, eleven of the sixteen carried totals in excess of that estimated for Richard Shakespeare's goods, with the average figure—£47—well in excess.[8]

On the face of it, then, the marriage around 1557 of Richard Shakespeare's son, John, to his former landlord's daughter, Mary, was a good one—even opportunistic given that her father had only recently died, after settling on her the Asbyes property as described above. Later evidence makes it clear that Mary brought with her a small reversionary interest in one of the Snitterfield estates as well. But the timing too is consistent with the impression of a man resolved to improve the family's prospects by moving to town and setting himself up in business. By 1552, John was living in Stratford-upon-Avon and in March 1556 was styled a glover, later in the year acquiring two houses in the town, one in Henley Street and the other in Greenhill Street.[9] An apprenticeship from the mid-1540s is therefore likely. Given that John and Mary's first child was baptised on 15 September 1558[10] (and assuming that Mary were not already pregnant),

5. Eccles, *Shakespeare in Warwickshire*, p. 16.

6. Gray, *Shakespeare's Marriage*, pp. 261–2.

7. Gray, *Shakespeare's Marriage*, pp. 259–60, 262–3.

8. Jones, ed., *Stratford-upon-Avon Inventories*, i, nos. 21, 24, 31, 45, 52, 57, 60, 61, 63, 76, 79, 91, 100, 102, 109, 124. The inventories of six Stratford yeomen, 1556–1601 (including a 'rogue' £6 15s. 2d. for Humfrey Plymley in 1594) have an average valuation of around £113 (nos. 6, 30, 33, 43, 75, 115). Published inventories of thirty-two Worcestershire gentry and esquires over the period 1556–1620 have an average of £268 (Wanklyn, ed., *Inventories of Worcestershire Landed Gentry*, pp. 21–142).

9. Halliwell, *Outlines*, ii, pp. 215–16.

10. Savage, ed., *Registers of Stratford-on-Avon, Baptisms, 1558–1652*, p. 1.

their marriage may be taken to date to some time in 1557, by which time John had both achieved freedom from his apprenticeship and, as would have been expected, acquired an establishment of his own wherein to raise a family and conduct his business. His father, Richard, continued to farm until his death late in 1560 or early in 1561 and John, who is on occasion termed a yeoman or *agricola* (as he was when nominated as one of the administrators of Richard's estate[11]) may then have taken over these responsibilities. In any event, his intention was clearly to advance the family from the status of minor lease-holding husbandmen by developing an associated business in a neighbouring town. The trade of glover provided an opening into the profitable world of wool-dealing, through the sale of fell wool—wool plucked from the skins purchased for glove manufacture—but which could develop into a trade in fleece wool thought to equal the business transacted by recognized wool dealers. By at least 1568 John was deeply involved in this trade. In that year he was allegedly party to a sale of twenty-one tods (42 stones) of wool and, three years later, to two transactions said to involve a further 300 tods (600 stones).[12] Such figures, especially when incorporated into an allegation, need to be treated with caution, but even so, trading on anything like this scale would have placed him well to the fore in the ranks of Midlands dealers. Other evidence from this period also points to a man engaged in extensive business activity. In 1568 he was said to have lent £180 to a business colleague, in 1572 he began legal proceedings to recover a debt of £50 owed to him by a fellow glover, John Luther of Banbury, and in 1573 he himself was faced with a claim made against him for a debt of £30.[13] In 1575 he bought another house in Stratford and negotiated a more favourable lease of grazing land at Over Ingon Meadow in Snitterfield.[14]

It was common practice for prominent members of the business community to enter the ranks of the civic elite who made up the Stratford

11. Gray, *Shakespeare's Marriage*, pp. 259–60.
12. Hotson, *Shakespeare's Sonnets Dated*, pp. 231–3; Thomas and Evans, 'John Shakespeare in the Exchequer', pp. 317–18.
13. Thomas and Evans, 'John Shakespeare in the Exchequer', pp. 317–18; Hotson, *Shakespeare versus Shallow*, p. 38; Fripp and others, eds., *Minutes and Accounts*, ii, pp. 70–1.
14. Halliwell, *Outlines*, i, pp. 283–4; SCLA, ER 24/6. The only surviving record for the purchase of the house is a final concord where the property is in fact described as two messuages, but it is generally assumed that they were adjacent and became part of the family's Henley Street property.

Corporation, a twenty-eight-man, self-perpetuating oligarchy established by the Corporation's founding charter of 1553. John was no exception to the rule. After holding a number of civic posts, he was elected an alderman in July 1565, high bailiff in September 1568, and chief alderman in September 1571.[15] By the mid-1570s, then, John might well have felt that his move to Stratford and the broadening out of his family's activities from simple farming into a more ambitious trade in commodities had paid off, his standing in the town far outstripping his father's position as a modest tenant farmer. His son William, born in April 1564, would have been raised in an environment which would have reflected this affluence.

John Shakespeare's difficulties

By the end of the 1570s, however, this advance in the family fortunes had ground to a halt.[16] The most obvious outward manifestation of this was John's failure to attend any Corporation meetings from at least January 1577 until September 1586 when he was eventually dismissed from the ranks of aldermen. That this was due to financial embarrassment is fairly clear from the initial and sympathetic reaction of the Corporation. Unlike some of his non-attending colleagues, he was not fined for his failure to appear at meetings, no action was taken against him in 1579 for declining to pay his contribution to a levy for the musters (which had already been reduced from 5 shillings due from aldermen to 3s. 4d. from capital burgesses), and in the same year he was excused a contribution towards the relief of the poor.[17] His difficulties may have been precipitated by determined action against him by Henry Higford early in 1578 for the recovery of a debt of £30, contracted some seven or eight years earlier. In 1573, Higford had gone no further than alleging the debt in the Court of Common Pleas at which John Shakespeare twice failed to appear. Presumably, as often happened, the parties reached agreement to extend credit but in 1578 Higford renewed his attack. By 9 February, John had already been unsuccessfully summoned four times to attend the court, resulting in

15. Fripp and others, eds., *Minutes and Accounts*, i, p. 146; ii, pp. 12, 52.
16. For a more detailed treatment of what follows, see Bearman, 'John Shakespeare: a Papist or just penniless?', pp. 411–33, esp. pp. 415–23.
17. Fripp and others, eds., *Minutes and Accounts*, iii, pp. 11, 24, 31.

the standard writ to the sheriff for his arrest. By early May he had still failed to appear, leading to a writ of outlawry and an order for the production of his person in the autumn.[18] Such procedures sound more draconian than they actually were, but some action on the part of the defendant would still have been required. In most civil actions, he or she could simply stay at home as the court's officers had no authority to enter a private dwelling in order to make an arrest. Such a strategy on John Shakespeare's part may therefore explain his absence from Corporation meetings from around this time. However, this was hardly a long-term solution and by the autumn we have good evidence that John had resorted to mortgaging or selling his freehold estates. On 14 November 1578 he mortgaged to Edmund Lambert the land at Wilmcote which his wife had brought with her on her marriage to raise £40, at the same time entering into a complicated agreement with George Gibbs for a twenty-one year lease of the same land virtually rent free, suggesting that Gibbs had come up with another lump sum.[19] A year later he sold his interest in land at Snitterfield which had again come to him on his marriage.[20] The house in Greenhill Street, which he had purchased in 1556, does not thereafter feature in the family's possession and may have been parted with at around this time, together with his copyhold land at Snitterfield which his father had farmed. Finally, in July 1582 arbitrators had decided that John should restore to William Burbage a sum of £7 10s. 0d. advanced on the security of a house in Stratford.[21] Intriguingly, instructions were given that the money should be repaid at the sign of the Maidenhead (*apud signum de le maiden hedd*) in Stratford, the name by which the inn established within part of the Shakespeares' Henley Street property was later known.[22]

18. TNA, CP 40/1352, m. 69; 1355, m.7v; 1356, m. 1123v. See also Fripp, *Shakespeare Man and Artist*, i, p. 71n.
19. Chambers, *William Shakespeare*, ii, pp. 35–7; Halliwell, *Outlines*, ii, pp. 202–3.
20. *Outlines*, ii, pp. 179–82.
21. Hotson, *Shakespeare's Sonnets Dated*, pp. 233–8; Fripp and others, eds., *Minutes and Accounts*, iv, pp. 57–60, 150–1.
22. It is tempting to speculate that the family home had, at least in part, already been leased out as a means of generating income, but in 1597 the name Maidenhead was used to describe another building in the town with no obvious connection to the Shakespeare family (SCLA, BRU 15/3/177). This does not the preclude the possibility that John had raised money on the security of the family home, although it might equally have been the elusive Greenhill Street property which he had bought in 1556 but of which there is no further record.

There is also evidence of other financial difficulties. In Trinity Term 1580, heavy fines are recorded against John's name in the records of the court of Queen's Bench: £20 for not having appeared in court himself and a further £20 for failing to secure the appearance of a hat-maker from Nottingham by the name of John Audley.[23] Audley was similarly fined £40 for not appearing himself and a further £10 for not securing John Shakespeare's appearance. Their names occur on the *Coram Regina* roll in a list of some 220 people from across the country fined similar sums for similar offences. Attempts have been made to represent this as evidence of punishment inflicted on recusants but, in fact, lists of this kind occur on rolls of previous years and have a simpler explanation, namely as a cumulative countrywide record of those who forfeited their sureties, having been bound over, probably by local magistrates, to keep the peace. Such binding over usually took the form of requiring offenders to attend the next holding of quarter sessions. If they failed to appear, they and their sureties forfeited the sums in which they had been bound and the matter was referred to the central courts. It was not, then, their failure to appear in Queen's Bench which had attracted the fines but their refusal to observe the conditions imposed by a lower court. And a common reason for failing to appear was to avoid arrest for debt and subsequent harassment in the civil courts.

For John Shakespeare's and John Audley's case we lack any record of the nature of the offence which had led to their being bound over, if indeed one was committed; for it was possible for a person to be bound over and sureties taken on the mere suspicion that an individual's behaviour was likely to cause a breach of the peace. Be that as it may, the most likely interpretation of the available evidence is that both John Shakespeare and John Audley had been bound over to appear at quarter sessions, each standing pledge for the other. Having failed to appear, notification of their default was sent to Queen's Bench and their forfeitures noted. There is some indication of the seriousness of John's original offence compared with that of John Audley: whereas John had been bound over in £20 simply to keep the queen's peace, Audley was bound over in twice that sum for the more serious requirement of 'bearing himself well' towards the queen

---

23. Fripp and others, eds., *Minutes and Accounts*, iii, pp. 68–9. For a fuller discussion, see Bearman, 'John Shakespeare: a Papist of just penniless?', pp. 420–2.

and her people.[24] Exactly what had happened to lead to this breach, or threatened breach, of the peace is not known, but one likely explanation would be some sort of quarrel arising out of John's financial plight. Threatening behaviour by a creditor, for example, could be a sufficient pretext for the victim to apply to the justices for his persecutors to be bound over. This was probably what lay behind a case, two years later, when John himself was on the receiving end. In this instance, he had appealed directly to Queen's Bench that four men, Ralph Cawdrey, William Russell, Thomas Loggin, and Robert Young, be bound over to save him from 'fear of death and mutilation of his limbs' (*ob metum mortis et mutulatione membrorum suorum*).[25] Why John had taken his case to Queen's Bench is unclear, but one explanation could be that Ralph Cawdrey, as high bailiff that year, and thus presiding over the local court of record, had been involved in measures to bring John to account for outstanding debts which John sought to evade by taking refuge in a higher court.[26]

As further evidence of John's serious plight, we also have, in 1585/6, and 1586/7, cases in this court of record, set up under Stratford's 1553 charter for the settlement of civil actions up to the value of £30. In the first of these, begun on 27 October 1585, John Brown brought an action against John Shakespeare to recover a debt of an unspecified amount. On his failure to appear, a writ of distraint on John's goods was issued, the first stage in enforcing attendance, but on 19 January the serjeants at mace reported back that they had been unable to execute the writ because John 'had nothing of which he could be distrained' (*nihil habet unde distringi potest*). A writ of *capias*, that is, for John's arrest, was therefore issued, but the case then petered out, Brown it seems, being reluctant to incur the fees which these processes involved without any guarantee that he would recover his debt.[27] James Halliwell, the scholar who discovered these entries, commented that the words *nihil habet unde distringi potest* 'are not to be taken literally, and that they merely belong to a formula that was in use when a writ of distringas failed in enforcing an appearance.' Nevertheless, in the context of the workings of the Stratford court, for things to have gone this far was

24. Jacob, *The Law Dictionary*, ii (unpaginated), *sub* Surety of the Peace.
25. Hotson, *Shakespeare's Sonnets Dated*, pp. 224–9.
26. By securing a writ of *habeas corpus cum causa*, as explained below, p. 14. This cannot be checked as Stratford's court of record proceedings are missing for this period.
27. Halliwell, *Outlines*, ii, p. 238.

unusual. For instance, this particular action was only one of seven which John Brown—perhaps in failing health (he was buried ten months later) and anxious to settle his affairs—filed in October 1585. The other six, for one reason or another, were quickly settled or dropped, whilst only the case against John was pursued to the point of arrest.[28] Nor does a wider investigation of the court's proceedings substantiate Halliwell's claim that the formula used in John Shakespeare's case was a common one. Amongst the scores of writs of distraint issued in the years 1585 and 1586, themselves arising out of over a hundred cases, only twice did the serjeants at mace return a *nihil*. It therefore cannot be assumed that the legal formulae of the common law do not, in this case, reflect a real situation.

The second case had its origin in a debt of £22 owed by John Shakespeare's brother, Henry, to Nicholas Lane.[29] By an arrangement made in June 1586, John, it was claimed, had stood surety for his brother Henry for the repayment of £10 of the debt by Michaelmas next. When Henry defaulted, Lane therefore took action against John, claiming a total, including damages, of £20. A final judgment is not recorded, but John, sensing that it would go against him, produced a writ of *habeas corpus cum causa*, transferring the case to a superior court.[30] To which court John had applied, or whether Lane pursued his claim there, we do not know: but the evidence of John's indebtedness is clear and an inability to pay implicit.

This cumulative evidence of John's financial difficulties—realization of assets, pursuit in local and national courts for the repayment of debts, and evidence of fines imposed for his failure to appear—calls for an explanation, and some have not been slow to attribute this to his supposed recusancy. The sale or mortgaging of his Wilmcote and Snitterfield land, for example, has been linked to contemporary complaints that recusants were conveying their lands and goods to friends in order to escape forfeiture and confiscation.[31] However, John's comparatively small-scale dealings do not have that air about them. The

28. Of the amount, we know nothing, but in Brown's inventory, drawn up in August, he had sums owing to him of £356 6s. 7d., of which £157 1s. 2d. were described as 'desperate': Jones, ed., *Stratford-upon-Avon Inventories, 1538–1699*, i, p. 74.
29. Halliwell, *Outlines*, ii, pp. 241–3.
30. This was often used as a purely evasive tactic and legislation of James I's reign restricted the frivolous removal of cases in this way: Jacob, *Law Dictionary*, i, *sub* Habeas Corpus. See also Baker, *The Oxford History of the Laws of England, 1483–1558*, pp. 91–4.
31. For example, Fripp in *Minutes and Accounts*, iii, pp. xxxiv–xxxvi.

disposal of his Snitterfield land coincided neatly with a policy actively pursued by his nephew Robert Webbe of buying up the various shares into which the inheritance had been divided. His Wilmcote transactions are also clearly mortgages, not 'friendly conveyances', and were designed to secure identifiable sums of money which, when John could not repay them, led, first, to the forfeiture of the estate and then, as we shall see, to legal wrangling over many years as first John, and then his son, William, struggled to get it back.[32] Indeed, in the course of these arguments, the Lamberts were alleged to have claimed that they had lent John more than just the £40.[33] Moreover, in the will of Roger Sadler, drawn up on the very day that the mortgage to Lambert was made, there is listed a debt of £5 due from John Shakespeare for which Lambert was acting as one of the sureties.[34] All the evidence, then, indicates that John was engaged in these transactions, not with any intention of concealing his ownership, but because he was indeed in genuine need of ready cash.

Others have attempted to interpret John's absenteeism from Corporation meetings as further evidence of his adherence to the old religion, and in particular the result of an early drive against recusancy. It is certainly the case that Bishop Whitgift, the newly appointed bishop of Worcester, in whose diocese Stratford then lay, had, with his brother bishops, received a request in October 1577 to make a return of all those who were refusing to attend church.[35] However, despite his best efforts, he was able, for Warwickshire, to come up with only three persons who had actually been cited—all Warwick town residents—to which he added in frustration a further seven, but not including John Shakespeare, who were not actually cited but 'by common reporte are noted to bee great myslikers of the religion nowe professed and do absente themselves from the churche.'[36] Two years later he was rebuked by the Privy Council for the deficiency of this return.[37] This does not support the notion of a crackdown on non-conformity severe enough to push John Shakespeare

32. Below, pp. 87–90.
33. Halliwell, *Outlines*, ii, pp. 16–17.
34. Vine Hall, *Testamentary Papers II; Wills from Shakespeare's Town and Time*, p. 13.
35. *CSPD, 1547–80*, p. 558.
36. For his letter to the Privy Council, see Fripp and others, eds., *Minutes and Accounts*, iii, pp. 6–7. For the paucity of names see Ryan, 'Diocesan Returns of Recusants for England and Wales. 1577', pp. 64–6, citing TNA, SP 12/118/11/5.
37. Strype, *The Life and Acts of...John Whitgift*, i, pp. 181–2.

into retirement from the deliberations of the Corporation. By way of comparison, Alderman Ralph Cawdrey, whose wife and daughters were later cited as wilful recusants, and whose son became a seminary priest,[38] had no difficulty in maintaining his regular attendance. Undeterred, advocates of John's recusancy, relying on copies of a document which no longer survives—John Shakespeare's so-called 'spiritual testament'—have argued that he remained a staunch Catholic and that this was what led to his financial difficulties. However, there are real problems over the authenticity of this evidence, linked as it is with other suspicious Shakespearean tales circulating in Stratford at the end of the eighteenth century when the 'spiritual testament' first came to light, nor is there any further document to substantiate recusancy on John Shakespeare's part.[39] It would hardly be surprising, of course, if John Shakespeare, reared in the old faith, had cherished some memories of traditional church worship. But to argue, on the basis of no reliable evidence, that he pushed such loyalty to the point that it threatened his livelihood, remains essentially unconvincing, given that until the mid-1570s John's conduct was typical of an ambitious man simply pursuing a business career. It is not impossible, of course, that John Shakespeare's quarrels had originated in high words over religious views, or that religious difference could have manifested itself in quarrels of a more general nature. But, in fact, the cause of most litigation, whether actions remained civil or degenerated into direct action and criminal offences, lay in the problems of enforcing payment for goods supplied or repayment of debts. Stratford's court of record, meeting fortnightly and specifically charged with sorting out disputes of this nature, and serving a population of perhaps less than 2000, could, at each session, in the mid-1580s, typically hear thirty cases, five or six of which would be new claims.

A favoured means of avoiding arrest in such circumstances, as already explained, was to remain closeted within one's home, a sufficiently persuasive reason for John's initial failure to attend Corporation meetings. This was also the reason that was given as late as 1592 for his non-attendance at church, another piece of evidence seized upon by those looking for evidence of recusancy. His name occurs twice in lists

---

38. Below, p. 17.
39. This issue is discussed in more detail in Bearman, 'John Shakespeare's "Spiritual Testament": a reappraisal', and McCoog and Davidson, 'Edmund Campion and William Shakespeare.'

compiled as the result of a nationwide drive against suspected Catholic sympathizers launched in the late autumn of 1591.[40] This required bodies of commissioners in each county to report those who were suspected of recusancy, as evidenced not only by the serious crime of harbouring Jesuits and seminary priests but also simply by not going to church. In the case of large parishes and market towns, these returns were to be based on the report of select, honest, and loyal persons. For Warwickshire, a first list appeared in the early spring, of which only a draft survives.[41] However, following further instructions, the commissioners produced in October a second, and official, list of those people 'presented to them Or haue bene otherwise fownde owt by the Endevoire of the sayd commissioners, To be Jhesuites, Seminarye preestes, fugitiues Or Recusantes... Or vehementelye suspected to be sutche.'[42]

John Shakespeare's name occurs in both these lists, which at first would seem to provide a lead on his religious views. The official list is divided into five sections. The first deals with those who 'yet wilfullye persiste in thear Recusancye', and includes three Stratford names.[43] The second section comprises 'The names of sutch daungerous and seditious Papistes and Recusantes As haue bene presented to vs or founde out by our endevoire to haue bene att any tyme heretofore of, or in this cowntye of warwick And now either beyonde the Seas or vagrante within this Realme.' Under Stratford, only one person fell into this category, George Cooke, alias Cawdrey, Ralph Cawdrey's son. The third section comprised 'all sutch Recusantes As haue beene hearetofore preasented within this Countye of Warwicke, And are now either Dwelling in other Counties, or gone oute of this Countye vppon their iust occasions, or to lurke vnknowen in other Contryes', including, from Stratford, John Buswell and the wife of Philip More. Fifthly, are those who, since the first return, had either conformed or were thought likely to do so, including sixteen from Stratford. But preceding these,

---

40. Parry, 'The context of John Shakespeare's "Recusancy" re-examined', esp. pp. 8–27.
41. It survives amongst the papers of Fulk Greville, one of the commissioners (WCRO, CR 1886/BL/2662) and has been edited by Tobias, 'New Light on Recusancy in Warwickshire, 1592', pp. 8–27, esp. pp. 20–1. Precise dating is impossible, but it must pre-date 25 April, when one of those listed, William Clopton, was buried.
42. TNA, SP 12/243/76, edited in its entirety, with modernized spelling, by Hodgetts as 'A Certificate of Warwickshire Recusants, 1592.' For a better transcript of the Stratford entries, see Fripp and others, eds., *Minutes and Accounts*, iv, pp. 159–62.
43. Frances Jefferies, Richard Dibdale, and Richard Jeanes.

in the fourth category, are those who had been presented for not attending church monthly, 'yet are thoughte to forbeare the Church for debtte and for feare of processe, Or for soom other worse faultes, Or for Age, sicknes or impotencye of body.' Under Stratford, these are further subdivided into nine (including John Shakespeare) who feared 'processe' for debt, and six whose presenters said 'that all or the most of theese cannot coom to the Church for age and other infirmities.'

It can hardly be claimed, then, that this establishes with any degree of certainty that John Shakespeare was an obdurate recusant if instead he had been included in the one category out of the five which was designed to cover those who were not, merely listing him as one who feared he might be arrested for debt if he ventured abroad. In fact, it was at the time of the first return (early spring 1592) that this might well have been the case, as it was then that Burbage was successfully pressing his suit against John in the Court of Common Pleas.[44] Others bracketed with him, Nicholas Barnhurst, John Wheeler the elder, George Bardell, and Thomas Jones, alias Giles, can similarly be shown to be in some financial difficulty.[45] That the reasons given for non-attendance were generally true is further suggested by looking more closely at the six who were said to have been too old or infirm to attend. Of these, Griffen ap Roberts died between the two surveys; Matilda Barber was buried on 15 September, a few days before the survey was sent in; Juliana Court died in May 1593; and Margaret Jefferies in February 1594.[46] Finally we may note that, in later returns of recusants, the same Stratford families as were cited for their open recusancy in 1592 are still found persisting in their faith—the Cawdreys, the Burmans, the Dibdales, and the Reynolds—whilst, with the exception of John Wheeler the younger and Mary his wife, there is no mention of families associated with the 1592 debtors.[47]

This does not establish beyond doubt that the words of the survey can be taken at face value, but surely the balance of probability is firmly in favour of accepting John's categorization as valid. Otherwise, one

44. Above, p. 11.
45. For details, see Bearman, 'Papist or just Penniless?', p. 429.
46. Savage, ed., *Registers of Stratford-on-Avon:. . . Burials, 1558–1652/3*, pp. 49, 51–2.
47. For these returns, see TNA, E 377/6, mm 15v, 20v; E 377/15, m. 15v; Guise-Berrow and Hodgson, 'Return of recusants in Kineton and Barlichway hundreds, 1605–6', pp. 19, 31; Fripp and others, eds., *Minutes and Accounts*, v, pp. 350–2. For those presented at the local church court or at visitations, see Brinkworth, *Shakespeare and the Bawdy Court*, pp. 131–2, 134; SCLA, ER 1/115/7; ER 1/115/15.

must ask why, if the town authorities were prepared to cite some twenty-five of their fellow townsmen for recusancy of varying degrees of seriousness, they should collude to protect fifteen others. The local men compiling the lists would have been aware that they would be looked over not only by government officials in London but also by zealous local commissioners and justices of the peace who would already be familiar with the situation locally and who would not look kindly on any deliberate attempt to mislead.[48]

However, if recusancy was not the cause of John Shakespeare's troubles, another must be sought. Incapacity of some sort would be one explanation for John's abrupt disappearance from Corporation records: Robert Bratt, who, like John, was excused the poor rate levy in November 1578, had made the smallest contribution in a similar assessment of August 1564, and almost certainly died soon after his last attendance in October 1578.[49] In John's case, however, illness is never hinted at during the legal wrangles which characterized his subsequent career, and the fact that he died in 1601, probably aged over seventy, indicates a robust constitution. More convincingly, Park Honan has drawn attention to the attempted clampdown on wool dealers in the late 1570s.[50] John, as we have seen, was deeply involved in this trade, and any measures to curtail his activities in this respect would not have been welcome. The wool trade had always needed middlemen and, in the days when most wool had gone for export, the Merchants of the Staple had achieved a near monopoly in this respect. However, there was a growing body of local entrepreneurs engaged in the trade, accused of raising prices to artificially high levels. Efforts were therefore periodically made to limit the scale of their operations.[51] Many were glovers, drawn into the trade via the money they already made through the sale of fell wool—wool plucked from the skins which they had purchased for glove manufacture—and some were thought to be conducting a trade in fleece wool equal to that of some Staplers. John's alleged sale of twenty-five stones of wool in 1568 would be a sizeable one when set against the business transacted

48. Parry, 'The context of John Shakespeare's "Recusancy" re-examined', pp. 8–27.
49. Fripp and others, eds., *Minutes and Accounts*, i, p. 130; iii, pp. 21, 23–4. His death is not recorded in the burial register, but his name had been removed from the lists of burgesses by the time of the next recorded meeting of the Corporation on 23 April 1579.
50. Honan, *Shakespeare: a Life*, pp. 37–40.
51. Bowden, *Wool Trade*, especially Chapters IV and V.

by small-scale retailers, or wool-broggers as they were known; and his purchases in 1571 of 400 and 200 stones, if true, would, as already explained, have placed him well up in the ranks of Midlands dealers.[52] This was despite an Act of Parliament of 1553, restricting the buying and selling of wool to all but manufacturers and Merchants of the Staple.[53]

There was renewed agitation against the middlemen in the mid-1570s when wool prices, held down for a few years in the early 1570s due to a suspension of trade between England and the Netherlands, began to rise in response to the expansion in cloth exports. Under a proclamation of November 1576 the purchase of wool under licence was suspended for a year and even the Merchants of the Staple were ordered to cease trading for three months.[54] A further instruction in late May 1577 required local justices of the peace to secure sureties in £100 from the wool-broggers that they would stop trading.[55] As this was pursued less than half-heartedly in the provinces, the government, during the summer, instituted an inquiry, which confirmed, but on the evidence of the wealthy clothiers and the Staplers only, that the middlemen were indeed to blame. Armed with this information, the government once again urged local justices to ensure observance of the regulations, and in August ninety-one commissioners were appointed to oversee enforcement.[56]

These measures against a trade in which John Shakespeare was clearly involved would certainly have had implications even though they were, in general terms, largely ineffectual and not pursued with any determination. Although continuing high wool prices provoked a further proclamation, in 1579, suspending licensed dealings,[57] this was soon reversed and from 1581 the government became less and less interested in enforcement. Nor is there any evidence that John was singled out

52. Bowden, *Wool Trade*, p. 82. However, the details of these transactions, depending on the evidence of a paid informer, must be treated with caution.
53. This legislation was neither widely observed nor vigorously enforced, but in fact it was contravention of this that had led to the allegations against John Shakespeare of illegal wool-dealing in 1562.
54. Hughes and Larkin, eds., *Tudor Royal Proclamations*, ii, pp. 414–15; and see Bowden, *Wool Trade*, p. 135.
55. TNA, SP 12/113/21 (*CSPD, 1547–1580*, p. 547); Bowden, *Wool Trade*, p. 135.
56. TNA, SP 12/115/14 (*CSPD, 1547–1580*, p. 554); *Acts of the Privy Council 1575–73*, pp. 366, 386.
57. Hughes and Larkin, eds., *Tudor Royal Proclamations*, ii, pp. 440–1.

as a brogger. For instance, his name does not occur in a list of seventeen Warwickshire broggers submitted to the Privy Council at that time by the Mayor of the Staple,[58] nor in a list, compiled by the Staplers, of twelve Warwickshire broggers accused of illicit trading at Cirencester market.[59] We cannot automatically assume, then, that John would have been seriously affected by this move against the broggers and we also need to bear in mind that wool dealing was not his only business. In contemporary documents he is described as a yeoman as often as he is a glover, and twice he occurs as a whittawer. Even if there were a temporary restriction on his wool-dealing activities in the late 1570s, his other interests might therefore well be thought sufficient to tide him over a difficult period.

However, if these particular measures against wool-broggers were not by themselves the immediate cause of John's difficulties, then another must be sought; and the most likely is that he had simply overreached himself. Business, then as now, was conducted largely on credit, with the result that a few bad debtors, or sudden demands on limited cash reserves, could have serious consequences. Those on the fringes of the wool-brogging trade, by buying on generous credit and selling for cash (or for a shorter term of credit), could even get by without any capital at all. We know that on occasion John did appear to have cash in hand—in 1570, for example, the year he lent John Mussheii £170 at interest:[60] but his general background—the son of a local husbandman who had set himself up in business in a local market town, working himself at the same time into the civic elite—suggests an over-ambitious man of limited means whose venture into the world of business, and especially large-scale wool dealing, had involved taking risks which in the end over-stretched his resources. The agitation of the late 1570s against middlemen would certainly have had an effect but perhaps only to the extent of pushing him to the brink. Then, as now, the loss of credit would spell the end of profitable business dealings, leaving the victim harassed by his impatient creditors and struggling, from a position of weakness, to gather in any debts owing to him. Legal records of the time are peppered with references to the desperate straits to which small-scale traders could be reduced as

58. TNA, SP 12/114/31. These include John Brooks and Thomas Wheeler of Stratford.
59. TNA, SP 12/114/39. Thomas Wheeler is again listed, but as of Henley-in-Arden.
60. Above, p. 9.

the result of a loss of credit, including the glover, John Lee, arrested in the open market at Cirencester to satisfy claims made against him by a Warwick wool-dealer, and Humphrey Grigg of Beaudesert, allegedly ruined through loss of credit by proceedings against him by Robert Wheeler of Tanworth-in-Arden.[61] In John Shakespeare's case, misfortune might at first have prompted a sympathetic response from civic colleagues but loss of credit, accompanied by unseemly behaviour, would in the longer term have brought disgrace in the eyes of the community, jeopardizing his civic standing and any future role in local governance, and leaving him under the constant fear of legal process.[62]

In the present context, there are two aspects of this downward trajectory in John Shakespeare's fortunes which would have affected his son William. In general terms it would have demonstrated the uncertainties facing those deeply involved in business based on credit. Over a period of twenty-five years or so a young husbandman from a small village had built up for himself, even during his father's lifetime, a profitable business in a local market town, reflected in his prominent role in civic affairs, serving as bailiff in 1568/9 and chief alderman in 1571/2. Within a decade, however, things had unravelled almost to the point of no return. Why this happened continues to be matter of debate but, rather than attributing the crisis in his affairs to an obstinate adherence to Catholic dogma, to ill health, or specifically to the government's moves against wool-broggers, a more realistic assessment would indicate that it was simply due to insufficient credit reserves and that a combination of bad luck and over-ambitious dealing in the increasingly unfavourable environment of the late 1570s had led to a collapse in his ability to meet his obligations. We cannot be sure that his son William consciously took this lesson on board, but, as will become apparent, his subsequent career was not characterized by any such crises, rather by a steady rise to a position of more than adequate sufficiency. This does not mean that he never had to borrow money, especially, as will be proposed, in the early years, only that his credit was never threatened. And, although absence of evidence must not be allowed to mislead, the fact that, unlike so many of his contemporaries, he was never known to have been pursued for debt and is only rarely found pursuing others suggests a man who had learned to be cautious

61. Everitt, 'The marketing of agricultural produce', pp. 567–8.
62. See, for instance, Barry, 'Civility and Civic Culture in Early Modern England.'

in his business dealings. More directly, of course, his father's misfortunes may simply have led to a wish on Shakespeare's part to recover the situation—but only after he had initially made things worse.

Education and marriage

This crisis in John's affairs occurred at a crucial period in William's life. We do not know what ambitions John had for his eldest son, but we can at least assume with some confidence that he was sent to the town's recently re-founded grammar school. This cannot be proved beyond all doubt as no formal records survive documenting the admission of pupils. Instead, we have to make do with passing references to the schoolmasters and payments towards the maintenance of the school buildings. But many have argued, on the evidence of incidental passages in Shakespeare's writings, that he underwent a standard grammar school education and, given that in the early 1570s his father was a leading Stratford burgess, it would be unreasonable to argue that this was not instilled at the local grammar school. For a boy with the necessary aptitude, and the backing of his father, this would typically have opened up the possibility of attendance at one of the universities or Inns of Court, leading on in turn to a career in teaching, in the church or in the law. This was the case with two of Alderman William Smith's sons, near Stratford contemporaries of Shakespeare, Richard, born around 1555 and William in 1564. Richard, to whom the Stratford vicar, John Bretchgirdle, on his death in 1565, bequeathed books in both English and Latin, went on to serve as vicar of Mottistone on the Isle of Wight.[63] His brother William, who entered Winchester College in 1580, at the age of sixteen, matriculated at Exeter College, Oxford, aged eighteen, in October 1583, and in 1589 is found acting as a schoolmaster at Loughton, in Essex.[64] Later, Richard Quiney, whose eldest son Richard, aged eleven, wrote to his father in Latin,[65] sent another son, George, to Balliol College, where he graduated in 1620, before returning to Stratford to serve as usher and curate. Abraham Sturley,

---

63. Fripp, *Shakespeare Studies*, p. 26; SCLA, DR 237/1b. He can probably be identified with the Richard Smith of Christchurch, Oxford, awarded his BA on 19 February 1576, and MA on 12 July 1578.
64. Hotson, *Shakespeare's Sonnets Dated*, pp. 131–2; Eccles, *Shakespeare in Warwickshire*, p. 59.
65. For the letter, see Fripp, *Shakespeare Man and Artist*, ii, p. 498.

who settled in Stratford early in the 1580s with two pre-school sons, Henry and Richard, sent them both to Oxford. Henry graduated in 1599 and, like George Quiney, returned to Stratford to serve as curate and usher before becoming vicar of Chipping Campden, in Gloucestershire.[66] Richard was awarded his BA in 1601.[67] Other Stratford boys known to have enjoyed a university education were John Parsons, son of the mercer William Parsons, who matriculated at Balliol in May 1597 at the age of fifteen; Edward, son of Richard Lane, who matriculated at Exeter College, Oxford, in March 1605, aged sixteen; and William, the son of another mercer, William Chandler, who matriculated at St John's College, Oxford, in 1624, aged nineteen;[68] and mention should also be made of George Cawdry, son of Arthur Cawdry, baptised in December 1565, who, at the age of eighteen, entered the English seminary at Rheims.[69] We may not be able to prove that any of these boys, or indeed Shakespeare, attended the town's grammar school, but cumulatively the evidence is persuasive that some at least must have done. Clearly, then, Stratford was no backwater as far as a boy's basic education was concerned and, equally clearly, Shakespeare, in common with other of his exact or near contemporaries, would have been more than adequately provided with the opportunity to pursue those careers open to university graduates.

To have stayed on at school after the age of fifteen or sixteen would have been unusual, in Shakespeare's case 1579 or 1580. This would have not been too young (indeed, as indicated above, would have been a quite normal age) to have matriculated at one of the universities. Lack of means was not an absolute bar to attendance at university, as demonstrated, for instance, in the case of Christopher Marlowe, son of a shoemaker. However, the fact that Shakespeare must clearly have pursued some other option until his marriage in November 1582 (which then ruled out a university education anyway) suggests that his father's financial embarrassment and social disgrace was such an overwhelmingly

66. Fripp, *Master Richard Quyny*, pp. 120–1; Fripp and others, eds., *Minutes and Accounts*, vi, p. 297.
67. Foster, *Alumni Oxonienses*, iv, p. 1441. Sturley himself was a university graduate who on at least one occasion wrote to Richard Quiney in Latin (Fripp, *Shakespeare Man and Artist*, ii, pp. 493–4).
68. Foster, *Alumni Oxonienses*, i, p. 216; iii, pp. 874, 1123.
69. Eccles, *Shakespeare in Warwickshire*, pp. 60–1.

dominant issue as to rule out any ambitious plans for his son's future. Perhaps John had cast his son in the more mundane role of rescuing the family fortunes by his following him into what was left of his family business. There may even have been attempts to apprentice him, though again, John's situation would have made this difficult.

Other suggestions have been made as to how he spent his immediate post-school years, but none is based on contemporary evidence. However, the tradition, first recorded in written form by John Aubrey in 1681, that 'in his younger yeares', he was a 'School-master in the Countrey', is worth our attention as it was related to him, so he claimed, by Christopher Beeston, the son of another Christopher who for a time was one of Shakespeare's colleagues in the Lord Chamberlain's Men.[70] Some have taken this as evidence that he can be identified with a William Shakeshafte known to have been employed at around this time in the household of Alexander Hoghton of Lea, in Lancashire.[71] Hoghton's family had Catholic associations, thus fuelling further speculation as to the Shakespeares' religious outlook. Again, however, detailed investigation of the relevant issues, not least that the surname Shakeshafte was very common in late sixteenth-century Lancashire, makes this a very unprofitable line of enquiry.[72] Nevertheless, it is certainly possible that the young Shakespeare, even without a university degree, could have been retained as a pupil-teacher at Stratford's grammar school or even as an unacknowledged usher—'a schoolmaster in the countrey' to anyone living in the capital.[73]

Matters were thrown into further confusion as the result of Shakespeare's marriage in November 1582 to Ann Hathaway, who was already some three or four months pregnant. This event has attracted more attention than almost any other event in his life, but rarely is it considered against the background of the expectations and usual practice of the time. The issue is made more complicated as the result of incomplete, and flawed, documentation. The couple did not marry in the bride's, or bridegroom's church, nor was the ceremony performed,

70. Chambers, *William Shakespeare*, ii, p. 254.
71. The idea had first been mooted in the 1930s but questioned by Douglas Hamer in 'Was William Shakespeare William Shakeshafte?'. In 1985, E.A.J. Honigmann, in *Shakespeare: the Lost Years*, enthusiastically revived the idea.
72. Bearman, '"Was William Shakespeare William Shakeshafte" revisited'; Parry, 'New Evidence on William Shakeshafte, and Edmund Campion'.
73. The latest to address this issue, and Shakespeare's education generally, is Ian Green, '"More polite learning": humanism and the new grammar school'.

as was usual, after the reading of banns three times in the couple's place (or places) of residence: instead the marriage took place by licence and was celebrated elsewhere, perhaps because of Ann's pregnancy. The licence itself has not survived nor is there an extant parish register which records the marriage. The waters are further muddied by the fact that, of the two documents concerning the marriage to have survived, one, a clerk's entry in the bishop of Worcester's register (in whose diocese Stratford then lay) simply records that such a licence was issued, naming the parties as William Shakespeare and Ann Whateley of Temple Grafton.[74] It has reasonably been argued that this is simply a scribal error on the grounds that the other surviving document, an original bond (and so more trustworthy) that there were no obstacles to the marriage and that Shakespeare would 'save harmles' the bishop and his officials from any subsequent difficulties through the issue of a licence, names them as William Shakespeare and Ann Hathaway of Stratford-upon-Avon.[75] Such a mundane explanation has not been universally accepted and elaborate, though largely unconvincing, theories have been put forward instead. One claim, however, does deserve serious consideration: namely, that the marriage may have been licensed to take place at Temple Grafton, a nearby (though not the nearest) parish in the Worcester diocese.

However, these details should not distract us from discussion of the real significance of the marriage and its effect on Shakespeare's circumstances. For, within the context of Elizabethan marriage, it was not characteristic. The marriage of Shakespeare's father, John, may be regarded as having followed a more usual pattern. This took place after he had completed his apprenticeship and had taken steps to provide himself with an income sufficient to support a family and to acquire an establishment where it could function as an independent unit. Inevitably such considerations would normally delay marriage until the bridegroom was in his mid-twenties. The bride would not be subject to these limitations and might therefore be a year or two younger. Such trends are reflected in a recent study of marriage patterns within Stratford over the period 1570 to 1640, where the average of first marriage for men has been calculated at twenty-six (though with the

---

74. Gray, *Shakespeare's Marriage*, pp. 224–6, printed alongside other typical entries from the registers.

75. Gray, *Shakespeare's Marriage*, pp. 202–4. For examples of other errors, see Gray, *Shakespeare's Marriage*, pp. 26–7.

biggest number occurring at the age of twenty-four) and for women twenty-four (with most occurring at the age of either twenty-one or seventeen).[76]

The circumstances of Shakespeare's marriage are therefore plainly unusual. He was still only eighteen, one of only three known teenage bridegrooms from Stratford marrying during the years 1570–1640.[77] On the other hand, Ann, daughter of Richard Hathaway, on the evidence of her age at death, was twenty-six, eight years older than William. She was also pregnant (she gave birth to her first child in May 1583) and fatherless (Richard had died the previous September). Though not penniless—her father, in his will, had arranged a marriage portion for her of £6 13s. 4d.—she was certainly no catch for the eldest son of one of Stratford's leading citizens, albeit currently in straitened circumstances.[78] This does not mean that Shakespeare's marriage was not a love match, but, given its far from typical characteristics, one is left wondering whether it would ever have taken place had Shakespeare not made Ann Hathaway pregnant.

Career choices

Shakespeare's hasty marriage in November 1582 finally ruled out both a formal apprenticeship, at least outside the family, and a university education. Unable to support himself and his dependants, he had simultaneously added to the burdens on his own family at an already difficult time. At what point he decided to try his hand at earning a living through acting and/or writing is unknown, although the conception of his twin children, Judith and Hamnet, in the early summer of 1584 implies intermittent residence in Stratford until at least that date.[79] However, the fact that, after the birth of twins in February 1585, he had no more children—when Shakespeare himself was still only in his early twenties and Ann thirty or so—would certainly suggest that thereafter he did not spend long periods at home during the

76. Jones, *Family Life in Shakespeare's England*, pp. 89–90.
77. Jones, *Family Life in Shakespeare's England*, p. 90. The others were George Davis, aged seventeen, and William Baylis, aged eighteen.
78. For Richard Hathaway's will, see Halliwell, *Outlines*, ii, pp. 195–6. It was dated 1 September and Richard was buried on 7 September.
79. The twins were baptised on 2 February 1585.

remaining years that Ann was most likely to conceive—or, in other words, that he had decided to be absent from home for long periods in an effort to earn a living.

To some extent this is speculative, but until that point the couple's fertility had clearly not been in question. It is possible, of course, that the carrying and birth of twins, especially to full term, might have led to complications and that as a result Ann later suffered a series of early miscarriages. It is even possible that Shakespeare deliberately intended to limit the size of his family although this would be against normal practice. Calculating the number of children born into Stratford families during this period is not straightforward, as final numbers born to a couple would remain unknown if they moved into or out of the town during the family's formation. Moreover, the early death of one of the parents could bring a sudden end to the same process. Even so, a detailed study of children born into Stratford families studied by Jeanne Jones puts the average at 5.56 children in the years up to 1599, falling back to 5.12 for some thirty years thereafter.[80] These figures are explained, of course, by the high mortality rates among the very young—9 per cent within a week, 11 per cent within a month, and 32 per cent before the age of sixteen.[81] Deliberately to restrict one's family to three, if we accept that this is what Shakespeare did, would therefore have been very unusual and, as it turned out in his case, unfortunate if he had set his sights on a male heir. More likely, then, is surely the scenario that after 1585 Shakespeare spent so little time in Ann's company, that she did not again conceive, or at least that, perhaps as the result of complications following the birth of twins, miscarried early on in those pregnancies which did occur.

The so-called 'lost years' extend only from 1585 to 1592 during which Shakespeare clearly established a firm foothold in the theatrical world. The earliest evidence we have for this is a barbed attack, allegedly from the poet and playwright, Robert Greene, on his deathbed, addressed to three fellow playwrights, unnamed but since convincingly

80. Jones, *Family Life in Shakespeare's Stratford*, p. 96. However, the table provided, covering all known baptisms, is misleading in not taking account of migration. J.M. Martin ('A Warwickshire Town in Adversity', p. 29) in a tighter study of fourteen completed families in Old Stratford for the years, 1580–99, puts the average at 6.42, falling to 5.61 for twenty-six families for the years 1600–24.

81. Jones, *Family Life in Shakespeare's Stratford*, p. 93. For Martin's similar figures for Old Stratford see 'A Warwickshire Town in Adversity', p. 29.

identified as Christopher Marlowe, Thomas Nashe, and George Peele. The complaint, attributed to Greene but almost certainly the work of another playwright, Henry Chettle, is included in a pamphlet entitled *Greene's Groats-worth of witte, bought with a million of Repentance* published in September 1592 and begins with a general attack on actors—'those Puppets... that spake from our mouths'—but going on, by mutilating a quotation from a play (*The True Tragedy of Richard Duke of York*, known to us as *3 Henry VI*) later attributed to Shakespeare, to draw attention to a particular threat, an actor who was also laying claim to being a playwright.[82] Shakespeare is not quite named, but the object of the attack could hardly have been anyone else, not only because of the mutilated quote but because the writer concludes with the observation that this intruder 'is in his owne conceit the onely Shake-scene in a countrey.' Some have sought to question that this represents Shakespeare in the dual role of actor and playwright, arguing that the attack was principally against actors, including the famous 'vpstart Crow [ie Shakespeare], beautified with our feathers', who were achieving fame merely by acting out blank verse which had been written for them. However, the phrase 'bombast out a blanke verse as the best of you', when addressed to fellow playwrights not known to have been actors, can only be a reference to a greater menace, namely an actor who was also trying out his hand as a playwright. The equally slighting description of him as '*Iohannes factotum*' (Jack-of-all-trades) might also reflect Shakespeare's role in these early years as someone who was expected to undertake other minor theatrical duties. But with whatever nuances we might interpret the 1592 attack, the overall implication is clear: given that we know from later sources that Shakespeare acted in some at least of his plays, then it was probably as an actor that he had been able to attach himself to one of the theatrical companies based in London at that time; and further that he had also turned his hand to the writing of plays. He had had ample opportunity to learn the craft of writing in verse from his immersion in the classics whilst at grammar school. Translating dramatic and poetic Latin verse into English was a standard feature of a grammar school education, which could be further honed for those who went on to university by similar study of ancient Greek authors. Certainly, those who went to university

82. Chambers, *William Shakespeare*, ii, pp. 188–9. The whole issue has recently been comprehensively analysed by Schoone-Jongen, *Shakespeare's Companies*, pp. 17–39.

did broaden their horizons in this way, but others, like Thomas Kyd, Thomas Dekker, John Webster, and Ben Jonson, were able to pursue the career of playwright with the benefit of only a grammar school education. Nevertheless, many of these writers, whether or not they had been educated at university, lived in a state of uncertainty, especially in their early careers, obliged to sell their scripts to playhouse managers and theatrical companies for whatever price they could get.[83] Shakespeare, intentionally or otherwise, did not follow this course. Barred, as the result of his marriage, from admission to university, he was still sufficiently equipped, mainly as the result of an intensive but typical study of the Latin classics, to develop his skills as a writer of verse: but he chose to do this from inside, rather than outside, the acting profession. Indeed, given his financial situation, this may have been a course of action forced upon him. Much has been written about the visits to Stratford during Shakespeare's youth by companies of players: from 1573 these occurred on a more or less annual basis, peaking in 1587 when no fewer than five different companies are known to have visited the town.[84] The mere fact of watching such performances might have led Shakespeare to consider that here was an opportunity to earn a living. Indeed, if Stratford's grammar school was typical of its grander contemporaries in or near the capital, the performance of plays by groups of boys was an accepted part of their education, bringing to some of them an awareness of their acting abilities; and in Shakespeare's case, it would have been his promise as an actor, rather than a writer, which led to his initial recruitment by one of the commercial troupes.

At the time, though, it would not have presented itself as a road to riches. Travelling players were not popular with the authorities, either civil or ecclesiastical, and were generally tolerated only because they enjoyed the protection of royal or aristocratic patrons, keen to ensure the livelihood of a body of men who could be called on from time to time to provide them with entertainment. There was also no permanent purpose-built theatre in London before 1576 where a habit of

---

83. But see below, p. 39, where evidence from the late 1590s indicates that a hard-working dramatist could earn a good living.

84. Most recently analysed by J.R. Mulryne, 'Professional Theatre in the Guildhall 1568–1620.'

play-going could be more easily fostered.[85] On the other hand, amongst the public generally, there proved to be an immense appetite for entertainment of this sort. Deprived of those theatrical spectacles which, because of their religious connotations, had been scaled back following the Reformation, the public responded eagerly to this new, secular form of entertainment. Even by the mid-1560s the idea of commercial drama had firmly taken root, and it would be misleading to argue that to embark on an acting career was in itself a daring venture. Around 1580, we now know of around forty different professional acting companies operating across the country, not necessarily always welcomed by the authorities but a regular feature of Elizabethan town life, including Stratford's.[86] On the other hand, when Shakespeare decided to try and provide for his family by involving himself in this unconventional way of making a living, there would have been no guarantee that he would succeed. Prevented through his marriage from seeking an alternative and with his father enmeshed in financial difficulties, he may, however, have thought he had little choice. With the benefit of hindsight, we know, of course, that he did succeed, to the extent of ending his days in some comfort. But that should not obscure the fact that he started from a very low base. His father had also been financially successful, at least into the 1570s, but had achieved this by building on his family's modest but stable resources and setting himself up in business in Stratford, marrying, and starting a family only when he had the means to support such moves. His son's path was a very different one. In his mid-teens he witnessed the collapse of his father's business, the sale or mortgage of the family's real estate to meet the demands of creditors, and the spectacle of a father fearful of leaving the house for fear of arrest for debt. Shakespeare himself had only made a bad situation worse by marrying at the age of eighteen and within three years producing three extra mouths to feed without the means to provide for them. At the same time, his marriage ruled out any remaining chance he had of further education. For a few years he may have struggled to earn a living in his native town, or at least to help rescue what remained of the family business, but in the end decided to make the best use he could of those dramatic talents

85. The much smaller Red Lion, built by John Brayne in 1567, lasted less than a year (Berry, 'The first public playhouses, especially the Red Lion').
86. On this subject generally, see Ingram, *Business of Playing*, especially Chapter 2, and pp. 239–42.

brought out during his years at school even though there was no reason to think that this would be a route to riches. Nevertheless, the
memory of these early experiences may have remained with him for
life, sufficient explanation not only for the cautious management of
his business affairs thereafter but also of a dogged determination to
rescue his family from its parlous state.

3

Laying the foundations

Early years in the theatre

It is not easy to flesh out the precise route by which Shakespeare made his way into the theatrical world. There are only two firm facts to go on, Greene's (or Chettle's) attack on his growing reputation, discussed in Chapter 2, made in September 1592, and his emergence as a sharer in the Chamberlain's Men shortly after its formation in May 1594.[1] By the end of that year it is also generally agreed that he had written, or at least contributed to, some eight or nine plays, the earliest dating from about 1591.[2] Clearly, then, he was building a base on which to secure his and his family's future, not simply by writing plays, which by itself would not necessarily have proved very profitable, but by combining this with the development of links with a particular acting company.

Those seeking entry to a theatrical company, at least by the later 1590s, might typically have served out some time as an apprentice, usually to individual actors rather than to a particular company, and by an arrangement more flexible and less formal than existed for a recognized trading company. The preferred mechanism was for an existing member of a theatrical company, already a freeman of one of the

1. In March 1595 payments were authorized to Shakespeare, William Kemp, and Richard Burbage, 'servaunts to the Lord Chamberleyne' for court performances at Christmas 1594 (Thomas, *Shakespeare in the Public Records*, pp. 10–11).
2. The chronology of the plays is much discussed and, in some respects, is controversial. For the chronology proposed by the editors of the Oxford Shakespeare, see Dobson and Wells, eds., *The Oxford Companion*, p. 78, but this should be compared with Martin Wiggins' more recent and authoritative proposals (Wiggins, *British Drama: a Catalogue*, iii, 92, 119, 155, 180, 206, 219, 227). This includes assumed collaboration in *Edward III* but excludes *3 Henry VI* on the grounds that Shakespeare's contribution was not made until at least 1594 (pp. 161–2).

London livery companies, to bind a boy in that trade, regardless of the fact that he was to be prepared for an acting career.[3] However, in the late 1580s, this was not a well-established practice. Richard Tarlton, as a freeman of the Haberdashers, and later of the Vintners, may have bound two boys in the early 1580s, but neither is currently known to have followed him on to the stage.[4] It is only by the mid-1590s, when John Heminges, of the Lord Chamberlain's Men but also a freeman of the Grocers' Company, bound two later boy actors as apprentices, that we have the first firm evidence of the system in operation.[5] However, given Shakespeare's age by the mid-1580s, and the embryonic state of theatrical apprenticeship, this was not an option open to him, leaving us to assume that he had sought initial employment with one of the playing companies as a 'hired man', as distinct from a sharer in the company's profits, contracted to take on minor roles on stage and also other non-theatrical jobs on the company's behalf (and not forgetting that such a company might also spend long periods on tour). In any event, he must have soon demonstrated remarkable abilities to have acquired by September 1592 enough of a reputation as both actor and playwright to have attracted the unwelcome attention of Robert Greene (or Henry Chettle), even though his playwriting, at least initially, was almost certainly carried out in collaboration with others. His other role as an actor, even at the level of a hired man, would naturally have led him to write for the benefit of the company that was offering him regular employment: indeed, this might even have been expected of him. Fixing on a likely company has, however, proved very difficult.

Before 1594, when Shakespeare emerges as a sharer in the newly formed Chamberlain's Men, the only evidence we have is to be found on title pages of editions of plays later regarded, at least in part, as his work, which name the companies that had staged them. There were three of these, Strange's (later Derby's) Men, Pembroke's Men, and Sussex's Men. Added to the mix is the likelihood that the play now known to us as 1 Henry VI (certainly collaborative) was played by Strange's Men in March 1592—if we accept, that is, that we can safely identify this as the 'harey the vi' entered in Henslowe's diary as one of

3. Kathman, 'Grocers, Goldsmiths and Drapers: freemen and apprenticeships in the Elizabethan theatre'.
4. Kathman, 'Richard Tarlton and the Haberdashers', pp. 440–2.
5. Kathman, 'Players, Livery, Companies, and Apprentices', pp. 416–20.

a series of plays performed then by 'my lord Stranges men' at the Rose.[6] To complicate matters further, it has been strongly argued that Shakespeare's contribution to this play was only made in 1594, perhaps even later, after the play had come into the possession of the Lord Chamberlain's Men.[7]

Strange's Men had been active from at least the late 1570s and remained a leading troupe until the death of its patron in April 1594. The 1594 title page of another early play attributed to Shakespeare—*Titus Andronicus* (written, it is now generally agreed, in collaboration with George Peele)—provides a further link with Strange's Men, declaring it to have been played by Derby's Men (formerly Strange's Men, but renamed when its patron Lord Strange became earl of Derby). But it is here that the complications begin as the title page goes on to claim that the play had also been recently staged by two other troupes, namely Pembroke's Men and Sussex's Men.[8] Furthermore, the play *Richard Duke of York* (now known to us as *3 Henry VI*), again in some scholars' view partly collaborative, was also said, when published in 1595, to have been played solely by Pembroke's Men.[9] This being an acknowledged continuation of *The First Part of the Contention of the Two Famous Houses of York and Lancaster* (our *2 Henry VI*), again generally accepted as partly collaborative, would imply that the latter might too have been written specifically for Pembroke's. *The Taming of a Shrew*, published in May 1594 (not certainly Shakespeare's *Taming of the Shrew*, but either an earlier version, or drawing from it) was also said to be from the Pembroke stable.[10]

Pembroke's Men was a company that enjoyed only a brief documented flourish over the winter period 1592/93, when restrictions

6. Foakes, ed., *Henslowe's Diary*, pp. 16–17. In August 1592, Thomas Nashe apparently referred to this play when he commented that Lord Talbot, a principal character, 'after he had lyne two hundred yeares in his Tombe, he should triumphe againe on the Stage': Chambers, *William Shakespeare*, ii, p. 188, citing a passage from Thomas Nashe, *Pierce Penilesse his Supplication to the Diuell*, published in 1592.

7. Wiggins, *British Drama: a Catalogue*, iii, pp. 161–2.

8. Gurr, *Shakespeare Company, 1594–1642*, p. 290. The Sussex connection is confirmed in entries in Henslowe's diary for January 1594 (Foakes, ed., *Henslowe's Diary*, p. 21). It was entered in the Stationers' Register on 6 February 1594.

9. Gurr, *Shakespeare Company*, p. 290.

10. Gurr, *Shakespeare Company*, p. 290. It has also been vigorously argued that *Richard III*, dating from 1591/92 at the latest but not published until 1598, was also written for Strange's Men (Honigmann, *Shakespeare: the Lost Years*, pp. 63–4) but see Schoone-Jongen, *Shakespeare's Companies*, p. 113.

against playing in the capital due to plague were briefly lifted. It has been reasonably argued, however, that the company had been formed in May 1591 following a quarrel between James Burbage and Edward Alleyn which had left Burbage's Theatre in Shoreditch without tenants.[11] Assuming that Shakespeare joined this troupe, this would have allowed him sufficient time to have written the *First Part of the Contention* (*2 Henry VI*) and *Richard Duke of York* (*3 Henry VI*) before the publication of Greene's (or Chettle's) parody of a line from the latter, published in September 1592, as part of his attack on Shakespeare; also for the drafting of *Taming of a Shrew*, which, according to its title page, had been 'sundry times' acted by Pembroke's Men. On the renewed closure of the theatres at the end of January, Pembroke's Men embarked on a tour which appears to have ended in near financial disaster.[12] Strange's Men went on a more successful tour but similarly fell apart following the death of its patron in February 1594. Both companies were in effect replaced by a new company, the Chamberlain's Men, formed when the theatres eventually reopened early in 1594, who were generally able to lay claim to the ownership of those early plays written for them by Shakespeare and other playwrights, often in collaboration.

Sussex's Men, the third company said to have performed *Titus Andronicus*, is indeed on record, in Henslowe's Diary, as having played it at the Rose on three occasions in January and February 1594, but again only a few months before it was recorded in the Chamberlain's Men repertory.[13] Sussex's Men had been well established since the mid-1570s, although its appearance at court over the winter of 1592/3 was the first recorded in the capital since 1581. Nevertheless there is a clear implication that it was London-based when it was granted permission to travel in April 1593, as was Strange's Men, following the plague closure. However, after its brief reappearance at the Rose early in 1594, it too disappears from the records for some ten years.

This chaotic period, then, triggered by the closure of the theatres due to plague over the period 1592 to 1594, was characterized by the splitting up, dissolution, amalgamation, and re-formation of various troupes which, deprived of their London patronage, were struggling

---

11. Gurr, *Shakespearian Playing Companies*, p. 267.
12. But that this was not as terminal as is sometimes argued, see Somerset, 'Not just Sir Oliver Owlet: from Patrons to "Patronage" of early modern theatre', pp. 345–7.
13. Foakes, ed., *Henslowe's Diary*, p. 21.

to meet the challenge of a serious drop in income. Sorting out quite what was happening is made worse by an almost complete lack of reliable information at this time on the personnel of both Pembroke's and Sussex's Men. Attempts have been made to reconstruct Pembroke's personnel, drawing mainly on the names of legatees in the will of August 1592 of Simon Jewell, a member of the Queen's Men thought to have had links with Pembroke's, but this has by no means been accepted.[14] Such uncertainty is not the case with Strange's. When licensed to go on tour in May 1593, six members (almost certainly its sharers) were specifically named—Edward Alleyn, William Kemp, Thomas Pope, John Heminges, Augustine Phillips, and George Bryan. The fact that five of these six men went on to form the nucleus of the Chamberlain's Men certainly suggests continuity between the two companies. However, this does not establish that any of Shakespeare's plays were written specifically for them. If we accept, for reasons already given, that Shakespeare's contribution to *3 Henry VI* post-dated the formation of the Chamberlain's Men, and that otherwise the indications are that Shakespeare wrote several plays specifically for Pembroke's (or so the title pages would suggest), then his earlier attachment to Strange's Men is far from certain. There is also the consideration that Henslowe's diary, which provides a more or less complete record of the Strange's Men's repertory for the year 1592, and by inference much of 1591, included none of Shakespeare's plays.[15]

In terms of Shakespeare's allegiance to any one of these companies at any one time, this discussion is to some extent academic, as the plays he had written, or contributed to, were almost certainly not his property. At that date the ownership of any play would normally have become vested in the commissioner or purchaser of the script—usually the dramatic company by whom it was then performed. When a company broke, or re-formed, as frequently happened in the years before the Chamberlain's Men emerged, ownership of its plays would presumably either have been sold to another company or simply taken by the majority of the shareholders who went on to form, or amalgamate

---

14. George, 'Shakespeare and Pembroke's Men'; Gurr, *Shakespearian Playing Companies*, pp. 267–9.
15. I am grateful to Martin Wiggins for pointing this out. However, for a recent and strongly argued case that Shakespeare initially wrote for Strange's Men, see Manley and MacLean, *Lord Strange's Men*, esp. pp. 280–320.

with, another company. As a result, even if it could be established that official ownership of the 'Shakespeare' plays was vested either in Pembroke's Men or Strange's Men, to be taken by them into the Chamberlain's Men, it does not follow that Shakespeare himself was only ever attached to those two companies. Indeed, another company in the running is the once-influential Queen's Men, but which by the late 1580s had split into two troupes and by 1591/92 had lost any claim to pre-eminence. The claim that Shakespeare might have been attached to this company stems largely from the fact that several of its playbooks found their way into the hands of the Chamberlain's Men, including four, dating from the late 1580s, which Shakespeare, it has been argued, drew on, or even revised, as *Richard III*, *Henry V*, *King Lear*, and *King John*.[16]

Such uncertainties, not to say speculation, only serve to underline Shakespeare's minor standing during this period. If he were still only a hired man, he would not necessarily have figured in lists of sharers anyway and it could even be that, in this period of crisis, his services as actor and writer were no longer required, leading him to seek alternative means of support, as discussed below (pp. 40–2). Turning, then, to the issue of Shakespeare's income during this early period, it is not unlikely that, even as late as 1592/93, he may still have routinely enjoyed only the wage of a hired man, not more than around 6 shillings a week, but often much less if daily takings had been bad, or none at all when the theatres were closed as the result of plague. As for his work as a playwright, if, like his contemporaries, he had simply been selling his scripts to the company which employed him as an actor, he is unlikely to have earned more than other freelance writers selling their work from outside. We can get some idea of how much this might have been from a later source, Philip Henslowe's so-called 'Diary', recording, later in the decade and as manager of the Rose and Fortune Theatres, his income and outgoings as middleman between the companies and playwrights, paying out, at the former's request, specific sums for the purchase of plays by named writers. In 1598, the first complete year for which details survive, Henslowe bought forty-three scripts in this way, paying for the vast majority £7 or less.[17] Moreover, as nearly all these plays were collaborative

16. This is discussed in McMillin and MacLean, *Queen's Men*, pp. 160–6.
17. Foakes, ed., *Henslowe's Diary*, pp. 85–103.

efforts, the fees often had to be divided between three, sometimes more, contributors. This did not prevent prolific writers from earning a good wage: Thomas Dekker, involved in the writing of seventeen of these plays (of two of which, *Triplicity of Cuckolds* and *Phaeton*, he was sole author) pocketed at least £43 in 1598.[18] This was a very substantial sum, though it did not prevent his imprisonment for debt that year, a fate shared by his prolific colleague Henry Chettle.[19] We cannot be sure, of course, that this method and rate of payment in the late 1590s was generally typical of the situation a decade earlier but, if Shakespeare, over the five or so years up to 1594, had been paid for only the seven or eight scripts of plays to which his name was later attached, it is hard to believe that this would have netted him a living wage, especially as three, or possibly four, were collaborations.[20] His closer association as an actor with one of the playing companies, even as a hired man, was therefore, financially speaking, probably more important to him. This would suggest in turn that he would have written for that same company too: otherwise, he would in effect have been freelancing to the benefit of potential rivals. Given that the corpus of Strange's Men went on to form the Chamberlain's, Shakespeare's link with them may at first sight be proposed with some degree of confidence. On the other hand, the close link between Pembroke's Men and at least four of Shakespeare's early plays, as discussed above (pp. 35–6), would have put him in a different camp from at least the summer of 1591. Either way, and given that in any case his links with a particular company might have been temporarily broken during the plague closure period, his skills as a writer had clearly been sufficiently demonstrated to encourage the group of largely ex-Strange players to recruit him in the late spring of 1594 as their 'resident playwright' and a sharer in the profits of their new company, the Chamberlain's Men.

---

18. Bearing in mind that a playwright might be earning money from other sources but on the other hand that 1598 was a year which witnessed something of a spike in the number of new plays acquired (Wiggins, *British Drama, 1533–1642: a Catalogue*, iii, pp. xii–xiii; iv, pp. xi–xiii).

19. Foakes, ed., *Henslowe's Diary*, pp. 86, 103.

20. The extent of Shakespeare's collaborations in these early years is conveniently summarized by John Jowett in 'Shakespeare as Collaborator', esp. pp. 88–92, who considers that *Edward III* (published in 1595) is a play to which Shakespeare may have contributed but does not endorse the argument that *3 Henry VI* was collaborative.

A search for patronage?

Whether or not, before 1594, Shakespeare enjoyed formal sharer status in any company, his income would have been severely curtailed during much of the early 1590s due to the closure of the London theatres whilst the plague was rampant. Even though the first official order to close the London theatres was not issued until January 1593, there is very little evidence of public performances in London after the end of June the previous year, several companies, including Pembroke's and Strange's Men, as already explained, then preferring to go on tour. If Shakespeare had been invited to accompany them, or any other company, he would have benefited from an income of some sort but generally lower than in the capital, to the extent, as in the case of Pembroke's, of drying up altogether. If he had not gone on tour, this would have happened anyway. The London theatres reopened briefly at Christmas 1593 but were again ordered to close the following February. It was only in April 1594 that normality returned.[21]

During this difficult period there are indications that Shakespeare turned his hand to another means of raising money, that is by the writing and arranging for the publication of two substantial poems, *Venus and Adonis*, entered in the Stationers' Register on 18 April 1593, dedicated to the nineteen-year-old Henry Wriothesley, earl of Southampton, and *The Rape of Lucrece*, which appeared in May the following year, also dedicated to the earl. This has led some to propose that Southampton became Shakespeare's patron, especially as the second dedication is in a warmer vein than the first. No doubt some financial advantage would have been in Shakespeare's mind when he took the liberty of requesting permission to make these dedications. The young earl's father had died in 1581, the wardship of his under-age heir passing soon afterwards to Lord Burghley. By 1592 Southampton was on the verge of coming of age and, given that he is known to have had (or at least developed) an interest in poetry and the theatre,[22] he might well have been thought a likely source of future patronage, once he had assumed

21. Chambers, *Elizabethan Stage*, iv, pp. 310–15; Gurr, *The Shakespearian Playing Companies*, pp. 91, 274, 276.
22. Based largely, it seems, on evidence of 1599: Duncan-Jones, *Ungentle Shakespeare*, p. 108.

control of his estates. This had clearly also occurred to Thomas Nashe whose book, *The Unfortunate Traveller*, entered in the Stationers' Register in September 1593, a few months after *Venus and Adonis*, was also dedicated to the young earl whom he hailed flatteringly, and perhaps hopefully, as a 'dere louer and cherisher...as well of the louers of Poets, as of Poets themselues.'[23] Any hopes of practical help cannot, however, be shown to have been fulfilled. Southampton proved never to have had large sums of money to hand, due partly to the adverse effect on the family's resources caused by his father's recusancy but compounded by a considerable fine which Burghley, as his guardian, is thought to have demanded from him on his refusal to marry a bride of Burghley's choosing, namely his own granddaughter. The queen's grave displeasure provoked by his marriage instead to Elizabeth Vernon, one of her maids of honour, and his later association with Essex's rebellion and his (Southampton's) subsequent imprisonment, would in any case have rendered him a liability as a patron rather than an asset. It can certainly be argued that John Florio enjoyed the earl's direct patronage: in his dedication to *A Worlde of Wordes*, an Italian-English dictionary, eventually published in 1598, Florio paid tribute to the earl 'in whose paie and patronage I haue lived some yeeres.'[24] But to argue from this, in the absence of other contemporary evidence, that Shakespeare enjoyed similar favour, remains pure speculation. The warmer tone of the dedication to the *Rape of Lucrece* of 1594 certainly does suggest personal contact between the two men since the publication of *Venus and Adonis* the year before. It has also been argued, far less convincingly, that the theme of the early Sonnets 1–17, that of urging a young man to marry, might reflect the pressure on Southampton at that time to take to wife the girl that Burghley had chosen for him—though whether a commoner might ever have presumed to have offered such unwelcome advice to a peer of the realm whose patronage he was intending to seek is surely very unlikely. In any event, whatever the relationship between the two men in 1593–94, there is no evidence that it was perpetuated. As to any immediate financial advantage, there is a similar dearth. Nearly seventy years later there was talk of Southampton having given Shakespeare the preposterously large sum

23. STC 18380.
24. Publication had been mooted as early as March 1596, with Southampton named as the sole patron, though when published three others were included: STC 11098; Akrigg, *Shakespeare and the Earl of Southampton*, p. 53.

of £1000 to set him up in his career, but it is not difficult to see how, over the years, such a story could have evolved simply through an imaginative misinterpretation of the dedications.[25] He would have received payment from Stratford-born Richard Field, his printer and initially his publisher, on handing over his manuscripts, but, before the days of author copyright, it would have been Field and his successors, as owners of the publication rights, and not Shakespeare, who would benefit from the extraordinary success of *Venus and Adonis* in particular, which was reprinted five times before the decade was out. We might wonder whether Shakespeare would have been able to negotiate a better price for *Lucrece* if he had waited for the commercial value of *Venus and Adonis* to have become fully apparent. But the sequence of events suggests a less considered process. Early in 1594, it seems, he handed over his new poem to Field, who then enlisted John Harrison, the bookseller, to act as publisher, the latter registering its title on 9 May 1594. Then, on 25 June, Field assigned the copyright of *Venus and Adonis* to Harrison as well,[26] and it was he who published it in its second edition in the summer, though still acknowledging Field as printer. Perhaps if Shakespeare had waited on this second edition, it would have turned *Lucrece* into a more valuable product. On the other hand, that he did not do so may indicate a more immediate need for funds and that, if Southampton had made a practical response to Shakespeare's dedications, it had been only a token one. In short, it is unlikely that this venture actually netted Shakespeare much in the way of ready money or secured him any long-term guarantee of patronage.[27] Indeed, as already explained, the instability which characterized Southampton's later behaviour would have considerably reduced his potential as a patron. By the time of Southampton's release from prison, at the start of James I's reign, Shakespeare in any case had no need of direct aristocratic patronage. Nevertheless, this would not rule out the idea that Shakespeare used any money he did receive, either from Southampton or Field, to help him with the expense of buying himself into the Chamberlain's Men.

25. The story is first recorded by Nicholas Rowe in 1709, having been handed down, he was assured, by William Davenant: Chambers, *William Shakespeare*, ii, pp. 266–7.
26. Arber, *Registers of the Company of Stationers*, ii, p. 655.
27. It cannot even be argued that Field remained a sympathetic supporter of Shakespeare's interests. Instead, two years later, he signed the petition against the extension of the Chamberlain's (Hunsdon's) Men's operations into Blackfriars (below, p. 101).

As a Chamberlain's Man

Shortly afterwards Shakespeare did feel the indirect benefit of aristocratic patronage when Henry Carey, the Lord Chamberlain, agreed
to act as patron of the new company of which Shakespeare was to
become a sharer, put together when the theatres reopened in the
spring of 1594. Henry Carey, Baron Hunsdon since 1559 and Lord
Chamberlain since 1585, had been patron of companies of players,
albeit intermittently, since 1564, the latest of which, on his appointment as Lord Chamberlain, had briefly taken on the name of the
Chamberlain's Men. However, this company is not known to have
been operational after 1588 and the body which emerged in the late
spring of 1594 was to all intents and purposes a new one. Whilst
Carey's theatrical interests were clearly of long standing, his willingness, in his late sixties, to take on this new commitment was probably
less to do with any wish to bestow particular favour on the members
of this new enterprise than it was to the requirement on him, as Lord
Chamberlain, to guarantee a source of good quality court entertainments, especially over the Christmas period. There had been particular difficulties over this in the early 1590s, exacerbated by the theatre
closures due to plague. Carey's decision to put this new company
under his protection, whether his own idea or in response to an
approach from the players themselves, is therefore better interpreted
as a practical and opportunistic solution to one of his governmental
duties rather than as an expression of favour to the company. This is
not to say, of course, that the Chamberlain's Men did not benefit
from Carey's protection. There was already a long history of struggle
between the City of London, keen to suppress the theatres, and the
Privy Council, mindful of the need to nurture theatrical companies
if it were to meet its obligation to provide the court with entertainment.
In the periodic outburst of activity on this front Carey's patronage
must therefore have been a welcome shield, especially when it additionally involved regular and profitable invitations to perform at
court. But the unreliability of such arrangements became quickly
apparent on Carey's death in July 1596. His son George did not
immediately succeed to the office of Lord Chamberlain which probably explains why, around November 1596, he felt able to sign the
petition against his own company, now known simply as Hunsdon's

Men, taking up residence in the Blackfriars Theatre.[28] It was only when he was appointed Lord Chamberlain in April 1597 that the need to protect the interests of the re-christened Chamberlain's Men once again became an issue for him. Four years later friends in high places might have been of particular value when the earl of Essex commissioned a performance of *Richard II* on the eve of his ill-fated attempt to overthrow the government and seize the queen. In the aftermath there was an investigation into the possibility that the company, in agreeing to perform this play at such a sensitive time, might in fact have been complicit in the plot. George Carey's favoured position at court may therefore well have been a factor in the company's subsequent exoneration.[29] But it is stretching the point to interpret protection of this sort as patronage in the sense that Shakespeare and his fellow sharers derived any immediate financial gain. The endorsement of the company by successive Lord Chamberlains, for practical reasons of their own, was no doubt useful, but it did not absolve the company from the need to make its own way.[30]

Once Shakespeare had become a sharer in the newly formed Chamberlain's Men, we can speak with a little more confidence about the income he might have derived from his theatrical work. If he had not been a full partner in one of the companies with which he had worked in the early 1590s, he certainly was by the end of 1594 when, with Richard Burbage (James Burbage's son) and other previous associates in both Strange's (Derby's) Men and Pembroke's Men, he emerges as a known sharer in the profits of the Chamberlain's Men. From what can be gleaned from the meagre evidence available, a sharer was normally required to buy himself into the company, thereby undertaking to help meet production costs, not least by acting in a number of roles. The precise sum involved for the investment in such a share at this time is not known, but an initial figure of between £50 and £80 has been proposed, based on occasional references to share values in other companies.[31] In return, such a purchaser would be entitled to a share in the receipts (once production costs and the rent of

28. Below, pp. 101–2.
29. Chambers, *William Shakespeare*, ii, pp. 323–7.
30. The issue of possible later patronage by the earls of Pembroke and Montgomery is discussed below, pp. 53–4.
31. Gurr, *Shakespeare Company*, pp. 89, 108.

premises had been met), the size depending on the number of share-holders. There are no surviving accounts for the Chamberlain's Men, nor even a record of the number of performances given or the size of the playhouse in which they initially performed. Nevertheless, from patchy records relating to other companies, it has been calculated that initially the eight sharers in the Chamberlain's Men might each year, in the period 1594 to 1597, have divided about £435 between them, that is, to have received about £50 each. This, then, might have been Shakespeare's annual income in the years immediately following the formation of the Chamberlain's Men.

There are, however, some unknowns. In the crisis years of 1592–94 there are, in fact, no records to establish that potential sharers were required to invest capital sums in a particular company in the way which later became standard practice. A proven track record as an actor or, additionally in Shakespeare's case, as a writer of income-generating plays, might have been more persuasive during negotiations over the formation of a new company, albeit one that inherited some of its costumes and stage furniture from those companies it replaced. But, whatever the understanding reached between the sharers, it clearly led to Shakespeare writing a succession of plays exclusively for the Chamberlain's Men at the rate, initially, of two or three a year. This could have been arranged by way of a formal contract under which Shakespeare, in return for writing a stipulated number of plays, was excused from having to buy himself in. Alternatively, as Shakespeare is unlikely to have had to hand the very large sum necessary to invest in a share, he could have raised it by borrowing on the security of the anticipated income derived not only from his share in the company profits but, in return for one-off fees, from writing plays for the company of which he had become a member. Either way, and this is hardly surprising, the writing of plays for his company was not some-thing he simply chose to do—thereby involving himself in more work than his fellow sharers—but was taken on as a means either of meeting contractual obligations as an 'in-house playwright', or of pay-ing off his creditors more quickly. In assessing which is more likely, it is important to remember, tempting though it might be with hind-sight to overlook this, that the company would never simply be a vehicle for Shakespeare's work. Even at the rate of two or three plays a year, this would have been a very small contribution to the company's repertory which in any one year might require the acquisition of twenty new scripts.[32] Shakespeare's work may have been felt to have brought the company greater prestige, particularly in the context of court performances, but this does not mean that as public spectacles they were any more successful (and therefore income-generating) than other plays, albeit that some of them have not even survived as published texts. Although it is still likely that Shakespeare's fellow sharers would urge him to continue to write and produce plays for what we might call the upper end of the market, this would have been on the understanding that he would only be paid for taking on this additional task at a rate thought by the company to be commercially realistic. This arrangement would not be quite so one-sided as it might at first appear. Shakespeare would have a more or less assured outlet for what plays he was able to write, and their commercial success would add to his income as a sharer in his company's profits. Also, his fellow sharers would not wish to drive him from their camp into a rival company's by declining to pay him a good rate for his work. Friction might arise, for instance, should it ever be thought that Shakespeare was not fulfilling his primary duty as an actor/sharer, namely that of taking leading parts in his company's repertory. There is evidence that he did play his part in this respect. Apart from the listing of his name in the First Folio of 1623 as one of 'the Principall Actors in all these Playes', he is twice cited as an actor in exactly contemporary sources.[33] However, later in his career he is not as well documented in this respect as many of his fellows at a time when his literary output was also in decline. This will be discussed later, but, in the early years, there is no evidence that a business agreement along the lines suggested above did not work well for both parties.

This arrangement—a sharer writing exclusively for his company over a long period—proved to be very unusual, indeed all but unique. It may have been that some playwrights for a period of time were tied to a company even though the best-known detailed contract to have survived between playwright and theatre company—binding Richard

32. For the known repertory until 1613, see Knutson, *Repertory of Shakespeare's Company*, esp. pp. 179–209; and, as part of a complete repertory, Gurr, *Shakespeare Company*, pp. 282–5. Only some eighty plays are known by their titles (estimates vary slightly and there would have been many more) but of these Shakespeare was the author of, or collaborator in, only some half.

33. The evidence, set against the record of his fellow sharers, is conveniently presented in Chambers, *William Shakespeare*, ii, pp. 71–7.

Brome to write exclusively for the manager of the indoor theatre, the Salisbury Court, at the rate of three plays a year for three years in return for an annual income of £39—dates only from 1635.[34] Evidence of earlier contracts do survive, one from 1572 binding Rowland Broughton to write no less than eighteen plays over two and half years,[35] and it is clear that some playwrights, at least for certain periods in their careers, must have had an understanding with particular companies which limited their ability to freelance.[36] In the case of Shakespeare's company, for instance, we have a succession of playwrights who wrote almost exclusively for the King's Men from the date of Shakespeare's retirement. But their careers do not provide an exact parallel with Shakespeare's for he was also a sharer (and actor) in the company for which he wrote. The closest parallel here is the case of Thomas Heywood, who was both a sharer in, and 'resident playwright' for, Worcester's Men (renamed the Queen's Men in 1603) for the first fifteen years or so of the seventeenth century. Less clear-cut are the careers of other actor/playwrights such as William Rowley, Samuel Rowley, and Nathan Field, but in no case can it be shown that they worked for one company over a prolonged period.[37]

This serves to emphasize what we might, somewhat anachronistically, term Shakespeare's essential professionalism. Of all the known authors of plays during the years 1590 to 1642, some had only one or two plays to their name, written with no commercial considerations in mind. Even the work of the better-known playwrights was written by men with other strings to their bows. Ben Jonson, from at least 1602, enjoyed the favour of wealthy patrons and from 1604 the benefits arising from his production of a series of lavish court entertainments. Francis Beaumont, from a family of landed gentry, might for a short period have written plays for the King's Men but married an heiress and then withdrew from the theatrical world. George Chapman showed similar short outbursts of theatrical activity but, like Jonson, enjoyed

34. For this, and the discussion of the implications for the earlier period, see Bentley, *Profession of Dramatist in Shakespeare's Time*, pp. 111–42.
35. Ioppolo, *Dramatists and their Manuscripts*, p. 20.
36. Exclusive contracts have also been proposed for Henry Porter, 28 February 1599, and Henry Chettle, 25 March 1602 (Knutson, *Playing Companies*, p. 55) based on brief entries in Henslowe's 'Diary' (pp. 105, 199). The second of these is suggestive, but the first seems linked to Porter's indebtedness to Henslowe (*Diary*, pp. 242, 265–6).
37. For Heywood and Field, and Robert Armin and Anthony Munday, see Johnson, *The Actor as Playwright in Early Modern Drama*.

sporadic aristocratic patronage and was as well known, and better respected, for his poetic output. John Marston, after a seven- or eight-year career in the theatre, withdrew from the scene around 1607, often attributed to his marriage to the daughter of one of James I's favourite chaplains, to pursue a safer option as a cleric. Even Thomas Middleton, though a prolific author of plays sold to a variety of companies, had other interests, and from 1620 an income as the City of London Chronologer. This leaves only some twenty-five writers who are known to have written regularly for established playing companies and of these, only eight, including Shakespeare, who can be regarded as dependent on such activity over long periods, characterized by a prolonged and professional attachment to particular companies.[38]

The Richard Brome contract, with the caveat that it dates from the 1630s, reveals another limitation of the exclusive agreement Brome reached with the theatre company, namely that during the period of the engagement he would not arrange for his plays to be printed without the consent of the company. As no other such specific contracts have survived we cannot safely argue that earlier playwrights were similarly bound, but the pattern of publication clearly implies that such limitations existed—or rather that a company, once the script had become its property, would not generally wish that play to be published whilst it was in production and thus a valuable commodity. With its run completed, however, the company might well decide that its sale to a publisher might raise some capital as well as serve as a form of general advertising if its name (and the author's) were included on the title page. In Shakespeare's case, his output was certainly thought to have had commercial potential: indeed, it has been calculated that over the period 1594–1600, he was theoretically the author of the highest proportion (25 per cent) of the new plays published during this period.[39] Some of these may have been unauthorized, but modern scholarship has moved steadily towards a general acceptance that the publication of playbooks was not a contentious issue but reflected instead mutually advantageous commercial arrangements between theatrical companies

---

38. Bentley, *Profession of Dramatist in Shakespeare's Time*. Bentley's views are now thought to have contributed to the impression that playwrights were generally exploited by the theatrical industry, but his statistical data would still seem to be valid.

39. Farmer and Lesser, 'The popularity of playbooks revisited', p. 11. Lukas Erne arrives at roughly the same figure (*Shakespeare as Literary Dramatist*, p. 271). For similar predominance, including reprints, see Erne, *Shakespeare and the Book Trade*, p. 43.

and stationers. In other words, given that revivals were by no means common, and that instances of one company performing a play that had originally been commissioned by another were rare, there was little point in standing in the way of a play's publication once it had ceased its run on stage—the contrary, in fact, if some money could be made by selling it.[40] Quite how Shakespeare might have benefited from this, however, is less clear. Thomas Heywood, who like Shakespeare was an actor/playwright and sharer, but in Worcester's (Queen Anne's) Men, implied, in 1608, that he could have derived direct benefit through having his plays printed, though he declined to do so; 'for though some haue vsed a double sale of their labours, first to the Stage, and after to the presse, For my owne part I heere proclaime my selfe euer faithfull in the first [in his case, the Queen Anne's company], and neuer guiltie of the last', going on to explain that any of his plays which had been printed had been done, 'corrupt and mangled, (copied onely by the eare)', without his knowledge.[41] Whether Heywood can always be taken at his word has been called into question,[42] but, on the other hand, if the company itself had decided to sell, then a playwright in Shakespeare's position (namely, a sharer in the company for which the play had been written) might well have taken a different view, expecting either a cut at the time of sale or, more likely, a higher fee for writing the play in the first place. Such a fee could rise over time if stationers continued to show an interest in a particular playwright's work or, of course, become more difficult to negotiate if such interest fell away.

To anticipate later developments, Shakespeare's 'bestselling' status might not, however, have been quite what it at first appears. His name does not occur on a title page until 1598 and, notwithstanding that over the next five years another nine of his plays appeared in print, there was a clear falling away thereafter. Precise calculations are not easy, but, of the plays written before 1601, about a dozen appeared in print[43] whilst only some six (including three of his earliest works)

---

40. Blayney, 'Publication of Playbooks', pp. 383–422. However, Martin Wiggins has reminded me that a few plays (for example, *Edward IV*, written in August 1599 and entered in the Stationer's Register the same month) were clearly published whilst still in production.
41. From the preface to his *Rape of Lucrece* (STC 13360).
42. Erne, *Shakespeare as Literary Dramatist*, pp. 147–50.
43. Erne, including *Edward III*, gives fourteen (*Shakespeare as Literary Dramatist*, p. 271).

remained unpublished. In the longer period from 1601 until his death, however, the figures are roughly reversed, with only some half dozen reaching the public in printed form, whilst twice that number remained unpublished until the appearance of the First Folio. Whilst it was once thought that this was the result of his company's wish to keep a tighter control of his plays, it would now seem more likely that stationers, after a period of willingness to buy scripts over the years 1598–1603—eight first editions of plays attributed to Shakespeare appeared during those years—no longer regarded the publication of his work as necessarily profitable. Only three plays, published by Andrew Wise in the initial flurry (*Henry IV, Part I*, in 1598, and *Richard II* and *Richard III* in 1597), with their multiple re-printings within twenty-five years, proved to be real money-spinners.[44] Of his other plays, only *Hamlet* ran to a second printing within a year. Even if subsequent scripts had been offered for publication, there was therefore no guarantee that the offer would be enthusiastically taken up. Nor were large sums of money at stake, if the estimate is correct that a publisher is unlikely to have paid more than £2 for copy for a print run of 800.[45] More likely, then, that Shakespeare, though he may have been well paid for the scripts which he produced, especially in the early part of his career, was always aware that it was his status as sharer/housekeeper in the most financially successful company of his day which over the years was going to yield the most important and consistent element of his income. If the going rate for a script was £7, which could perhaps be negotiated upwards if his company thought it of high commercial value, but which would also fall if, as later proved the case, it was written in collaboration, then this would be dwarfed by the profits he was to receive as a sharer/householder (as much as £200 a year), discussed in more detail later.[46]

Recent scholarship has also reminded us that in these early years playwrights were not necessarily regarded as the 'authors' of the plays. The play as presented on the public stage, or at court, was a collaborative effort coordinated by the company which performed it and

44. Blayney, 'Publication of playbooks', pp. 387–8. For Wise, see Hooks, 'Wise Ventures: Shakespeare and Thomas Playfere'.
45. Blayney, 'Publication of playbooks', p. 396. For the view that the publication of play-books was never a stationer's main source of income see also Syme, 'Thomas Creede, William Barley, and the venture of printing plays', pp. 44–6.
46. Below, pp. 147–50. In particular, it had become apparent that by the time of Shakespeare's death, the going rate for a playwright's fee had more than doubled.

thus reaped the principal financial (and reputational) benefit. The person who provided the script was therefore but a cog in the machine, in Shakespeare's case certainly an important cog as he would have also acted in most of them and assisted in their production, but a cog nevertheless. In particular, it has been shown, by a close study of the imperfectly printed versions of his plays, that the altered and untidy state of the manuscripts on which many of these were based must have reflected his close involvement in the production process.[47] But this does not mean that he necessarily cherished the idea that he was the author of the play, in the sense that we would understand it, and thus that he deserved particular credit. Ben Jonson's well-known determination in 1616 to publish in book form his 'complete' dramatic and poetic works to date may have struck the first obvious blow in the growing recognition of playwrights as the 'authors' of the plays for which they had provided the scripts. There is no material evidence, however, that Shakespeare shared such views or that he ever regarded himself as occupying a more elevated position in the company than that of a fellow actor/sharer who took on the additional role of contributing a good proportion of scripts to the company's repertory.[48] It has been strongly argued, based on the clear evidence that some plays, in the form they have come down to us, were too long to be performed within the generally agreed two to three hours available at the public theatres, that Shakespeare increasingly wrote with his eye on eventual publication and his reputation as a literary dramatist, and that how his plays would be read on the page was as important to him as how they would be interpreted within the constraints of a performance on the public stage.[49] However, whilst it is generally accepted that the abridgement of many of the longer texts would have to have taken place to fit them into a two- to three-hour performance slot (as is still the case), it is by no means as easy to establish that this stemmed from a deliberate policy on Shakespeare's part to create a literary text worthy of publication in its own right irrespective of whether or not it had to be cut down for performance. Indeed, there is no evidence that Shakespeare took any interest at all in the publication of his texts

47. See in particular, Ioppolo, *Dramatists and their Manuscripts*, pp. 174–84.
48. Research on this issue is summarized by Heather Hirschfeld, in '"For the Author's Credit": issues of authorship in English Renaissance Drama', pp. 441–55, esp. pp. 445–7, but see also Johnson, *The Actor as Playwright in Early Modern Drama*, esp. pp. 152–67.
49. Erne, *Shakespeare as Literary Dramatist*, reaffirmed in his *Shakespeare and the Book Trade*.

which his company might have sold to the stationers. Some dramatists, clearly working more closely with their publishers, were, increasingly from the early seventeenth century, at some pains to have dedications and other prefatory material included to emphasize their authorship. Ben Jonson and John Marston were the leaders in the field in this respect with a succession of addresses to the readers from 1602, followed by Thomas Dekker from 1604 and Thomas Heywood from 1608.[50] Shakespeare's colleagues were to do the same for him, of course, but not until the early 1620s, when they put his plays together in the posthumous First Folio. However, during his lifetime, Shakespeare's indifference to the publication process is to a great extent implied— though not universally accepted[51]—by the textual imperfections of the versions of the plays which were allowed to reach the public in printed form and by the absence of any evidence of his personal involvement. None is dedicated to a patron and only one, *Troilus and Cressida*, which appeared in 1609, carries an address to the reader. This was not by Shakespeare, however, but presumably by one of his publishers (it is not signed off) who goes to some length to distance his publication from a mere play which would have been 'clapper-clawd with the palmes of the vulger' and 'sullied with the smoaky breath of the multitude.' Even if Shakespeare had become frustrated at the limitations imposed by writing play texts, it is hardly likely, in this particular instance, that he would have connived at insulting his theatrical audience. And in the context of this present discussion—what effect did this have on his income—it is largely an irrelevance. If, as the publication data clearly indicate, Shakespeare's play texts did not generally sell in sufficient numbers to justify more than one edition and that after 1603 there was in any case a clear falling away of the number of his plays published, any financial advantages must also have been compromised as well. It was only in 1623, seven years after his death, that his friends and colleagues were to publish his plays, in what seemed to them the most satisfactory manner, as proof of his literary genius and as an expression of their debt. Whether Shakespeare would have thought this tribute was well overdue remains a matter of speculation but, however well known and better appreciated Shakespeare might

---

50. Helpfully tabulated in Bergeron, *Textual Patronage in English Drama*, pp. 216–20.
51. See, for instance, Bruster, 'Shakespeare the Stationer', esp. pp. 124–30, where it is argued that Shakespeare was actively involved in efforts to sell his scripts.

have become during his lifetime—becoming thereby a better risk for the publisher—evidence that he ever tried to capitalize on this is singularly lacking.

The dedication of the First Folio, however, does again raise the issue of patronage. Here we read that John Heminges and Henry Condell, the effectual editors, chose to seek the particular support of William Herbert, earl of Pembroke, and his brother Philip, earl of Montgomery, as two lords who have thought 'these trifles [Shakespeare's plays] something, heeretofore; and haue prosequuted both them, and their Authour liuing, with so much favour' that 'you will vse the like indulgence toward them [the plays], [as] you have done vnto their parent... For, so much were your L.L. [Lordships] likings of the seuerall parts, when they were acted, as before they were published, the Volume ask'd to be yours.' Can this be interpreted as evidence that Shakespeare received any direct assistance from either man? Pembroke was the foremost literary patron of his day with more works dedicated to him than to any other during the early years of the seventeenth century and who, with his brother, Philip, and mother, Mary Lady Herbert, maintained the family residence, Wilton House, as a centre of distinguished literary and cultural activity. Indeed, in December 1603, the King's Men had been summoned to perform there, in the presence of James I, though whether a Shakespeare play was presented is not known.[52] On his appointment as Lord Chamberlain in December 1615, Pembroke had become directly responsible for the provision and supervision of court entertainment, so important to the King's Men's finances. Amongst those to whom he is also known to have provided direct financial assistance was Ben Jonson, who received an annuity of £20 to buy books, and other writers and artists thought to have been actively patronized were George Chapman, Edward Alleyn, and, important in this discussion, Richard Burbage: on Burbage's death, in March 1619, Pembroke excused himself from attending a play at court 'so soone after the loss of my old acquaintance Burbadg'.[53] His younger brother, Philip Herbert, another of James I's leading courtiers (he was appointed a Gentleman of the Bedchamber in 1603) and earl of Montgomery since 1605, was also a noted literary patron, with a total of forty works dedicated to him, ten in conjunction with Pembroke, whom he was to

52. Below, p. 118; and Chambers, *William Shakespeare*, ii, p. 329.
53. Quoted by Mary Edmond in 'Burbage, Richard', *ODNB*, viii, p. 718.

succeed as Lord Chamberlain in 1626. Clearly, then, both men would have been well acquainted with the King's Men, and the work of its principal dramatist, and Pembroke's continuing favour as Lord Chamberlain would also be critical to the company's fortunes, most notably in ensuring regular invitations to perform at court. In 1619 Herbert had also written to the Stationers Company to the effect that none of the plays performed by the King's Men should be printed 'wthout the consent of some of them.'[54] Whether or not this was in specific response to the flurry of Shakespeare texts then being published by Thomas Pavier—so compromising the 'First Folio' project—has been much debated, but, whatever its origin, it was clearly an intervention on the company's behalf to protect its interests in some way. Looked at in this way, the dedication can be read at least in part as a means of keeping Pembroke and his brother well disposed towards the company, exploiting their fond remembrances of the work of its principal writer as a means of holding on to their goodwill. This was not their only motive, of course, and Heminges and Condell were no doubt sincere in their wish to offer a tribute to the man who had done so much for them. However, reminding Pembroke and his brother of their favourable reception of Shakespeare's work does not establish that in his lifetime they ever treated Shakespeare with any marked favour and that they can therefore be seen as 'patrons'—except in the limited sense that, as with James I's 'patronage', the protection of, and promotion by, those moving in the highest circles of government was bound to be of benefit.

A suggestion has also been made that, prior to publication, some of Shakespeare's plays might have circulated in manuscript which, if commissioned by a wealthy patron, could have brought in substantial fees, though to whose benefit—Shakespeare's or the Chamberlain's (King's) Men—is not made clear.[55] There is some evidence of this practice at a later date, at least in the case of other playwrights, but the only hint that one of Shakespeare's plays might have been circulating in this way is Gabriel Harvey's reference to 'Shakespeares... Hamlet' in a note which was seemingly made at some point between 1598 and 1601, that is, at a time when it was not yet in print.[56] If Harvey had not seen the

54. See Erne, Shakespeare and the Book Trade, p. 176, and the books and articles there cited.
55. Erne, Shakespeare as Literary Dramatist, pp. 114, 284–6.
56. Chambers, William Shakespeare, ii, pp. 196–8.

play or was not relying on the hearsay of 'the wiser sort' who *had* seen it, then a manuscript copy could have prompted such a remark. But to go beyond this and suggest that Harvey had had access to a manuscript copy sufficiently prestigious to have been commissioned by a wealthy patron, is, to say the least, unconvincing.

A freelance writer?

Returning, then, to the 1590s, and the nature of any contractual understanding between Shakespeare and his company, we have still to consider whether this would have allowed him to augment his income through further freelance writing. However, of this there is little persuasive evidence. There is no reason, for instance, to think that he was involved in, let alone profited by, the publication of *The Passionate Pilgrim*, a collection of twenty poems published in 1599 which on its title page the printer, William Jaggard, attributed to Shakespeare.[57] In fact, only five were certainly his, three of which were simply lifted from *Love's Labour's Lost*, a quarto version of which had been published in 1598. Of the others, at least five are known to have been the work of other poets, whilst the remainder, of which no other versions are known, are only very tentatively, if ever, attributed to Shakespeare by modern editors. Of more significance is the inclusion of two poems which certainly were his, namely versions of Sonnets 138 and 144, which resurfaced in the publication of the full sequence in 1609. Their existence as early as 1599 is therefore a nice confirmation of Francis Meres' reference, in 1598, to Shakespeare's 'sugred Sonnets' circulating 'among his private friends',[58] but the notion that he gave permission for these to be used is now almost universally rejected. Most editors argue that Jaggard had somehow secured possession of manuscript versions of these poems, or copies of them, and, aware of Shakespeare's increasing reputation, had published them under Shakespeare's name together with a batch of other poems on which he had managed to lay his hands. It is just possible that this was the result of a genuine misunderstanding but more likely was simply sharp practice, made easier at a

---

57. For a balanced and scholarly analysis of the issues surrounding this publication, see Burrow, ed., *William Shakespeare: Complete Sonnets*, pp. 74–82.
58. Chambers, *William Shakespeare*, ii, p. 194.

time when an author's copyright in his work was not recognized. In any event, when an expanded third edition appeared in 1612, Thomas Heywood lodged a vigorous complaint concerning the unauthorized and unattributed inclusion of eleven poems of his own, implying at the same time that Shakespeare was also 'much offended' at Jaggard's behaviour.[59] But, whatever were Shakespeare's feelings about the exploitation of his name over this period, it cannot convincingly be argued that he derived any financial advantage from it.

The case of the poem beginning 'Let the bird of lowdest lay', attributed to Shakespeare when published in 1601, is less straightforward. It is one of what the printer or publisher had set out as fifteen separate poems appended to a long narrative poem by Robert Chester, entitled *Loves Martyr*, dedicated to his employer, Sir John Salusbury of Denbighshire. Its theme is allegorical, 'shadowing the truth of Love in the constant Fate of the Phoenix and Turtle' [i.e. the turtle dove].[60] The authenticity of Shakespeare's contribution is not generally questioned even though its meaning remains elusive. From a biographical standpoint, however, the main point of interest is why Shakespeare agreed to its inclusion—if, indeed, he did. The section containing his, and the fourteen other subsidiary poems, has its own separate title page, declaring them to be 'Poeticall Essaies on the former Subject; viz. the Turtle and Phoenix. Done by the best and chiefest of our moderne writers, with their names subscribed to their particular workes...' In fact, only five of these poems are specifically attributed—two to Ben Jonson and one apiece to Shakespeare, John Marston, and George Chapman, although the assumption is usually made that six of those not so identified can be attributed to the poets whose names next occur after the 'anonymous' ones.[61] This is of some relevance here as the reader, already uncertain as to who had written these six, would also have been left in considerable doubt as to quite which section was Shakespeare's work. A five-verse poem (in triplets), entitled 'Threnos' (Lament) occupying p. 172, with printer's banners at the top and bottom of the page, does

---

59. In fairness, the wording of the title page of the third edition, though not attributing the new material to Heywood, does not specifically attribute them to Shakespeare either. The argument that, in light of Heywood's complaint, the title page was cancelled in favour of one which omits Shakespeare's, rests on shaky ground (Burrow, ed., *William Shakespeare: Complete Sonnets*, pp. 77–9).
60. STC 5119.
61. On this basis Marston and Jonson are counted as the authors of four apiece, rather than one.

carry Shakespeare's name and at first sight appears largely self-contained (Figure 1). However, it is usual to regard the thirteen quatrains on the previous two pages (pp. 170–1) as Shakespeare's work as well, principally on the grounds, it would seem, that the final quatrain makes reference to 'this Threne' which follows on p. 172. Be this as it may, the layout of the work does not encourage the reader to assume this and, if the preceding quatrains really were Shakespeare's work, he might well have felt aggrieved that the editorial process had all but obscured the fact.[62] More to the point, there is no material evidence to link Shakespeare with either Salusbury or Chester and thus to explain why, with three other poets of the day, he had been persuaded to write these supporting verses. The first two poems, signed 'Vatum Chorus' (Chorus of the Bards), certainly were in honour of Salusbury and personally addressed to him, but one suspects they were simply Chester's composition, giving his patron the impression that those whom he had recruited to add their own verses shared his sentiments.[63] But, amidst all this uncertainty, it does at least seem clear that Shakespeare would have derived very little, if any, direct financial benefit from his involvement in this project and that, given Salusbury's modest status, Shakespeare would ever have considered him as a likely source of patronage.[64]

If we can discount any financial gain from his involvement, with or without his consent, in the publication of *Passionate Pilgrim* and *Loves Martyr*, it has nevertheless been increasingly argued that, around this time, he was a collaborator in the play, 'Sir Thomas More'.[65] This might well have contributed to his income if undertaken outside any contractual arrangement with the Chamberlain's Men, also opening up the possibility that he contributed to other plays which were never

---

62. The reader might also have been struck by the beautiful simplicity of the 'Threnos', standing in marked, if not startling, contrast to the complex, inscrutable, and obscure quatrains which precede it and which, unlike all the other poems included in the appendix, appeared with no heading.

63. However, for a strongly argued view that the appendix was carefully planned, see Bednarz, *Shakespeare and the Truth of Love*.

64. Ernst Honigmann (*Shakespeare the 'Lost Years'*, pp. 90–113) has argued for the mid-1580s as the date both for the original composition of Chester's poem and also of Shakespeare's commendatory verse, when a quest for patronage on Shakespeare's part would have been more understandable. The argument, however, is purely hypothetical.

65. In 2013 John Jowett felt able to claim that 'there is no longer any need to treat the question as controversial' (Jowett, 'A collaboration: Shakespeare and Hand C in *Sir Thomas More*', p. 255).

172

Threnos.

BEautie, Truth, and Raritie,
Grace in all simplicitie,
Here enclosde, in cinders lie.

Death is now the *Phœnix* nest,
And the *Turtles* loyall brest,
To eternitie doth rest.

Leauing no posteritie,
Twas not their infirmitie,
It was married Chastitie.

Truth may seeme, but cannot be,
Beautie bragge, but tis not she,
Truth and Beautie buried be.

To this vrne let those repaire,
That are either true or faire,
For these dead Birds, sigh a prayer.

William Shake-speare.

Figure 1. Page from the appendix to Robert Chester's *Loves Martyr*, published in 1601, with the poem *Threnos,* attributed to William Shakespeare

Source: It is usual also to attribute to Shakespeare the 'unsigned' poem on the preceding two pages, beginning 'Let the bird of lowdest lay', but the printer's layout of p. 172, including the two banners, does not encourage the reader to assume this.

Folger Shakespeare Library

published. There are, however, serious obstacles to overcome. This is not the place to discuss in detail the ongoing complex arguments concerning the date of the play's composition and the part played in it by the known collaborators, rather simply to ask how likely is it that Shakespeare could have become involved in this project and, if so, what contribution this might have made to his income. For many years, 'Sir Thomas More' survived in manuscript form only and close study revealed contributions in at least six different hands. On the evidence of the only certain examples of Shakespeare's handwriting—his six signatures which themselves show inconsistencies—it was surely too bold to claim, as some had done, that one of these six hands was Shakespeare's. Arguments based on more recent analysis of spelling and stylistic elements are more persuasive,[66] but these still need to be weighed in the balance against another consideration, namely, that, if the other collaborators in the project have been correctly identified— Arthur Munday, Henry Chettle, Thomas Dekker, and, perhaps, Thomas Heywood—then the play would have very much the flavour of one of those written for the Admiral's Men by this same group of writers to whom, in various combinations, Philip Henslowe, during the years 1598–1603, is known to have made payments on the company's behalf, for the purchase of their 'books'. The contribution by the anonymous annotator, known as 'Hand C', whose collaboration in the production phase of three other plays is on record, also has to be added to the mix.[67] Lack of evidence as to how other companies operated renders hazardous any wider deductions, but, on the face of it, Shakespeare's active involvement with a group of men known to have written regularly for the Admiral's Men—the Chamberlain's (King's Men's) principal commercial rival—would suggest a serious conflict of interest.[68] After all, Shakespeare, apart from his role as quasi-resident playwright, was also a sharer in the profits of the Chamberlain's Men and probably by then, as is discussed below (p. 102), one of the 'housekeepers' of its theatre, the Globe. It is true that Thomas Dekker can be shown to have sold a play, *Satiro-mastix*, to the Chamberlain's Men by November 1601

66. For a full summary, see Jowett, ed., *Sir Thomas More*, pp. 437–58.
67. Jowett, ed., *Sir Thomas More*, pp. 28, 102. At least one of these, *Fortune's Tennis*, Part 2, was a Lord Admiral's play: Foakes, ed., *Henslowe's Diary*, p. 331.
68. If the play were written for the Admiral's Men, it would not have been during the period 1598–1603, i.e. the period for which Henslowe's payments for 'books' survive (cf., Jowett, ed., *Sir Thomas More*, p. 100).

(albeit whilst he had temporarily broken the exclusive link with the 'Henslowe group'), but to assume from this one example that the Chamberlain's Men's leading writer would at an earlier date have cooperated with a group of writers generally associated with another company would surely be going too far.

There are counter-arguments to this. The original play, initially largely the work of Munday and Chettle perhaps for the Admiral's Men, could have been rejected on Henslowe's advice after critical intervention by Edmund Tilney, Master of the Revels, whose instructions to cut certain passages also survive as fascinating additions to the manuscript.[69] It could then have been sold on to another company, perhaps the Chamberlain's Men, thus allowing Dekker and Shakespeare to modify it. Alternatively, perhaps Munday and Chettle had put the original work together, not for the Admiral's Men at all but for some other company and that, after Tilney's intervention, other collaborators, including Shakespeare, worked on modifications. This then raises the issue of which company they would have been working for: if the Chamberlain's (King's) Men, then this would have placed another of the collaborators, Thomas Heywood, a sharer in Worcester's Men, in a compromising position, but conversely, if the Worcester's Men, then Shakespeare would have been equally open to a charge of conflict of interest.

Amidst all this uncertainty, what can we conclude concerning the more limited issue of Shakespeare's income? Firstly, we would need to accept, of course, that Shakespeare's hand has indeed been correctly identified, and on this there is still not unanimity. But, whether or not originally written for, or commissioned by, the Admiral's Men, would Shakespeare's limited contribution to the subsequent reworking—165 lines and possibly two shorter passages—have earned him any money? If this were done for the Chamberlain's (King's) Men, the work would then have been carried out as part of Shakespeare's working arrangement with his own company and therefore not likely to have led to significant additional payment. If, instead, he agreed to collaborate with a project associated with a competing company, then the payment for such a limited contribution is not likely to have been substantial.

---

69. If so, this would need to have happened before 1598, assuming Henslowe's recorded payments, which survive only after that date, are complete.

Early residences in London

On the assumption, then, that at this stage continuing freelance work would not have made a noticeable contribution to Shakespeare's income, we return to the annual sum of around £50 which it is thought likely he was drawing as a sharer in the Chamberlain's Men. This was a considerable sum (more than twice that of the annual salary of either Stratford's schoolmaster or vicar), but it would not have made Shakespeare or his family affluent, not least because he had to allow for his own expenses in London. From the little evidence we have—national tax returns—he appears, in the mid-1590s, to have been lodging respectably, but not extravagantly, in St Helen's parish in Bishopsgate Ward, within easy reach of the Theatre in Shoreditch where his company, the Chamberlain's Men, was then based. Here he was twice assessed for national subsidies on the value of his goods, once in October 1596 at 1 shilling in the pound, with payment due in February 1597, and secondly in October 1598, at 2s. 8d. in the pound.[70] On both occasions, his goods were assessed at £5, thus creating liabilities of 5 shillings and 13s. 4d. respectively. On both occasions, he failed to pay. The document listing the defaulters on the first occasion, dated 15 November 1597, places him in a group who were either dead, had left the ward, or had arranged to secrete their goods so that the sum due could not be levied. That Shakespeare appears to have fallen into the second of these categories is confirmed on the second occasion that he defaulted when, in the lists of other non-payers, it was explained that the debt would be recorded in the sheriff's accounts (the pipe roll) of 1597/8, under 'London'. Here, however, we find that Shakespeare's continuing failure to pay was to be carried over to the pipe roll of 1598/9, under the counties of Sussex and Surrey. Finally, on this later roll, we are informed that the sheriff had referred collection to the bishop of Winchester. This sequence can convincingly be interpreted to mean that Shakespeare had moved to Sussex or Surrey (for instance, simply by crossing the River Thames to Southwark) but more specifically to an area within Southwark where the county sheriff's authority did not

---

70. There are five documents in all, authoritatively discussed in Giuseppi, 'The Exchequer documents relative to Shakespeare's residence in Southwark'. See also Thomas, *Shakespeare in the Public Records*, pp. 6–8.

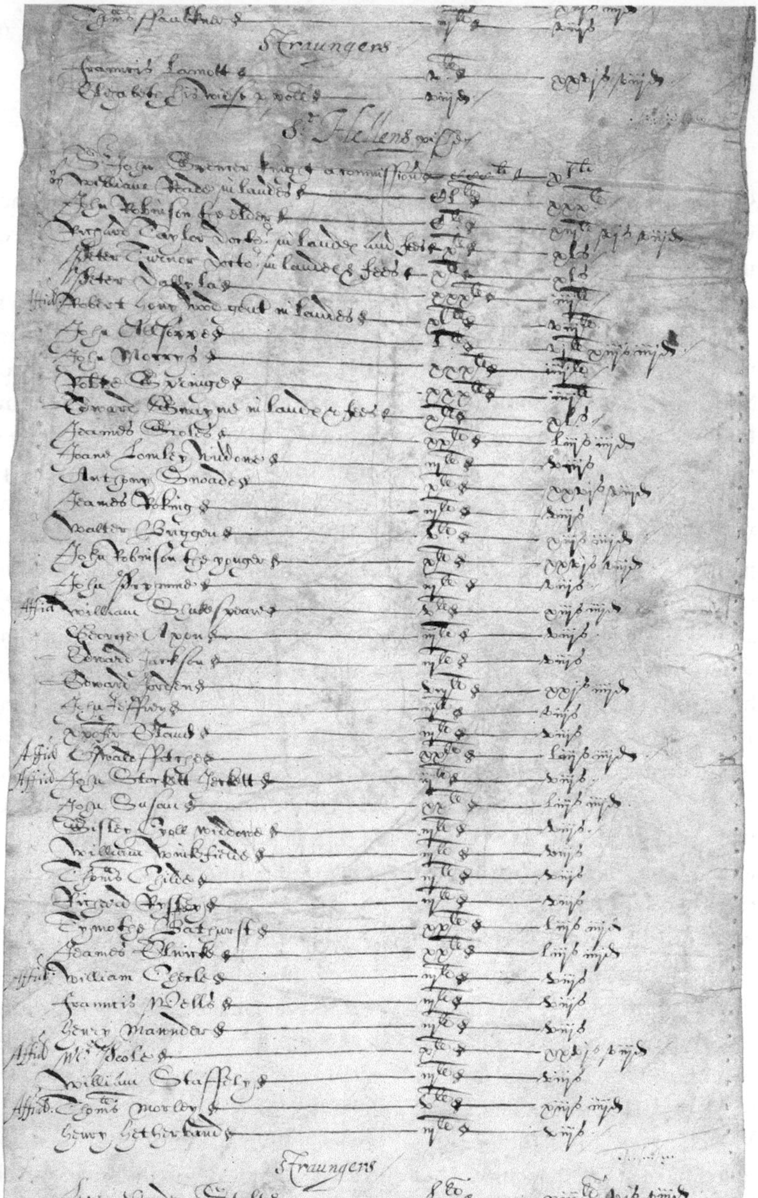

Figure 2. The forty regular householders in the parish of St Helen's, Bishopsgate, assessed on the value of their moveable goods as liable to contribute to a government subsidy, 1 October 1598

Source: This is one of the few surviving records which show William Shakespeare alongside his neighbours. His goods, and that of two others, were valued at £5 and seventeen others had goods valued at £3. Above him were twenty others, topped by Sir John Spencer, with goods valued at £300, but with most falling between £8 and £20. The word 'Affid' against Shakespeare's name indicates that the collectors had declared that he had not paid.

The National Archives, E 179/146/369

extend, almost certainly the bishop of Winchester's liberty of the Clink where the Rose Theatre already stood and where the Globe was to be built nearby in 1599.[71]

These assessments cannot be accepted at their face value due to the age-old practice of understating the value of property in order to reduce tax liability. However, though in many cases they may represent an under-estimate of any one person's individual wealth, it may still be valid to use these figures as an indicator of comparative social standing. On the second occasion that Shakespeare defaulted, the assessment, dated 1 October 1598, lists all forty of the regular tax-paying residents in the parish of St Helen's (Figure 2).[72] The valuation of Shakespeare's goods, at £5, was shared by two others, but it was not the lowest: seventeen other residents, by far the biggest single category, had goods valued at only £3. Above him, one resident's goods were valued at £8, six at £10, five at £20, and three at £30. Above that again was a smattering of the 'super-rich', topped by one valuation of £300. On the one hand such comparisons certainly suggest a man of fairly comfortable means, and a cut slightly above many other residents, but on the other not a man possessed of any great wealth; or, putting it another way, his income as a sharer in the Chamberlain's Men since 1594 had clearly brought with it a comfortable sufficiency.

It has proved impossible to establish Shakespeare's tenancy of this property in St Helen's at an earlier date. However, his first recorded default, in February 1597, was for a second instalment of the last of three subsidies originally granted by Parliament back in 1593. No documentation is extant to establish whether or not he defaulted, or was even assessed, on those previous occasions, but, given that he did default by 1597, his name may well have been carried over from earlier listings, suggesting in turn that he had been resident there for the previous two or three years.

These defaults do not establish with certainty that Shakespeare had moved to Southwark before the collection of his debt was referred to the sheriff of Sussex and Surrey in November 1597. However, that he may have moved to Southwark as early as 1596 is implied by his

71. It would not be true to claim that Shakespeare thereby escaped payment. His debt was not the only one referred to the bishop of Winchester, who the following year paid into the exchequer a lump sum which almost exactly matched the outstanding liabilities.
72. TNA, E 179/146/369. For a full transcript, see Lewis, *Shakespeare Documents*, i, pp. 266–8.

involvement in a legal case of the autumn of that year when William Wayte petitioned to have William Shakespeare, Francis Langley, and two women, Dorothy wife of John Soer and Ann Lee, bound over to keep the peace, clearly as the result of some quarrel.[73] The writ to enforce this has not survived, only a note that it was issued. Nor do we know that Shakespeare and his co-defendants were subsequently bound over or precisely why. If the documentation were extant, it would, in any case, simply have complied with the standard formula that Wayte had entered his petition 'for fear of death and mutilation of limbs', not to be taken as evidence of actual physical violence but certainly of a quarrel which Wayte thought might lead to some public disturbance. Be this as it may, the fact that the writ to enforce this request was addressed to the sheriff of Surrey and that Francis Langley had been lord of the manor of Paris Garden, Southwark, since 1589 and had built the Swan Theatre there in 1594/5, indicates that the quarrel most probably originated in that parish.[74] The Soer family owned property in the vicinity of Paris Garden, providing further confirmation.[75]

The quarrel was the latest stage in a longer running dispute between Francis Langley and Wayte's stepfather, William Gardiner, a local justice of the peace, who lived in the neighbouring parish of Bermondsey.[76] How Shakespeare (and the two women) had got drawn into the dispute is obscure. It is tempting, given Langley's and Shakespeare's common link with the theatre, to assume that the argument was somehow linked to the Swan, but it would seem more likely that it related to Langley's other activities in Paris Garden, including the building of tenements some of which were clearly occupied by members of the acting profession. A dispute concerning such buildings, involving owners and tenants, would be relevant to our current purpose, suggesting that Shakespeare was not living in any great style. Paris Garden, however, was not in the Clink.[77] If Shakespeare, on crossing the river, had first found lodgings there, he must soon have moved again, to

73. This is exhaustively discussed by Leslie Hotson in *Shakespeare v Shallow*, esp. pp. 1–28.
74. For Langley, see Ingram, *A London Life in the Brazen Age*.
75. Hotson, *Shakespeare v Shallow*, pp. 127–8.
76. Hotson, *Shakespeare v Shallow*, pp. 25–8; Ingram, *A London Life in the Brazen Age*, pp. 146–7.
77. For the manor of Paris Garden, see *Survey of London*, vol. 22, pp. 94–100, and Plates 1, 2, 65, 66. The Clink was still within Southwark parish but further east.

the Clink, to account for the 1598/99 tax entry referred to above (p. 61).

There is one further piece of evidence to indicate that Shakespeare had moved to Southwark by 1596. Edmond Malone, writing in 1796, declared: 'From a paper now before me, which formerly belonged to Edward Alleyn, the player, our poet appears to have lived in Southwark, near the Bear-Garden, in 1596.'[78] This 'paper' has not survived, but, on the face of it, Malone's statement is credible. The Bear Garden was located in the Clink and Alleyn is known, on the evidence of several documents now in the Dulwich Archives, to have had considerable interests there as both the owner of the Bear Garden itself and of other neighbouring properties.[79] Malone continues with a reference to 'another curious document in my possession...[that] affords the strongest presumptive evidence that he continued to reside in Southwark to the year 1608.'[80] A listing of some sort, which included Shakespeare's name, is therefore not impossible despite the fact that his name does not occur in any of the so-called 'token books' for Southwark parish. These are extant for all but two years over the period 1596–1616, listing heads of household and, from the number of tokens purchased, how many in their households were obliged to take communion.[81] If Shakespeare were simply a lodger, however, then his name would not have appeared. On the other hand, there would seem to be no obvious reason why Shakespeare would have moved to Southwark as early as 1596. At that date, as a sharer in the Chamberlain's Men with its headquarters at James Burbage's Theatre in Shoreditch, his living in St Helen's Bishopsgate, as recorded in the tax assessments, is what we might have expected; and, although the company vacated the Theatre following the expiration of its lease in April 1597, the company is then thought, though it cannot be proved, to have used the nearby Curtain, in which Burbage also had an interest;[82] and it was not

78. Malone, *Inquiry into the Authenticity of Certain Miscellaneous Papers*, pp. 215–16.
79. Dulwich College Mss 1/47–51.
80. The water is muddied by John Payne Collier's notorious insertion of Shakespeare's name into a rate book of 1609 (Dulwich College Ms 1/49) and by a completely fabricated list of Southwark residents, including Shakespeare, of 1596 (1/20), both acts clearly inspired by Malone's earlier comments.
81. These are comprehensively indexed by William Ingram and Alan H. Nelson on their website, *The Token Books of St Saviour Southwark* (http://tokenbooks.lsa.umich.edu/index.php).
82. Below, p. 102.

until the winter of 1598/99 that the Theatre was famously dismantled
and re-erected in Southwark as the Globe. But in that case why would
Shakespeare have chosen to cross to Southwark as early as 1596? It
could be argued that the tax default records do not establish his residence there until towards the end of 1597 and that he may not have
been living there when he was named in the writ issued on William
Wayte's behalf. Even so (and ignoring Malone's testimony), his presence in Southwark before 1599 is not what we would have expected.
There is yet another consideration, however. Two of Shakespeare's
fellow sharers in the Chamberlain's Men, William Sly and Augustine
Phillips, do occur in the Southwark token books from 1593, equally
odd if we are to assume that players preferred to live near their centre
of operations.[83] In inconclusive summary, although the tax assessments
and the Wayte summons suggest that Shakespeare had moved to
Southwark, and specifically to the Clink, by 1596/97, this is not confirmed by the token books, even though these same books establish
that two of his fellow sharers in the Chamberlain's Men had made such
a move before the building of the Globe in 1599. Until we learn by
chance, from evidence presented in the Bellot/Mountjoy case, that
by 1604 Shakespeare was living as a lodger in Silver Street,[84] we can
only assume that until then he had been lodging equally quietly in
Southwark. This might perhaps be thought to reflect on his personal
circumstances, in effect a step back from a position which had attracted
the attentions of the tax collectors of the mid-1590s to one where he
disappears from any records which would have indicated that he maintained his own establishment in the capital. However, as we shall see in
Chapter 4, it was at exactly this time that he was able to raise substantial sums of money for other purposes and any decision to live in
London more simply may therefore reflect nothing more than his wish
to husband his resources.

83. This is by no means established, however. Many actors are known to have lived some
    distance from their theatres (Ingram, '"Near the Playe Howse": the Swan Theater and
    community blight', pp. 54–6).
84. Below, p. 118.

4

Consolidation

The grant of arms

From the mid-1590s surviving documentation begins to reflect
Shakespeare's improving financial position. First there is the approach
made to the College of Heralds for a grant of arms, a successful one as
it turned out with the grant apparently made on 20 October 1596.[1]
Shakespeare's father, John, was then still the titular head of the family
and it was to him, and not William, that the grant was actually made. It
could be argued that the application was John's idea and that he carried it through without his son's involvement. This, however, is very
unlikely. There is some evidence of John's re-engagement in business
dealings in the 1590s, but not at the level which had characterized his
activities earlier in life; and, anxious though he may have been to re-
establish his personal reputation, he is unlikely to have had the necessary means to pursue a grant of arms.[2] He must also have been at least
in his sixties, if not early seventies. That William was involved is therefore highly probable, not only because, based in London, he would
have been well placed to oversee negotiations, but also because he
now had the means to advance the family's status. This would not necessarily imply that he was personally eager for social advancement:
while his father was still alive and probably with his encouragement,
Shakespeare may merely have wished to make it clear that, whatever
misfortunes had befallen John Shakespeare in the early 1580s, the family had more than recovered its former position. If he had held himself
responsible, at least in part, for his family's troubles as the result of an

---

1. The grant survives in the form of two drafts only but both are so dated.
2. Bearman, 'John Shakespeare: a papist or just penniless?', pp. 427–8.

imprudent marriage, his family's reinstatement may also have acted as a salve to his conscience. There is a further reason we might question personal ambition on Shakespeare's part to establish a Shakespeare dynasty of gentle status. His only son, Hamnet, had died earlier in the year, in August 1596, and his wife Ann, then over forty years old, was unlikely to produce a replacement. Shakespeare may perhaps have considered the possibility of her death, his subsequent remarriage, and the birth of a son and heir, thus perpetuating his family name, and the gentle status that went with it, but this would hardly explain a decision to initiate proceedings at that particular time.

Whatever the motives of either John or William in approaching the College of Heralds, at least one of them, and probably both, understood that they were in effect simply purchasing a coat of arms. The man who sanctioned the grant was William Dethick, then Garter King of Arms, and the discussions which took place between the parties are nicely reflected in the surviving documentation. The wording of the final grant has not survived, but more revealing, perhaps, are two surviving drafts which demonstrate how the justification for it was gradually improved.[3] As first drafted, John Shakespeare's claim to gentry status depended solely on the claim that unnamed ancestors had been rewarded by Henry VII for their valiant service. This was improved by an interlineation in one of the drafts to the effect that it was his 'parentes & late antecessers' who had been so rewarded, the word parent not then limited to its modern restricted use but still an advance on ancestor. In the second draft this ancestor was transformed into John's grandfather, though still unnamed (Figure 3). A similar process can be traced in the description of his marriage. This was not mentioned at all when the grant was first drafted, but an interlineation improved the situation by a statement that he 'maryd Mary daughter & one of the heyres of Robert Arden of Wilmcotte...gent.' This addition was repeated in the second draft but then again enhanced by the visible deletion of 'gent' and substitution of 'esquire' to improve Robert Arden's status. This may not have been the end of the matter, for at the bottom of the second draft are notes of further material that might be used to bolster the claim, namely that John had produced a twenty-year-old 'patierne'[4] by Robert

3. The two drafts are conveniently printed in facsimile on facing pages in Schoenbaum, *William Shakespeare; a Documentary Life* (1975 edn), pp. 168–9. For transcripts, see Lewis, *Shakespeare Documents*, i, pp. 210–12.
4. Probably in the sense of a design.

Figure 3. Part of one of the drafts of the grant of arms to John Shakespeare, 20 October 1596

Source: The crucial section of this second draft is badly damaged at this point, but the interlineation of 'Grandfather' is clearly visible above the word 'antecessors.' Four lines below, the description of Robert Arden as a 'gent.' was deleted and 'esquire' substituted.

College of Arms MS Draft Grant of Arms to John Shakespeare 2

Cooke, then Clarenceaux King of Arms, of the arms to be claimed, that fifteen or sixteen years ago John had been bailiff of Stratford and a justice of the peace and that 'he hathe Llandes & tenementes of good wealth & Substance, 500^{li}.' The statement that he had married 'a daughter and heyre of Arden, a gent. of worship' was also repeated.[5] Whether or not all, or some, of these claims were incorporated into the final wording, they are all serious misrepresentations or exaggerations. It is difficult, for instance, in view of the status of John's father, Richard, as simply a leaseholder and/or copyholder, to place much credence in the statement that Henry VII had previously 'advanced & rewarded' the family. Nor had John himself married the daughter of a man who at any

---

5. The bottom of the page which once carried the final statement has since disintegrated but was recorded by Malone in his late eighteenth-century transcript, published in 1821 (Malone, *Plays and Poems of William Shakespeare*, ii, p. 89).

point had claimed the title of esquire; in fact, as already explained, he is never found styled more grandly than husbandman, with two intermediary social ranks—that of yeoman and gentleman—dividing him from the squirearchy. John may have been bailiff of Stratford (though more like thirty years ago than fifteen or sixteen), a small market town then of some 1500 souls, but this would hardly have elevated him into the ranks of those urban elites who dominated mercantile life in the big cities and some of whom were being admitted, albeit with the disapproval of traditionalists, into the armigerous class. The claim that John, as the owner of no more than his house in Henley Street, and a man who did not feature in the 1593/94 subsidy roll, was nevertheless worth £500 is therefore bordering on the absurd.[6] As for Cooke's sketch of a coat of arms, allegedly produced in the 1570s, this, or any reference to it in surviving records, has never been traced; nor, Cooke having conveniently died in 1593, could any check as to its authenticity have been easily undertaken. In 1563, Cooke, then a young man, had assisted in the earliest recorded visitation of Warwickshire[7] and John Shakespeare's recollection of this may simply have evolved into a claim that he himself had appeared before the heralds who conducted the inquiry.

All this, then, would imply that father and son had in effect colluded with Dethick to make the case that a grant of arms would be justified. Given Dethick's record, this should be no cause for surprise. In the course of his career, his fellow heralds made many allegations of personal misconduct against him, some implying venality in the granting of coats of arms.[8] In 1602, a brother herald, Ralph Brooke, brought a formal complaint against some of his colleagues, principally Dethick, but also naming William Segar and William Camden. Some twenty-three grants were eventually challenged, including that to John Shakespeare, apparently slimmed down from draft lists, one of over thirty-six and the other of twenty-nine names.[9] Against this background, it is hardly controversial to propose that Dethick, eager to get

6. TNA, E 179/193/235. This lists twenty-five burgesses with goods valued between £1 and £10.
7. *Visitation of the County of Warwick in the year 1619*, p. vi. Fragmentary evidence of this visitation is preserved in the College of Arms, F 7, G 11, and H 12, and BL, Harl. Ms 1563.
8. *ODNB*, xv, pp. 924–5; Duncan-Jones, *Ungentle Shakespeare*, pp. 99–100.
9. Folger Shakespeare Library, V.a.156; V.a.350. Dethick's involvement is recorded in at least twenty-seven of these. The second of these manuscripts (V.a.350) is a *c.*1700 copy but there is no reason to doubt its authenticity (Matus, *Shakespeare in Fact*, pp. 79–81).

his hands on the Shakespeares' fee, was willing to overlook any weaknesses in their claim, and perhaps even to advise them on how best to make their case. Such collusion would have been entirely typical of late Tudor England with many a rising family keen to manipulate the system in the pursuit of improved social status. That Shakespeare may have entered into such negotiations is not therefore remarkable, but, if any justification is required, a willingness to redeem the family name and console his father in old age is surely sufficient.

The fee which Dethick collected from the Shakespeares could have been in the region of £10–£20, then, of course, a very substantial sum. The Shakespeares were not Dethick's only clients from the business community. In the documentation arising out of the 1602 complaint, 'Parr the Embroderer whose father was a Pedler' was said to have paid Dethick £10 for his coat of arms, as had Robert Wythens, a London vintner. 'Sergiant [Peter] Warberton' was said to have paid £20.[10] Other 'base persons' whom Dethick was accused of elevating to gentry status included 'Tey the Hosier', 'Dungan Clarke…the plasterer' and 'one Smith, an Inn kep[er] in Huntingdon.'[11] The somewhat dismissive 'Shakespear the Player', by which the playwright is described in one of these lists (even though the grant had been made to his father) also suggests that the family's status was an issue.[12] Unluckily, although we have the draft lists of the disputed grants, we do not have the wording of the formal accusations against Dethick which were subsequently made. But we do have his, and Camden's, reply to it, which they describe as 'a Libellous Scrwole against certein Arms supposed to be wrongfully given.'[13] Amongst the twenty-three then cited, clearly digested from the drafts, must have been the grant to John Shakespeare, as Dethick went out of his way to defend it. One of the objections had clearly been that the arms so granted too closely resembled those of the deceased Lord Mauley.[14] Dethick dismissed this on the grounds that the inclusion of a spear on John Shakespeare's coat of arms made

10. Folger Shakespeare Library, V.a. 56, unpaginated; V.a. 350, pp. 9, 20, 22.
11. Folger Shakespeare Library, V.a. 56, unpaginated; V.a. 350, pp. 2, 5, 13.
12. As John had died in September 1601, the right to the arms in question had, by the date of the dispute, been inherited by William. It is a matter of some interest that Brooke appears either to have thought that the grant had been made to William, or to have known that 'Shakespeare the player' was John's son.
13. Lewis, *Shakespeare Documents*, ii, p. 344.
14. Chambers, *William Shakespeare*, ii, p. 22; Duncan-Jones, *Ungentle Shakespeare*, p. 101 and Plate 5.

it recognizably different. However, he also felt obliged to point out that John Shakespeare 'was A magestrat...A Justice of peace. He maryed A daughter and heyre of Ardern, and was of good substance and habelite', implying that the Shakespeares' social standing had also been challenged. These claims, of course, were no more than had been put forward when the grant was made and in reality, as already explained, fell far short of establishing gentle status, indicating instead that the Shakespeares' application, like others cited by Brooke, typified an attempt by a family of modest social background to improve its status by the simple expedient of purchasing the privilege.

On the other hand, it is clear that Brooke, motivated by malice arising out of quarrels reaching back to at least 1594/5, had grossly exaggerated the humble status of some of Dethick's recent clients. In his defence, Dethick went to some length to justify the grants he had made and, generally speaking, his statements can be verified.[15] Amongst those whom Brooke had singled out, John Clark of Ardington, for instance, Henry Hickman, and Thomas Peake were lawyers, and Michael Murgatrod was Fellow of Jesus College, Cambridge, and steward to the archbishop of Canterbury, all thus qualifying for gentry status by virtue of their professions.[16] As for those criticized for being mere tradesmen, 'John Whitmore a haberdasher of London' turns out to be closely related to, or perhaps even a mistake for, the wealthy London merchant, William Whitmore, who married the daughter of Alderman William Bond and fathered another William who occupies a niche in the *Dictionary of National Biography*.[17] 'Elkyn' and 'Lee', allegedly 'basse Tradesmen', were William Elkin and Robert Lee, both aldermen and sheriffs of London, Lee going on to be Lord Mayor in 1602/3, having purchased the manor of Billesley, in Warwickshire, for £5000 in 1600.[18] 'Pettous' was Thomas Pettus, mayor (1590) and

15. Bodl. Ashmole 846, ff. 59–59v.
16. For the Clarks of Ardington, see *Burkes Commoners*, 1836, i, p. 110, including John, died c. 1570, and John died c. 1596. Thomas Peake was probably the man of that name, of Lutterworth, at Trinity College, Cambridge, 1578–86, and admitted to Grays Inn, 7 February 1589 (Venn, *Alumni Cantabrigiensis*, iii, p. 327; Foster, *Register of Admissions to Gray's Inn*, p. 74). For 'M^r [Henry] Hykman...A Doctor in the Civil Lawes', see Foster, *Alumni Oxoniensis*, ii, p. 703; Hasler, ed., *History of Parliament, House of Commons, 1558–1603*, ii, p. 313. For Murgatrod, see *ODNB*, xxxix, pp. 824–5.
17. *ODNB*, lviii, 743.
18. Beaven, *Aldermen of the City of London*, ii, pp. 42, 45; *Victoria History of the County of Warwick*, iii, p. 60.

sheriff (1598) of Norwich, and 'M^r [Robert] Gibson', an alderman of the same city and sheriff in 1596.[19] Robert Wythens 'was no vintner but A Riche & worshipfull Citizen of good reputacions', borne out by his election as a London alderman in 1590.[20] Another alderman of London (and, according to Dethick, 'no Kannell raker') was Henry Hawarde (or Heyward), fishmonger (father of John Hawarde, the lawyer and Member of Parliament) who retired to Tandridge Hall, in Surrey, on the fortune he had made.[21] However, only in one instance was Dethick able to point to a landed estate as a justification for the grant, namely William Whitmore's 'faire Landes' in Shropshire, in effect backing up Brooke's case that, whatever their wealth, these men were tradesmen and thus not true gentry; though even here, Dethick argued that 'trades of Marchandize' did not 'derogate from Gentrie more in England Then it dothe in Venice, Genoua, Florence etc.' However, when possible, he did point out that some applicants had produced evidence. John Clark showed the arms he claimed 'engraved in an auncyent Seale of Sylver from his Antecessors', whilst Peake made 'good proofe' that his arms had been borne by his grandfather. Hickman's application was also approved 'uppon proofe by him produced' and, in Walter Cowley's case, 'it cannot be denyed that he is descended of that Name.' Generally speaking, then, Dethick was able to mount a reasonable defence of his actions, either on grounds of gentlemanly profession or sheer wealth, albeit of men 'in trade'. But this only serves to emphasize the weakness of John Shakespeare's claim which had neither lands, personal wealth, evidences, nor a gentlemanly profession to back it up. Moreover, to make out that his status as a magistrate and justice of the peace in a small market town bore comparison with aldermen and mayors of Norwich and London was, to put it mildly, clearly overstating the case.

We might also note that the grant of arms to two other 'players', Augustine Phillips and Thomas Pope, both of whom were Shakespeare's colleagues in the Chamberlain's (later King's) Men, had attracted criticism from another herald, William Smith, who appears to allege that

---

19. For Pettus, see Blomefield, *Essay towards a Topographical History of the County of Norfolk*, iii, p. 359. His son John Pettus was also sheriff (1598) and Member of Parliament for Norwich (1601 and 1604) but was not mayor until 1608: Hasler, ed., *History of Parliament, House of Commons, 1558–1603*, iii, p. 212.

20. Beaven, *Aldermen of the City of London*, ii, p. 44.

21. Ferris and Thrush, eds., *History of Parliament, House of Commons, 1604–29*, iv, p. 597.

Phillips and Pope had simply laid claim to the arms formerly borne by earlier distinguished persons with the same surnames.[22]

The Shakespeares' family ambitions did not rest there. Three years later, late in 1599 or early in 1600, there were clearly sufficient funds in hand to encourage another approach to the heralds, this time for permission to quarter the Arden arms with those granted to John Shakespeare in 1596. Again only a draft survives, drawn up in William Dethick's name.[23] Interestingly, the precise relationship of John Shakespeare's ancestor who had been advanced by Henry VII, given as grandfather in the previous grant, is here changed to great grandfather (and only in an interlineation), perhaps in recognition of the fact that, on investigation, the former claim was not found valid. John's marriage was again mentioned, to 'the daughter & one of the heyres of Robert Arden', though somewhat oddly his place of residence is given as 'Wellingcote' despite the fact that it had been more properly spelt in the 1596 application. On this occasion, John is also said to have produced 'his Auncient Cote of Armes heretofore Assigned to him, whilest he was her maiesties officer & Baylefe.' However, this is clearly a distorted account of what had happened earlier. We only know about the 'patierne' allegedly issued by Robert Cooke to John Shakespeare when he was bailiff, from the rough note attached to the latest draft of the 1596 grant. But, if the grant really had been made then, there would have been no need for the 1596 application. Here, then, is another example of Dethick making the most of what up to that point had only been a rumour, probably with the intent of pushing John's gentry status back as far as he could in order to distance this new application from the one made only three years before. By 1599 it might also have conveniently been forgotten that Mary, one of Arden's heirs, was, in fact, the youngest of the eight daughters of a husbandman, giving the claim that she was entitled to bear his arms dubious to say the least. As if to emphasize this, there was an embarrassing uncertainty as to what the 'Auncyent Arms of the said Arden of Wellingcote' actually were. At first the herald began to sketch in the arms of the Ardens of Park Hall

22. Lewis, *Shakespeare Documents*, ii, pp. 340–1. Sidney Lee (*Life of William Shakespeare*, pp. 286–7) also identified Richard Cowley, another of Shakespeare's theatrical colleagues, as the 'merchant in lynen' in Brook's list.
23. For a facsimile, see Schoenbaum, *William Shakespeare; a Documentary Life* (1975 ed.), p. 170. For transcript, see Chambers, *William Shakespeare*, ii, pp. 20–2. The incomplete date, 43 Elizabeth, 1599, limits it to the period 17 November 1599 to 24 March 1600.

before changing his mind, probably on realizing that this might be challenged, in favour of a coat based on that borne by Arden families thought to have branched off from the main line at a much earlier date. That there should have been any doubt indicates, of course, that Robert Arden had never borne a coat of arms at all and that any claim that would have entitled him to do so had to be virtually fabricated but in such a way that it would not cause difficulties with other armigerous families. It is generally assumed that this second application did not end in a formal grant. Whereas the arms granted to John Shakespeare in 1596 were subsequently used by the family, principally to commemorate William Shakespeare on his funerary monument,[24] there is no evidence that they were ever quartered with those of the Ardens. But the fact that the Shakespeares had been willing to initiate the process, involving the payment of further substantial fees, is another indication of rising social aspirations.

There is no evidence that the grant of arms conferred on John Shakespeare an elevated status recognized by the local community. On his death in September 1601, there was an opportunity for the clerk to describe him as a gentleman ('generosus') when he entered his name in the burial register. This he did not do, though members of the Combe, Reynolds, Nash, Trussell, and Woodward families occur fairly regularly in the registers with this suffix. This is hardly a scientific test, as the data are both limited and inconsistent, and John's traditional status, as a former high bailiff and prominent burgess, was at least recognized by the customary prefix 'Master'. However, the decision not to describe him by the title to which he had successfully laid claim does imply a general lack of awareness or acceptance of his status. On the other hand, William Shakespeare was not slow to allow the title of gentleman to be added to his name. On 7 October 1601, only a month after his father's death, he was styled gentleman when listed as one of eighteen tenants of Nicholas Brend's properties in Southwark.[25] This can hardly be held up as an example of personal sensitivity. Thirteen of the eighteen tenants are identified by their trades—two as watermen, two as tanners and two as brewers, for example—and some suitable

24. They are also found quartered on his daughter Susanna's gravestone (and his son-in-law's) and on Susanna's seal.
25. Kathman, 'Six biographical records "rediscovered": some neglected contemporary references to Shakespeare', pp. 73–8.

suffix was no doubt thought advisable for four others not in trade.[26] 'Gentleman' therefore presented itself as the obvious alternative. This acceptance that Shakespeare was not engaged in an accepted trade is, of course, of interest, but the greater significance of his inclusion in this list of tenants is the coupling of his name with Burbage—'Richard Burbage and William Shackspeare gent(lemen)' doubtless as occupiers of the Globe—but with no reference to other Globe householders who by that date we might also expect to have been named.[27]

It is worth mentioning in passing that the determined belief that John Shakespeare's marriage into the Arden family would bolster his claim to gentry status sits uneasily alongside the claim, often made, that his wife's family was related to the Ardens of Park Hall and that the arrest and execution late in 1583 of the then head of the family, Edward Arden, for his alleged involvement in the so-called Somerville conspiracy to murder the queen, brought the Shakespeare family itself under deep suspicion. However, despite intensive research, the relationship between these two Arden families has never been established. On the other hand, if they were related, it would surely have been unwise for the Shakespeares to have made anything of their Arden connections if, in the recent past, such a link had been with the disgraced Ardens of Park Hall. One might speculate that, when Edward Arden was arrested for treason, his family name might have caused the Shakespeares some embarrassment, but the notion that the relationship was close enough to have aroused the suspicion of the authorities is surely disproved by the hopeful use of Robert Arden's name in support of the application for the grant of arms.

The purchase of New Place

Hard on the heels of the grant of arms on 28 October 1596 came the second, and better known, indication of Shakespeare's improving financial position: his purchase of New Place, to all intents and purposes completed by May 1597. Discussion of the significance of this purchase has not always been helped by the attribution attached to it as the second largest house in the town. The College in Old Town,

26. One tenant, John Knolles, has no suffix.
27. Below, pp. 102–3.

which before the Reformation had housed the priests who served Holy Trinity Church, was certainly the biggest. New Place, on the other hand, was built within the confines of a medieval burgage, the size of which had been defined in the charter by which the bishop of Worcester laid out his new town of Stratford in 1196; namely 3½ by 12 perches (18 × 60 metres or 57¾ × 198 feet).[28] Each plot attracted a chief rent of 12 pence, still being paid to the lord of the manor, Ambrose Dudley, earl of Warwick, on his death in 1590. A survey of his property then taken indicates, on the evidence of the payment of fractions of these rents, that many of these burgages had been subdivided. Nevertheless, over thirty in the main town centre streets had not, including at least four in High Street and eight in Church Street and Chapel Street.[29] According to a drawing from memory the street range of New Place was timber-framed, and was of two stories topped with five gables:[30] in other words, rather like the five-gabled section of the Shakespeare Hotel, also in Chapel Street, or Nos 19–21 in High Street (once with four gables but now with only two). At least another twenty-seven would have been as wide along the street. There were, however, other features about New Place which made it particularly attractive: unusually, it was said to have been built, at least in part, in brick, then an expensive building material, with a range of buildings on the far side of a small courtyard entered through the front range. In the hearth tax returns of 1663–70, the only near contemporary, if imperfect, measure of size we have, New Place was said to have had ten hearths.[31] Only the College, regularly returned as having fifteen hearths, was clearly bigger, giving support to the claim that New Place was indeed the second largest house in the town. Two others, however, were generally rated at the same level as New Place, namely with ten hearths, two or three with nine hearths and two or three with eight. In the 1590 survey, some of the wealthier burgesses held more than one of these larger houses, liable to the full burgage rent of 12 pence. John Sadler, for example, held two and the heirs of William Smith another two. Richard Quiney and his father Adrian held one each between them as well as numerous smaller properties. William Walford, who

28. Slater, 'Domesday village to medieval town'.
29. Fripp and others, eds., *Minutes and Accounts*, iv, pp. 92–110.
30. Simpson, 'New Place: the only representation of Shakespeare's House from an unpublished manuscript', pp. 55–7.
31. Arkell, ed., *Warwickshire Hearth Tax Returns*, pp. 217–23.

occupied a major property in High Street (Nos 17–18), owned on his death in 1624 at least thirteen other houses in the town centre, including Nos 19–21 High Street.[32] By itself, then, Shakespeare's purchase of New Place, though one of the most impressive houses in the town, did not necessarily catapult him into the upper reaches of the town's hierarchy.

There are other features of the purchase which suggest the house was obtained at a good price.[33] It had been built by Hugh Clopton towards the end of the fifteenth century and then left, with all his other property, to his great-nephew, William Clopton, whose main residence was Clopton House, a mile out of town. There is no evidence that any member of the family subsequently lived at New Place. In 1532 Adrian Quiney was the tenant and from 1543 to 1549 Dr William Bentley, who left the house 'in great ruyne and decay and unrepayred.'[34] Another William Clopton, who inherited the freehold in 1560, spent a considerable length of time abroad due to his unwillingness to abandon the old faith. In his absence two unscrupulous plotters, Ludovic Greville of Milcote and William Bott, were accused of conspiring to deprive him of much of his inheritance, to which was incidentally conjoined, in a later legal case, the more serious, indeed extraordinary allegation that in 1563 Bott had poisoned his daughter soon after her marriage to John Harper of Henley-in-Arden.[35] In that same year Bott had been able, by a process not entirely clear, to obtain the freehold of New Place in which he was already living. Four years later, in 1567, he sold it to William Underhill, a younger son of landed gentry and an up-and-coming lawyer. In 1568 Underhill had sufficient capital in

32. TNA, PROB 11/143, ff. 380–81v. See also Vine Hall, *Testamentary Papers I: Wills from Shakespeare's Town and Time*, pp. 6–9.
33. For much of what follows, see Bearman, 'Shakespeare's purchase of New Place'. The references are not all repeated here.
34. Halliwell, *Outlines*, ii, p. 102.
35. This was an accusation made by Roland Wheler, some eight years after the event, in a complex case about the Clopton inheritance brought by Greville against Francis Alford. Many of the papers were brought together in TNA, SP 12/79 and Wheler's unsubstantiated allegation (on pp. 149–51) was included in one of his responses to a series of interrogatories put to him about Bott's activities. Whether or not this was simply a vindictive accusation also needs to be considered alongside evidence of an action brought by Bott against Wheler in 1564 for libelous remarks (SCLA, BRU 15/5/15, 186, 196) and suits in Star Chamber, in the mid-1560s, between Bott and John Harper (TNA, STAC 5/H9/22; H29/34; H40/4; H62/1; H79/28).

hand to buy the manors of Idlicote and Loxley but died young, in March 1570, leaving his son, also William, a minor.

William the younger failed to build on the base he inherited from his father: indeed, the estate which he in turn passed on to his son had shrunk in size. An underlying reason for his difficulties was his adherence to Catholicism. As early as 1576 there were moves to arrest him as a recusant, abandoned only after intervention by Lord Burghley, Elizabeth's principal secretary of state. A few years later, in 1580, after a further citation for his recusancy, he was committed to prison by the Privy Council followed by claims that he had suffered such a great calamity that he was being forced to sell some of his lands. He married, in 1577, his cousin Mary and lived at Idlicote for a year or two where his eldest son was born but then moved to Stratford, and thus presumably to New Place, for the period 1580 to 1588. By 1589, however, he had returned briefly to Idlicote.

In the early 1590s his troubles multiplied. In 1591, he vested his lands in trustees, who were to hold them for his benefit, almost certainly a device to evade forfeiture of his lands as a consequence of his recusancy. Indeed, in 1592 he was named in a return of recusants although it was reported that his whereabouts were unknown: since the burial of his wife on 17 November 1590, he had not been seen at Idlicote, nor, apparently, in Stratford. In 1596, he sold land at Shustoke to raise £980, and other land in Loxley.

The man with whom Shakespeare struck a deal in 1597, or perhaps the year earlier, for the purchase of New Place was thus in some difficulty. This would have been generally known about in Stratford as one of his creditors was the Stratford Corporation.[36] Back in 1568 Underhill's father had acquired the lease of the tithes of Little Wilmcote belonging to the Corporation as part of the possessions of the dissolved Guild of the Holy Cross, settled on the Corporation by its 'foundation' charter of 1553. For this he paid an annual rent until his death in 1570, as did his trustees until at least 1574 when his son came of age. In 1583 the Corporation agreed to renew this lease, but the following year two members of the Corporation were asked to call on Underhill to find out why the rent was not being paid. In later years there was intermittent difficulty on this same issue, and from 1592 no payments at all were made. In October 1595 the Corporation decided

36. For further details, see Bearman, 'Shakespeare's purchase of New Place', pp. 479–81.

on legal action to recover what was owing to them. In Easter Term
1596 the case reached the Court of Common Pleas, the Corporation
claiming £16 13s. 4d. in unpaid rent. In September of that same year,
the town's legal officers served subpoenas on Underhill and the surviving trustees of his father's will, and the Corporation also agreed to
pursue the case in Chancery where a petition was duly lodged. Early
in 1597, notices of this suit were served on Underhill 'at Banburi, at
Coventry & at his oune house by Coventry', this thoroughness no
doubt the result of an uncertainty as to his whereabouts, noted as early
as 1592 when cited for recusancy. Underhill's response, laid before the
Corporation in February 1597, was to claim that the case should not
have been brought as the Corporation was already prosecuting him in
the Court of Common Pleas. Clearly, then, at the very moment that
the sale to Shakespeare of New Place was under discussion, Underhill
was being pressed very hard by the Corporation.

There is good reason, too, to believe that Shakespeare knew of
Underhill's difficulties. From time to time the Corporation would dis-
patch one of its number to London on civic business.[37] In October
1593, its choice fell for the first time on Richard Quiney. In October
1595, when the Corporation decided to take action against Underhill,
Quiney was again sent to London to obtain a copy of the will of
William Underhill's father, in preparation for the coming legal battle.
Early in 1597, Quiney was back in London at the height of the struggle
with Underhill: in fact, it was he who laid before the Corporation 'the
answere of Mr Wm Vnderhyll whch he brought hoame wih hym ffrom
London to Mr Bayleefe.'[38] There is no material evidence to establish
that Quiney met Shakespeare during either of these visits, let alone
discussed the business which had brought him to London on those
occasions. On the other hand, we can say with near certainty that on
two other occasions in the late 1590s the two men did make contact.
These will be discussed later as they have a bearing on the perceived
improvement in Shakespeare's circumstances. Suffice to say at this
point that on 24 January 1598, Quiney, whilst in London on a subsequent visit, received a letter from his friend, Abraham Sturley in
Stratford in which he makes mention of talk in the town that
Shakespeare was looking around to purchase some land in or near the

37. For further details, see Bearman, 'Shakespeare's purchase of New Place', pp. 475–6.
38. Fripp and others, eds., *Minutes and Accounts*, v, p. 99.

town; Sturley then asks Quiney to persuade Shakespeare to purchase an interest in the Stratford tithes instead which would benefit the Corporation.[39] It was also in that year, but in October, that Quiney, on his next visit, sat down and penned his famous letter to Shakespeare, asking for his help in securing a loan of £30.[40] What these letters establish, then, is that on at least two occasions in the year following Shakespeare's purchase of New Place, Quiney, whilst in London, had direct dealings with Shakespeare and that he knew him well enough to ask for his help over money matters. What might also therefore be reasonably proposed is that Quiney met Shakespeare on the other occasions that he visited London, including those of 1595 and early 1597, and that they had discussed the business which had brought him to town; and, in particular, the Corporation's dispute with William Underhill which had reached a critical point at the very moment that Shakespeare made his bid to buy Underhill's Stratford home. To some extent this is speculative, but the convergence of the Corporation's, Underhill's, and Shakespeare's interests at exactly this time is very persuasive.

The documentation recording Shakespeare's purchase survives only in the form of a final concord and its exemplification.[41] Normally a transaction of this sort would have been recorded in a dated and signed title deed containing, in its simplest form, a clear statement of the amount of money which changed hands and a description of the property in sufficient detail, especially in a town, for it to be identified on the ground. But for Shakespeare's purchase of New Place only the less precise final concord, and its exemplification, exist. The final concord (or fine) evolved out of a late twelfth-century method of settling land disputes in the Court of Common Pleas which by Shakespeare's day had become a ritualized process but still a useful means of ensuring that the transfer of property was acknowledged in a court of law, with standard copies of the concord delivered to the purchaser and vendor. An 'exemplification'—consisting of a certified copy in the monarch's name and bearing the court's seal—served as an additional safeguard. For Shakespeare's purchase of New Place, we thus have the record of the final concord itself, amongst the surviving records of the Court of

---

39. Below, pp. 91–2.
40. Below, pp. 93–8.
41. SCLA, ER 27/4a.

Common Pleas, now in The National Archives,[42] and the less common elaborate certified copy, the 'exemplification', which was given to Shakespeare to be filed with his title deeds. Why Shakespeare was prepared to pay the extra fee required for an exemplification, rather than make do with the routine copy to which he was entitled, is not entirely clear, though it may be connected with the fact that he was dealing with a man known for the dubious manner in which he had conducted his affairs, especially in the matter of land conveyancing. In 1596 it had emerged in a Chancery case that Underhill had sold to one Thomas Huntbach land in Shustoke to raise £980, to be paid in instalments.[43] Three payments were made, totalling £520, but Underhill had then put obstacles in the way of completing the deal, holding onto the earlier deeds of title but at the same time suing Huntbach, who had begun to suspect that Underhill's title was unsound, for the payment of £800 on a forfeited bond. In a similar transaction of around the same date, Underhill had agreed to the sale of land at Loxley to Walter Clark for £360, over half of which was paid; but Clarke, having 'referred the making of the Indentures & other bookes of conveyance' to Underhill, was still waiting for his title deeds on Underhill's death in the summer of 1597; and it was not until 1604 or so that his son Hercules acknowledged the sale.[44] Suspicion on Shakespeare's part that Underhill might renege on the deal would therefore not have been without some substance and, more wary than Underhill's other clients, he therefore took steps to ensure that the agreement he had reached with Underhill by final concord was given additional weight by arranging for its exemplification. It may even be that no formal deed was ever drawn up, Shakespeare relying simply on the 'final concord' process, by which a freehold property could pass in law.[45] Any more formal arrangement was then frustrated by Underhill's death three months later, allegedly poisoned by his son Fulk. Fulk in turn died in March 1599 before attaining his majority, and was thus succeeded by his brother, Hercules, who came of age in June 1602. The law allowed for a challenge to final concords by heirs coming of age and so, within a month or two,

---

42. TNA, CP 24/1/15; TNA, CP 26/1/251; CP 25/2/237, East. 39 Eliz. 1.
43. TNA, C 2/Eliz/H8/53.
44. TNA, C 2/JasI/C9/22.
45. A standard deed of conveyance could simply, of course, have been lost, but for the argument that it may never have existed, see Bearman, 'Shakespeare's purchase of New Place', pp. 466–70.

Shakespeare took steps to ensure that his purchase of New Place from William Underhill would not be challenged by his son. Again no conventional deed appears to have been executed, Shakespeare relying on a simple fine. The court's record, the 'foot', still survives in its archives. As for the vendor's and purchaser's copies, instead of one copy passing to Underhill and the other to Shakespeare, they both ended up in Shakespeare's bundle of deeds where they resurfaced in the 1880s.[46] We may infer from this not only that Hercules Underhill was not concerned about the issue (and may hardly have been involved) but also that Shakespeare, aware that his title was not guaranteed by a formal conveyance from Hercules's father, had taken immediate steps on Hercules coming of age, to ensure that there would be no subsequent challenge.

The description of property in final concords is given in formulaic Latin and in the case of New Place, we read (in translation) simply of 'one messuage, two barns and two gardens with appurtenances in Stratford-upon-Avon.'[47] Nor can the sum of money said to have changed hands, £60, be taken at its face value, probably on the grounds that neither party wanted the true sum to be a matter of public record. In cases where a standard conveyance and a final concord survive, it was often the case that the purchase money was at least twice that recorded in the final concord. We do know that, when Clopton had sold the house to William Bott in 1563, £140 changed hands and in 1567, when sold to Underhill senior, the purchase price was at least £110.[48] A price of £120 in 1597 (that is, twice the sum mentioned in the fine) would therefore be a likely estimate. This would certainly have been a very considerable sum. At that time houses in Stratford could change hands for as little as £30: the so-called 'Hornby Cottage' in Henley Street was sold for £24 in 1614 and another in Middle Row, in Bridge Street, for as little as £19 in 1583.[49] Nevertheless, a substantial property in Henley Street was mortgaged for £195 in 1599 and another

46. TNA, CP 25/2/237, Mich. 44 & 45 Eliz. I, no. 15; Folger Shakespeare Library, Z.c.36 (110, 111).

47. For a facsimile, see Schoenbaum, *William Shakespeare: a Documentary Life* (1975 edn), p. 174. For a full transcript of the exemplification, see Lewis, *The Shakespeare Documents*, i, p. 237; of a partial copy of the foot, Chambers, *William Shakespeare*, ii, pp. 95–6.

48. Folger Shakespeare Library, Z.c.36 (100); Z.c.36 (103). The latter deed is damaged at the vital point.

49. SCLA, TR 46/6/3; BRU 9/1/1. The latter, however, was sold on for £30 in 1608 (ER 2/28). See also Jones, *Family Life in Shakespeare's England*, pp. 9–10.

in Wood Street was sold in 1611 for £131.[50] The £120 which Shakespeare might have paid for New Place was therefore not excessive for a house of its reputed size and indicates, firstly, that given its recent history it may not have been in good condition and, secondly, that he had been able to strike a good deal with Underhill due to the pressures on him at the time. And, as already pointed out, the ownership of more than one property in the town was the norm for its leading citizens, indicating that Shakespeare's investment would not automatically have brought him to the top of the pile. Nor does his purchase imply that he had £120 to hand, only that he now enjoyed sufficient credit to enable him to raise the necessary funds.

There is one further point to consider: was there a reason behind Shakespeare's decision to make this purchase at that particular time? At that point his own immediate family comprised only four members, one of whom, himself, was often absent. On the face of it, the purchase of New Place might therefore be thought of as somewhat beyond his present needs. However, he may have had in mind a wish to provide a home not only for his immediate dependants, who until that time had presumably been living in the Shakespeare home in Henley Street, but also for his wider family, the head of which, his father John, had just been recognized as of gentry status. Stratford had recently twice been affected by fire, in May 1594 and the summer of 1595. One of these fires affected Henley Street and, from surviving documentary evidence, several properties, on both sides of the street and all within a stone's throw of the Shakespeare family home, can be specifically identified as damaged.[51] That the Shakespeares may subsequently have been reviewing their landholding in the street is indicated by the sale in January 1597 by John Shakespeare to George Badger, his neighbour on his north-west boundary, of a strip of land not more than a yard wide, and at about the same time of another plot on the south-east boundary.[52] Both transactions suggest at the very least a reassessment of the family's real estate in Henley Street and also that this may have been prompted by redevelopment or rebuilding work following the fire and

50. SCLA, TR 46/7/1; ER 27/11.
51. For these fires, and their extent, including a plan, see Bearman, 'Stratford's Fires of 1594 and 1595 revisited'.
52. Wellstood, *Catalogue of the Books, Manuscripts, Works of Art . . . Exhibited in Shakespeare's Birthplace*, p. 28; Halliwell, *Outlines*, i, pp. 390–2.

the family's (or Shakespeare's) decision to move his dependants to Chapel Street.

There are a number of other indicators that this is what might have happened. By the time of Shakespeare's death in 1616, the Henley Street home had been divided into two units, one let to Lewis Hiccox for use as a tavern; in Hiccox's inventory of 1627 there is reference to a sixty-two-year lease of the property to him by William Shakespeare.[53] It has been assumed, but on no surviving evidence, that this lease was arranged following John Shakespeare's death in 1601. However, this was not necessarily what happened. It is equally plausible to argue, especially if the Henley Street house had been partly damaged by fire, that in 1597 the decision was made to relocate the whole family. Such a move would be consistent with another feature of the wider family at the time: namely that, Shakespeare apart, no member was ever of any noticeable social standing. Neither John Shakespeare nor his wife Mary is known to have made a will nor did the administrations of their estates require official endorsement. There is no evidence that his brothers who remained in Stratford—Gilbert and Richard—maintained their own establishments and neither of them married. Like their father, they are not known to have made wills or to have had their estates formally administered.[54] Shakespeare's sister Joan did eventually attract a partner, William Hart, but not until she was thirty and the renaissance of the family well under way.[55] All this would indicate not only that the family's recovery was due almost entirely to Shakespeare's own improving financial status but also that, although he was able to provide his dependants with a home, this did not extend to their automatic enrichment. His brother Edmund's decision to follow Shakespeare to London to pursue a career in the theatre is a timely reminder of his limited options—indeed, as limited as Shakespeare's

53. See below, pp. 86–7.
54. There is need for a caveat here as not all copies of wills known to have been made have survived. The wills of Stratford testators could be proved at the Prerogative Court of Canterbury, the diocesan court at Worcester, or (for two years out of three) at Stratford's Peculiar Court. The Stratford will register has not survived, though it was said to have included at least one will for which no original survives (SCLA, BRT, 2/1, p. 2). On the other hand, the year of John Shakespeare's death (1601/2) was one of the years when the Stratford court did not sit.
55. Their place of marriage has not been identified, but their first child was baptised on 28 August 1600. Joan was baptised on 15 April 1569. Hart, who died in April 1616, is also not known to have left a will.

had been.[56] Likewise, brother Gilbert, though he may have been apprenticed as an haberdasher and sought to try his hand at the trade in London in the mid-1590s,[57] is later found back in Stratford and standing in for Shakespeare to finalize a subsequent land purchase.

Early business dealings

New Place may have been a residence fit for a gentleman, but true gentry status required the enjoyment of an independent income, one, in other words, not derived from trade or business. In Elizabethan England such independence would almost invariably involve the ownership of property, the management of which would yield sufficient income to allow the gentleman and his family freedom from the necessity of earning a living. However, the newly created aspirant, John Shakespeare, even though possibly already installed in New Place, had no such estate. He, or his son soon afterwards, did let the old family home in Henley Street to Lewis Hiccox. When Hiccox died in 1627, the unexpired term of years in a lease of sixty-three years was valued at £65.[58] Assuming this lease was made in around 1600, the rental income may therefore have been in the region of £2 a year, if not less.[59] This may sound a poor return on a substantial urban property, perhaps with a street frontage of nearly ninety feet,[60] although it is possible that Hiccox had paid what was known as an entry fine when he became tenant. This was a process frequently employed by the Stratford Corporation as a way of raising a capital sum, or, by not requiring one, to avoid the costs of repair or renovation to a run-down property, albeit at the cost of a lower rent over long periods of years. As a result, in 1600, the highest rent paid by a Corporation tenant was

---

56. Eccles, *Shakespeare in Warwickshire*, p. 107.
57. Below, pp. 109–10.
58. Jones, ed., *Stratford-upon-Avon Inventories*, ii, p. 16.
59. i.e. it would have had thirty-six years to run, valued at £65.
60. John Shakespeare paid a chief rent of 17 pence on his Henley Street property in 1590, echoed by the 20 pence paid by the Hiccox family in 1637 for the same property (Fripp and others, eds., *Minutes and Accounts*, iv, p. 96; Maidstone, Centre for Kentish Studies, U269/E249/6). These rents derived from the 12 pence paid to the lord of the manor for each burgage into which the town had originally been divided. These measured fifty-eight feet on the street (above, p. 77).

44 shillings and this was exceptional.[61] If Shakespeare had charged such an entry fine for the lease of the Henley Street house, he may have done so to fund his New Place purchase.

At about the same time the Shakespeares also let a barn at the rear of their Henley Street property, facing out into Guild Street, to Robert Johnson, the proprietor of a substantial inn (later the White Lion) lying further along Henley Street to the north-west. On Johnson's death in the late summer of 1611 the unexpired (but unspecified) term of years in the lease was valued at £20 when the inventory of his estate was drawn up.[62] Given that his two leases of Corporation tenements, valued in the same inventory at £10 apiece, reflected the annual rents he paid for these (6s. 8d. and 5 shillings) it is probably safe to assume that he was not paying the Shakespeares any more simply for a barn.[63] In confirmation that together these two leases might have netted for Shakespeare less than £3, John Smith, a wealthy ironmonger, was receiving only £1 for a tenanted town property when he made his will in 1612.[64] In 1603, Richard Hornby leased out his house in Henley Street for twenty-one years at an annual rent of 30 shillings and there are other examples of returns smaller than this, even when no entry fines were paid.[65]

Ownership of farmland was always seen as a more appropriate component of a gentleman's estate, yet in the 1590s, John Shakespeare held no such property. This was not the case earlier in his career, but by the late 1580s, in order to meet a pressing need for funds, he had sold or mortgaged the property which he had acquired on his marriage to Mary Arden.[66] By November 1597, however, within six months of the purchase of New Place, we have the first indication of an effort to

---

61. Fripp and others, eds., *Minutes and Accounts*, vi, p. 91. Between 1600 and 1609, entry fines of more than £10 and £20 were very unusual.

62. This inventory, located at Worcester in 1908, can no longer be traced, but Richard Savage's manuscript copy is preserved at SCLA, ER 82/6/93/37. Savage announced the discovery in a short note in *Athenaeum*, 29 August 1908, p. 250.

63. The properties were a house in Henley Street, valued at £10 with thirty years to run, giving an annual rent of 6s. 8d. which is what he paid annually to the Corporation, and another in Windsor Street, valued at £10 with twenty years to run, giving an annual rent of 10 shillings, though in fact he was only paying 5 shillings.

64. Hall, *Testamentary Papers I: Wills from Shakespeare's Town and Time*, p. 23.

65. SCLA, TR 46/6/2. For another example, see SCLA, ER 1/1/40 (16 shillings per annum for a twenty-one-year lease of a house in Sheep Street, 1593).

66. The issue of the subsequent legal challenge is best treated by Eric Poole, 'John Shakespeare and the Aston Cantlow Mortgage'.

enhance further the family's status through the acquisition of landed property. This initially took the form of an attempt to regain possession of the very house and land in Wilmcote which John Shakespeare had mortgaged to his wife's brother-in-law, Edmund Lambert, back in 1578 as security for a loan of £40. The loan had been scheduled for repayment in September 1580, but John Shakespeare had clearly defaulted. If interest on the loan had at least been paid, it is unlikely that Lambert would have immediately exercised his right to claim the freehold, but the implication is that John had failed to do even this whereupon Lambert assumed outright possession. On his death in 1587, the property had therefore passed to his son, John.

At that point, John Shakespeare, clearly still in need of money but unable to redeem the original mortgage, had taken advantage of Lambert's uncertain title to ask for a further sum of £20 in return for giving up any claim to the property. As this was, in effect, John Shakespeare's wife's original marriage portion, and his son William's inheritance, they too were said to have been parties to this offer, tendered in Stratford on 26 September 1587, and to which Lambert allegedly agreed. However, when Lambert later reneged on the deal, John Shakespeare brought an action against him, seeking £30 in all for damages. In his defence, Lambert denied any such deal and the case appears to have petered out.[67]

By November 1597, however, the Shakespeares were in a stronger position and a decision was clearly made to revive the issue, especially in view of complexities associated with the original mortgage of 1578 whereby a twenty-one-year lease of part at least of the property had been granted to one George Gibbs, at a nominal rent, probably in return for an additional loan. By 1597 this lease was due to expire, opening up the possibility of a new lease at market rates. The case the Shakespeares now brought against Lambert in Chancery therefore differed markedly from the one of 1588.[68] The matter in dispute was still the house and land in Wilmcote mortgaged by John Shakespeare to Edmund Lambert, but this time round the claim that John Shakespeare had asked Lambert for an additional £20 in order for Lambert to

---

67. The documentation up to this point is mainly found in Halliwell, *Outlines*, ii, pp. 11–13; Chambers, *William Shakespeare*, ii, pp. 35–41. The argument, often put, that William Shakespeare was involved in this reported action beyond merely giving his consent, is unconvincing.

68. Halliwell, *Outlines*, ii, pp. 14–17.

obtain the undisputed right to the freehold was quietly dropped. Instead, John claimed that, before Edmund Lambert died, he had offered him £40 to redeem the mortgage, and that Lambert had refused the offer because John owed him other monies; and that he (John Shakespeare) had made the same offer to John Lambert after his father's death which had been similarly rejected. It was therefore argued that in equity the Shakespeares should be allowed to resume undisputed ownership. In reply, Lambert denied the claim, and on 5 July 1598, a commission was appointed to take evidence from witnesses on behalf of both parties.[69] The Shakespeares chose as commissioners Richard Lane and John Combe, substantial Stratford landowners and the sort of people to whom the Shakespeares now believed themselves allied. But here the process faltered, leading to complaints by Lambert's counsel nearly a year later that the plaintiff had taken no such evidence (whether Lambert had is not clear) and a new commission was therefore appointed on 27 June 1599. The last reference to the case is dated 23 October 1599 and is an order to the effect that, unless the defendant within seven days asked for a 'stay of publication', then 'publication is granted', i.e. the case would be heard. No further documentation survives to establish what, if anything, happened next; all that can be said with certainty is that no judgment could have been made in the Shakespeares' favour: Lambert, perhaps regarding the property as a poisoned chalice, sold it off in 1601.[70]

William Shakespeare is not mentioned as a party to this second suit but there can be little doubt that he would have played an important part in the proceedings, if only because he now had the means to meet the legal costs. Whether or not he knew of the true circumstances concerning the original mortgage, or of the subsequent efforts to squeeze more money out of the Lamberts, the recovery of lost patrimony would be a natural first step for a family anxious to establish that its recently acquired gentry status had something to back it up. Shakespeare might also have felt that the recovery of land which had been lost during a period of family misfortune would have been of particular comfort to his ageing father and mother. But whatever the

69. For this and the following papers in the case, see Lewis, *Shakespeare Documents*, i, pp. 145–6.
70. Eccles, *Shakespeare in Warwickshire*, p. 29; Alcock, *Topography and Land in Early Wilmcote, Warwickshire*, p. 10, citing an abstract of title at the Church of England Record Centre (copy at SCLA, PR 408/4).

motive, there is little doubt that this second lawsuit, coming just after the purchase of New Place, was part of a deliberate process of re-establishing the family's standing. However, after assessing the witness evidence collected by the commissioners (which must have been taken and disclosed to both sides in order for the latest court order to have been made), Shakespeare's lawyers presumably advised him that his, or his father's, case was insufficiently strong. Until the 1620s, the dice were heavily loaded against those who had resorted to the uncertain process of mortgaging their estates and for whom there was no easy escape from forfeiture if they failed to repay the loan on the date agreed. Over time, there evolved a right of 'equity of redemption' by which a mort-gagor, as long as he met his interest payments, could petition against foreclosure. However, certainly in the 1580s, when John had initially pledged his Wilmcote lands, and even by the late 1590s when the fam-ily renewed its attempts to reclaim the property, there was no such principle which could be invoked. Over the years the Lord Chancellor had become increasingly willing to intervene in cases of severe hard-ship or suspected fraud but it was not until the mid-1620s that 'equity of redemption' had developed into a recognized right. For the Shakespeares, a retrospective appeal from a family not by then in obvi-ous distress was therefore unlikely to succeed.

This dispute also raises questions over how Shakespeare viewed wider family relationships. Lambert, who succeeded his father in a sizeable estate at Barton-on-the-Heath, was, after all, his cousin but the fact that Shakespeare brought this case against him certainly implies that no love was lost between them. Unwise though it may be to use the plays as a source of biographical data, Shakespeare's unflattering portrayal, in the opening scenes of *The Taming of the Shrew*, written in the early 1590s, of Christopher Sly, the drunken tinker hailing from 'Burton Heath', would suggest at the very least that Barton-on-the-Heath, and by association the Lambert family, did not provoke kindly thoughts in the poet's mind.

Another strand to this revival of the family's interests must surely be the simultaneous effort to recover from John Walford, a wealthy cloth-ier of Marlborough, a debt of £21, allegedly still owing to John Shakespeare, despite frequent requests, following a sale some thirty years before of twenty-one tods of wool.[71] To this John added £10 in

71. Hotson, *Shakespeare's Sonnets Dated*, pp. 231–3.

damages. Only the opening plea survives, on the plea roll of the Court of Common Pleas for Trinity Term 1599, exactly contemporary with the final stages of the Lambert case and seemingly part and parcel of a coordinated effort to revive the family's status. The outcome is unknown as the later plea roll is missing and, on the face of it, is unlikely to have succeeded, given the considerable passage of time. Nevertheless it is this very timing, against the background of similar proceedings, which gives this episode particular relevance in any assessment of family ambition.

This is as good a point as any to make reference to the so-called 'Clayton suit', which was heard in Queen's Bench some six months later in which one William Shakespeare, through his attorney, Thomas Audley, brought a successful action against John Clayton of Willington, in Bedfordshire, for the recovery of a debt of £7, acknowledged under a bond dated at Cheapside on 22 May 1592, together with 20 shillings in costs.[72] The close proximity in date of this and the two other cases already discussed lends some plausibility to the idea that this William Shakespeare is to be identified with William Shakespeare the playwright, engaged in further action to promote family interests. However, in 1949 Leslie Hotson drew attention to entries in the Bedfordshire subsidy rolls for a John Clayton of Willington (1593) and a William Shakespeare of Campton (1596), eight miles to the south.[73] More recently, John Rollett has shown that Thomas Audley occurring in the subsidy roll for London for 1599 was, in all probability, the son of Thomas Audley of Henlow, two miles from Campton.[74] That William Shakespeare of the Clayton suit was William Shakespeare the playwright is therefore very unlikely.[75]

It was not only by laying claim to the lost Lambert inheritance that Shakespeare hoped to add to his property portfolio. On 24 January 1598, whilst the Lambert case was still in progress, Abraham Sturley, one of the town's leading aldermen, wrote a long letter to his friend and fellow alderman, Richard Quiney, then in London on Corporation

---

72. The documentation was apparently discovered by Halliwell (*Outlines*, i, pp. 185–6) and discussed by Stopes (*Shakespeare's Industry*, p. 259), both of whom thought the plaintiff was the playwright.
73. Hotson, *Shakespeare's Sonnets Dated*, pp. 229–30.
74. Rollett, 'William Shackspere vs. John Clayton'.
75. But see Diana Price, *Shakespeare's Unorthodox Biography*, revised edn, 2012, pp. 21–2, citing, for example, Honigmann, '"There is a World elsewhere": William Shakespeare, Businessman'.

business.[76] Crucial though it is for the light it throws on events in
Stratford at a time when high corn prices had pushed the population
to the verge of open protest, it has become better known for its passing
reference to Shakespeare: for Sturley tells Quiney that he had gathered
from his father, Adrian Quiney, that 'o[r] countriman M[r] Shakspeare is
willinge to disburse some monei upon some odd yardeland or other
att Shottri or neare about us.' Whether this was the land which
Shakespeare did eventually purchase will be discussed later but, according to Sturley, Adrian Quiney, clearly unimpressed by the news, was
keen instead that Shakespeare should be persuaded 'to deal in the matter of o[r] Tithes. Bi the instrucctions u can geve him theareof and bi the
frendes he can make therefore, we thinke it a faire marke for him to
shoote att & not unpossible to hitt. It obtained, would advance him
indeede & would do us much good.'[77] The history of the Stratford
tithes is a very complicated and intricate one and again this will be
discussed in more detail when considering Shakespeare's investment
eight years later in a half-share of part of them.[78] To explain Sturley's
use of 'our' and 'us', we need only be aware at this point that, under
Stratford's 1553 charter, a portion of these tithes had been granted to
the Corporation whose interests Adrian Quiney clearly had in mind.

Reports, then, were circulating early in 1598 of Shakespeare's serious
intention of investing in some further real estate in or near his native
town. In a sense this is hardly surprising, given that his purchase of
New Place in 1597 would almost inevitably have encouraged a belief
that he was now in a position to add to his property portfolio. It also
implies an early decision on Shakespeare's part that, despite the fact
that he was earning his money in London, he had decided to invest
any surplus capital, or at least money he could now raise on credit, in
his native town. Again we cannot be sure that this was intended to be
of comfort to a father whom Shakespeare felt he may have disap-
pointed, if not wronged, when he contracted a youthful and hasty
marriage at a time of financial difficulty. At the very least it is clear that

76. SCLA, BRU 15/1/135, printed in part, with modernized spelling, in Fripp, *Master
    Richard Quyny*, pp. 124–9. The original has since suffered water damage, but for an
    early nineteenth-century copy by James Saunders, used here, see SCLA, ER 1/97, ff.
    148–52v.
77. Quiney was currently one of the farmers of the Corporation tithes, held on lease by
    Ralph Hubaud, and this may have had a bearing on Sturley's remark (Fripp and others,
    eds., *Minutes and Accounts*, v, p. 94; vi, p. 60).
78. Below, pp. 118–21.

he never intended to turn his back on Stratford. The acquisition of a coat of arms, the purchase of a substantial town property, and news of the family's attempt to regain its mortgaged estate would all have served to make it easier for Shakespeare to raise sufficient capital for further investment when the opportunity arose.

Sturley's reference to Shakespeare's intention of purchasing land in Stratford may be the first evidence that his local contemporaries were aware of Shakespeare's improving financial position, but even better evidence of this is to be found in Richard Quiney's letter to Shakespeare dated 25 October 1598, written during another of Quiney's visits to London (Figure 4).[79] In it he seeks help for negotiating a loan of £30, ostensibly to help Quiney pay the debts he had incurred during his current visit to the capital but almost certainly made largely on behalf of Abraham Sturley who had written to Quiney on 16 October, bemoaning the fact that a bond for the repayment of £100 would become due on 22 November and that he was also in dire need of £25 to meet pressing creditors which he therefore hoped 'might bi u^r good labour & leisure be procured.'[80] That these financial embarrassments were linked to Quiney's plea to Shakespeare for help is more or less proved by the fact that on the day he wrote to Shakespeare, Quiney also let Sturley know that an approach to Shakespeare concerning a loan had indeed been made.[81] In other letters to Quiney, it is also clear that his nephew, Daniel Baker, and his father, Adrian, knew of the approach.[82] Indeed, Baker had already written to Quiney, on 17 October, asking him to 'procure monie to paie it [a debt to Edward Kempson] for mee', bringing additional pressure on Quiney to lay hands at short notice on some ready cash.[83] Whether or not Shakespeare responded to these requests is not known, but, in the context of the perceived notion of Shakespeare's financial position, it is at least clear

79. SCLA, ER 27/4.
80. SCLA, ER 1/97, f. 134.
81. His letter does not survive, only Sturley's reply, dated 4 November, written on receipt of Quiney's, the date of which he gives as 25 October: SCLA, BRU 15/1/136; Chambers, *William Shakespeare*, ii, p. 103.
82. Chambers, *William Shakespeare*, ii, p. 103. Adrian's letter (SCLA, BRU 15/1/131) is undated but includes mention of a matter also found in a letter of Sturley's dated 27 October (SCLA, BRU 15/1/145). Baker's (SCLA, BRU 15/1/124) is dated 24 November, he having picked up the news from Quiney's wife.
83. SCLA, BRU 15/5/149.

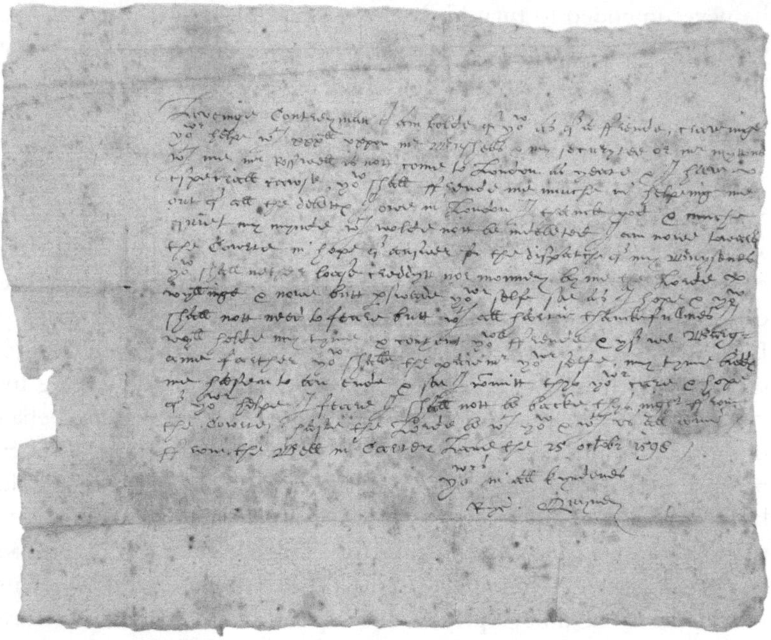

Figure 4. Richard Quiney's letter to William Shakespeare asking for his help in securing a loan of £30, 25 October 1598

Source: In this only surviving item of Shakespeare's correspondence, Quiney addresses him as 'Loveinge Contreyman' and signs himself off 'in all kyndenes', sure indications of an established relationship between the two men. Within three lines, he has set out the essentials of his request and named 'Mr Bushell', 'Mr Mytton', and 'Mr Rosswell', further evidence that Shakespeare needed no introduction to the business in hand.

Shakespeare Centre Library and Archive, ER 27/4

that to his Stratford contemporaries he was now seen as a man of sufficient means to help in the business of raising money.

Quite what was expected of Shakespeare is not entirely clear. The letter has been published many times, but it may help this discussion to set out again its essentials.

...I am bolde of yo^w as of a Frende, craveinge yo^{wr} helpe wth xxx^{ll} upon Mr Bushells & my securytee or Mr Myttons wth me. Mr Rosswell is nott come to London as yeate & I have especiall cawse. Yo^w shall Frende me muche in helpeing me out of all the debettes I owe in London, I thancke god, & muche quiet my mynde wch wolde nott be indebted. I am nowe towardes the Cowrte in hope of answer for the dispatche of my Buysenes. Yo^w shall nether loase creddytt nor monney by me, the Lorde wyllinge, & nowe butt perswade yo^{wr} selfe soe as I hope & yo^w shall nott need to feare butt wth all hartie thanckfullnes

I wyll holde my tyme & content y^wr Frende, & yf we Bargaine farther yo^w
shalbe the paie m^r yo^wr selfe ...

£30 was then a very considerable sum, £10 more than the annual
salary of either Stratford's vicar or the town's schoolmaster. From the
evidence of some 160 inventory valuations drawn up in Stratford
between 1556 and 1620, the personal estate of eighty-two townsmen
and women was valued at £30 or less, with a further thirty-three falling within the £31–£50 range. In the years 1570–1630 around half of
the properties for which purchase prices have been traced changed
hands for £30 or less.[84] To interpret Quiney's plea for help as a direct
request for a loan of £30 would therefore imply that Shakespeare had
an almost impossibly large sum of disposable income to hand. Moreover
Shakespeare, having just raised £120 for the purchase of New Place
and pondering on the uncertainty facing the Chamberlain's Men on
the expiration, in April 1597, of the lease of its home at the Theatre, to
be discussed later,[85] would hardly have been in a position to think of
making very substantial personal loans. In any case, that he was being
asked to do so is not consistent with Quiney's actual wording. The
crux of his request is that Shakespeare should 'helpe with' a loan of this
£30 'uppon Mr Bushells & my securytee or Mr Myttons wth me.' These
men have been persuasively identified as Thomas Bushell (father or
son) of Pebworth, in Gloucestershire, and Richard Mytton, both associated with Stratford's lord of the manor, Edward Greville.[86] The reason
for Quiney's approach to Shakespeare is then explained, namely that
'Mr Rosswell is nott come to London as yeate & I have especiall cawse.'
This is a reference to Peter Rosswell, yet another of Greville's associates.[87] Normal practice at this time would require two men to enter
into a bond to act as sureties that the borrower would repay his debt
by a specified date. Quiney's phrasing is a little ambiguous but needs to
be taken in the context of some twenty other letters, dated to the

84. Only twenty-three prices have so far been traced, four for the decade 1571–80, two
   each for the decades 1581–90, 1591–1600, and 1601–10, eight for 1611–20, and five for
   1621–30.
85. Below, pp. 101–2.
86. Eccles, *Shakespeare in Warwickshire*, pp. 93–4, citing in particular SCLA, BRU 15/7/138;
   Fripp and others, eds., *Minutes and Accounts*, iv, 118. Thomas Bushell junior had married Greville's sister by 1593 (*Visitation of Warwickshire, 1619*, pp. 29, 139; *Visitation of
   Worcestershire, 1569*, p. 29).
87. Eccles, *Shakespeare in Warwickshire*, pp. 93–4, 109–10; Fripp and others, eds., *Minutes and
   Accounts*, vi, pp. 132–4, 139, 142.

period October–December 1598, which Quiney received in London, concerning not only his negotiations on the Corporation's behalf but also his personal business and financial affairs.[88] Both these issues involved Edward Greville, firstly because, as lord of the manor, his agreement was required if the Corporation's ambition to secure a new charter were to be realized; but, secondly, the letters reveal that Greville, and his wife, were also involved in a web of financial dealings with Stratford townsmen. In January 1598, we learn that Quiney's wife, Elizabeth, was in pursuit of Lady Greville for arrears over a business transaction involving malt 'w^c hindreth & trowbleth her not a littell.'[89] In the autumn, Quiney was to hear from both his father and Sturley that this dispute was ongoing ('Yesterdaye y^r wyffe was w^t my laydy Grevelle but can have no moneye').[90] Daniel Baker, in letters of 26 October and 13 November, also seems to have been confident that Greville would pay off his debts in London to the tune of £70 in recognition of money that Greville owed him, this to be expedited, according to the earlier of the two letters, through the efforts of Greville's agent Peter Rosswell.[91] At the end of his letter, he also asks to be remembered to Richard Mytton, as we have seen, another of Greville's associates already in London, who he is sure will help him out with a further loan if necessary. The implication here, then, is surely that Quiney, to meet his and his friends' immediate needs, was hoping to get some money out of Rosswell too, in recognition of the fact that his master also owed money to the Quineys.[92] However, as Rosswell 'is nott come to London as yeate', Quiney decided to make an approach to Shakespeare instead, asking him to borrow £30 with Quiney and Thomas Bushell or Richard Mytton, acting as sureties. His follow-up—'Yo^w shall nether loase creddytt nor monney by me, the Lorde wyllinge'—is then clearly designed to reassure Shakespeare that, should he agree to help, he would be taking no undue risk. He ends this main part of his letter with an intriguing reassurance that Shakespeare should not 'feare butt wth all hartie thanckfullnes I wyll holde my

---

88. These letters are partially transcribed by Fripp in *Master Richard Quyny*, pp. 133–54, 157–60, and discussed by Alan Stewart in *Shakespeare's Letters*, pp. 117–31, 157–65.

89. SCLA, ER 1/97, f. 156v, from BRU 15/1/135 (see n. 76).

90. SCLA, BRU 15/1/133, 145.

91. SCLA, BRU 15/1/126, 128.

92. Lena Orlin, who in 'Anne by Indirection' discusses in detail these letters as they affected the Quineys, draws attention to a letter of 23 November implying that Greville was about to pay Quiney £20 (p. 445).

tyme [i.e. repay the debt at a date to be agreed] & content y^wr Frende.'
This is presumably a reference to the actual money-lender or his agent,
here not named but known to Shakespeare, implying that the matter
had already been discussed between the two men: indeed, Quiney's
letter indicates that the names of all the parties (Rosswell, Bushell, and
Mytton) must have been already well known to Shakespeare and that
some discussion of Quiney's affairs must have previously taken place.
Quiney's next remark—'yf we Bargaine farther yo^w shalbe the paie m^r
yo^wrselfe'—is far from clear unless it is to confirm that, if the transaction goes ahead, it will be Shakespeare who will be in control of the
situation. But that Shakespeare is indeed being asked to take on the
risk of the loan is supported by Abraham Sturley's response when he
heard that an approach to Shakespeare had been made ('that o^r countriman Mr William Shak*speare* would procure us monei, w^c I will like
of as I shall heare when & wheare & howe').[93] He then continues with
the remark that 'if monei might be had for 30 or 40^l, a lease &c might
be procured. Oh howe can u make dowbt of monei who will not
beare xxx^tie or xl^s towards sutch a match?' Quiney's letter to which
Sturley was replying has not survived so we cannot be sure to what
Sturley is alluding. Perhaps Sturley is saying that, if Shakespeare suc-
ceeds in his negotiations, he might be rewarded in part with the grant
of a favourable lease of the Corporation tithes, an issue which the two
men had discussed previously in the year.[94] Clearly the rate of interest
(but at only a shilling in the pound, or 5 per cent, half of what was
legally allowed) must also have been raised, though whether or not
Shakespeare was directly involved in this is not made clear.

This letter, though folded and sealed, may not in fact have been
sent, as it was later found in Quiney's own papers. But, as already
noted, that Quiney made an approach to Shakespeare in some form is
established by Sturley's later remarks; and, even if Shakespeare did not
see these exact words addressed to him, this does not invalidate the
clear evidence that Quiney saw Shakespeare as a man of some substance and influence. However, if the above interpretation is accepted,
the letter does not establish that Quiney thought Shakespeare had
sufficient capital in hand to lend him £30, simply that he thought

93. SCLA, ER 1/97, f. 144v, from BRU 15/1/136 (above, n. 76); Chambers, *William Shakespeare*, ii, p. 103.
94. Above, p. 92.

him a man of sufficient credit in London to negotiate, and then secure,
the money on Quiney's (and Sturley's behalf)—not, then, a man of
wealth but certainly creditworthy. And, indeed, a man thought to be of
a generous disposition, given that, if Shakespeare really was being asked
to borrow £30 on Quiney's behalf (perhaps because Quiney currently
lacked sufficient credit in London to raise the money himself), then he
would have been thought of as a man prepared to accept an assurance
from an old acquaintance that he would be repaid promptly. And it is
also clear, of course, that Shakespeare was already thoroughly versed in
the mechanics of borrowing and lending money based essentially on
creditworthiness which, if undermined through a failure to meet obligations, could lead on to financial difficulties.[95] Indeed, taken together,
Quiney's correspondence over this period forcibly reminds us that,
then as now, all those involved in business both owed money and had
money owing to them, and that the key to success, or at least to the
avoidance of failure, was to ensure that one's obligations did not
exceed expected returns. It has been proposed above (pp. 10–23) that
Shakespeare's father John got the balance wrong and paid the penalty.
Shakespeare, however, retained his creditworthiness throughout his
career. Indeed, as Quiney's letter reassures him, he would not 'loase
creddytt' were he to come to his friend's help.

Quiney's view of Shakespeare's financial position at the time would
have been influenced by a further consideration. As the result of a succession of bad harvests beginning in 1595, the price of corn had been
pushed up to record levels leading to serious disturbances in many
parts of the country. The government was not unresponsive and took
measures to restrict the use of barley for malting and to enquire into
accusations of the hoarding of grain by unscrupulous profiteers. In
Stratford, an initial survey of the holders of grain and malt was carried
out in 1595, before Shakespeare's purchase of New Place, and he was
therefore not included. Nor, more significantly, was his father.[96] But
his name does appear in a second survey, conducted in February 1598,

---

95. As a postscript, we might note that, in a letter of 18 November, Adrian Quiney implies
that Greville had indeed given Quiney £20 which Lady Greville had earlier hoped
might be set against her debt to the Quineys (SCLA, BRU 15/1/129, 133). Shakespeare's
help may therefore not have been required.

96. Printed in part in Fripp and others, eds., *Minutes and Accounts*, v, pp. 48–70, but with
significant and inexplicable omissions, not least almost the entire return for the borough of Stratford. The full survey is at WCRO, CR 1886/BB711/2663.

nearly a year after he had acquired New Place.[97] There is every reason to suppose that the quantities recorded on this occasion were underestimates. The earlier survey had listed Richard Quiney as one who 'usethe the trades of buyinge and sellinge of Corne for greate sommes And makinge of mallte' and his holdings, said to comprise forty-seven quarters of barley and thirty-two of malt, were the highest in the town.[98] By the time of the second survey, of February 1598, written up by Quiney himself, these holdings had miraculously dwindled to just over sixteen quarters.[99] Some massaging of the figures might therefore be suspected. Nevertheless they can still be used, with the necessary caution, to indicate the relative wealth of the seventy-one burgesses whose holdings are listed in the return. Occasionally holdings of beans, peas, and fletches are also recorded, but, taking account of malt and other grains of various types only, Shakespeare's recorded holding of ten quarters of malt certainly places him fairly high in the rankings with only sixteen holding more than that, two the same, and fifty-two fewer (Figure 5). In addition to these personal holdings, twenty-eight burgesses were also storing in their barns considerable quantities of malt belonging to men living outside the town, including Sir Thomas Lucy of Charlecote and Sir John Conway, with whom they were presumably in some business relationship. John Sadler, for instance, holding only three quarters of his own, also had custody of a further 24½ quarters belonging to men from outside the town.[100]

Shakespeare, then, was clearly not dealing in malt in the same way as those who were taking in these considerable quantities from elsewhere. On the other hand, his personal holdings were considerable, well above the average and placing him in the upper reaches of local society. Though he may be acquitted of any charge of deliberate hoarding, and the associated intent of releasing malt onto the market at inflated prices, his holdings were clearly in excess of immediate household needs; and, as we shall see, he is later found selling surplus holdings to at least one fellow townsman.[101] In other words, he had the means of

97. Fripp and others, eds., *Minutes and Accounts*, v, pp. 135–40.
98. WCRO, BB711/266, f.1, transcribed with modernized spelling in Fripp and others, eds., *Minutes and Accounts*, v, p. 48.
99. However, he was holding a further eighteen quarters of 'straingers malte' (Fripp and others, eds., *Minutes and Accounts*, v, pp. 138, 140).
100. In the published version (see n. 98), this 'Straingers Malte' is grouped together at the end of the survey, whereas the original lists the holdings at the end of each ward.
101. Below, pp. 131–3.

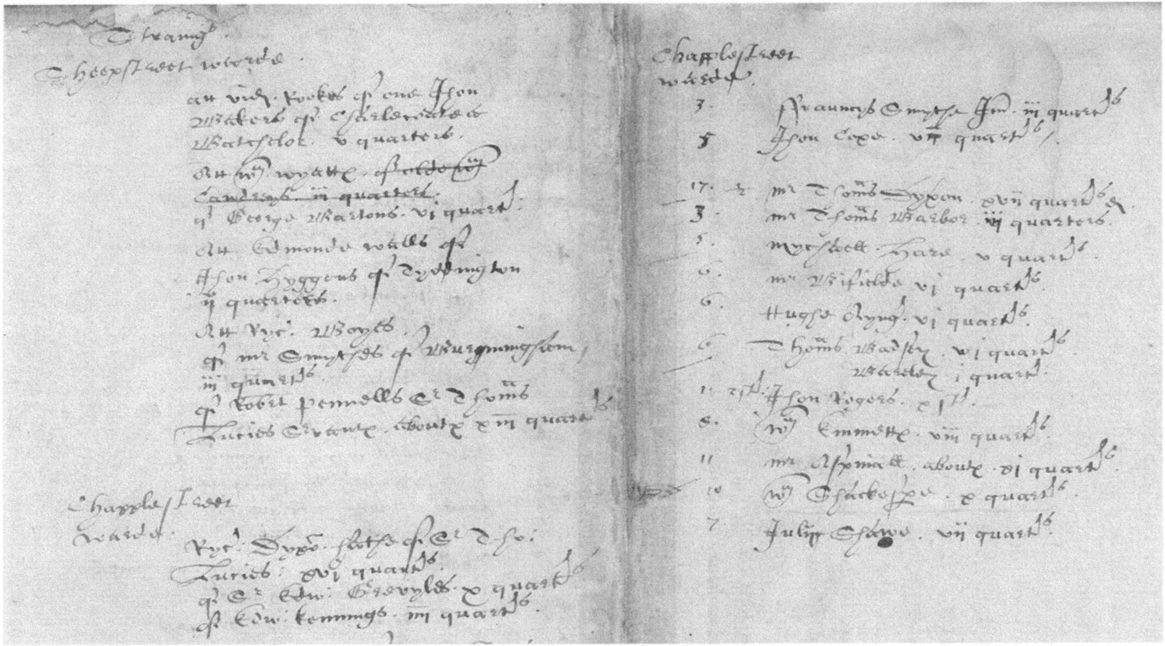

Figure 5. Extract from the 'noate of Corne & malte' stored in Stratford-upon-Avon, 4 February 1598, recording William Shakespeare's holding of ten quarters (eighty bushels) of malt

Source: Shakespeare's name is listed under Chapel Street ward (to the right) in which his recently purchased house, New Place, was situated. His holding was substantial but not the largest in his ward: both Thomas Dixon and the schoolmaster, Alexander Aspinall held more. However, another fifty-two of the seventy-one burgesses listed in the survey held less, an indication of Shakespeare's relative means. On the other hand, he was not engaged in the large-scale dealings of those townsmen who also stored malt belonging to local landowners ('Straingers Malte'). On the left are listed those holdings stored in Richard Boyce's barn in Sheep Street ward, including three quarters belonging to 'Mr Smyth' of Birmingham and thirteen to Sir Thomas Lucy's servant, Robert Pennell.

Shakespeare Centre Library and Archive, BRU 15/1/106

laying in stocks of an expensive material and Quiney, closely involved in the compilation of the report, would have had this information to hand when he thought fit to approach Shakespeare for help with a loan.

The property portfolio expands

The rumours circulating in January 1598 that Shakespeare was intending to purchase land in the neighbourhood of Stratford did not immediately become a reality. This may have been due to the unexpected expense which had fallen on him and his fellow-sharers in the Chamberlain's Men following the expiration of the twenty-one-year lease on their first home, the Theatre, in April 1597.[102] This lease had been granted to James Burbage by Giles Allen back in 1575 and, in probable anticipation of future uncertainty, Burbage had recently invested £600 in the purchase of part of the old Blackfriars Priory, previously used for theatrical performances by a company of boy players, signing the deed of conveyance on 4 February 1596. He is then said to have spent a further £400 on turning it into an indoor theatre for the Chamberlain's Men. However, in November of that year residents in the near vicinity, apparently led by the Dowager Countess Russell, and even including George Lord Hunsdon who in July had succeeded his father Henry as the company's nominal patron, successfully petitioned the Privy Council to prevent the new theatre from opening. Burbage died early in the New Year—he was buried on 2 February—failing to leave a will. His estate in effect passed to his sons, Richard and Cuthbert, who now found themselves in a difficult position. With the lease of the Theatre due to expire in April but with the Chamberlain's Men unable to take up occupancy of Blackfriars into which their father had recently sunk significant capital, the company was in need of a new venue. There is a temptation to over-dramatize the situation. A clause had been included in the original lease that, if within ten years Burbage had spent £200 on the old buildings on the site, then the lease could be extended by a further ten years from the date of that

102. For the documents, with commentary, for the Theatre, see Wickham, Berry, and Ingram, eds., *English Professional Theatre*, pp. 330–87, and for the Blackfriars, pp. 501–8.

expenditure. For some eighteen months after its expiration there were protracted negotiations over renewal, during which time the Chamberlain's Men was apparently allowed continued use of the Theatre. Allen was not totally opposed to an extension but on conditions that the Burbages eventually found unacceptable and it was they who in September 1598 broke off talks. Though it might be misleading to regard these events as a major crisis in the company's affairs, clearly some serious thought nevertheless had to be given to the future. Assuming that on the breakdown of talks in the autumn of 1598, the company was evicted, there is some slight evidence that, as a stop-gap measure, it transferred to the nearby Curtain, in which James Burbage is earlier known to have had an interest although quite what this was has never been fully established.[103] Almost immediately, however, in a bold and contentious move, the Burbage brothers oversaw the demolition of the Theatre, carrying away what material they could to erect a new theatre, the Globe, on a site in the Bankside, leased from Nicholas Brend.[104]

To push this project through, the Burbage brothers, no doubt short of capital, gave five of the Company sharers, of whom Shakespeare was one, the opportunity to buy into the project at a cost, if we can accept claims made much later, of around £100 each.[105] The members of this syndicate, since dubbed 'housekeepers', now freed from the obligation to pay more than a ground rent to a landlord, could look forward to an increased income once their initial outlay had been recouped. The original documentation for the lease, dated 21 February 1599, has not survived though, being twice cited in legal cases, is not in doubt.[106] Its main provision was to set up a lease of the property to the seven members of the company who would hold half to the use of Richard and Cuthbert Burbage, who would pay half the annual rent of £7 5s. 0d., and the other half to the use of Shakespeare and his four fellow sharers, also paying £7 5s. 0d. divided between them. What is less easy to interpret is the arrangement, said in one of these

---

103. Wickham, Berry, and Ingram, eds., *English Professional Theatre*, pp. 404–6, 411–12.
104. Gurr, *Shakespeare Company*, pp. 10, 251.
105. This can only be an estimate inferred from evidence submitted in a legal case much later during which an initial estimate was reduced from £1000 to £700 (Berry, *Shakespeare's Playhouses*, pp. 182–3, 198, 221–2). The Burbages would have paid half the cost and the five sharers the other half between them (Chambers, *William Shakespeare*, ii, pp. 58–61).
106. Chambers, *William Shakespeare*, ii, pp. 53, 58.

legal cases to have taken place 'shortelie after', whereby Shakespeare
and his fellow sharers of their half interest assigned it to two London
financiers, Thomas Savage and William Leveson, who then apparently
granted a fifth of it back to each sharer in five separate transactions
('who regraunted & reassigned to euerye of them seuerally a fift parte
of the said moitie'). This has been interpreted as a friendly mechanism
by which a joint tenancy was converted into a tenancy in common,
the difference being that, whereas a share in a tenancy in common
could be treated as a separate estate to be sold on or bequeathed, a
share in a joint tenancy was inalienable and liable to pass on death or
surrender to the other joint tenants. Indeed, this distinction is spelt
out in the surviving documentation where a share in the company's
takings is described as a joint tenancy and a share in the lease, after the
negotiations with Savage and Leveson, as a tenancy in common.
However, that the two financiers had simply come forward in an
effort to be helpful is far from certain. Unlike the lease from Brend,
cited by its exact date in two separate cases and thus likely to reflect
the true situation, the arrangements with Savage and Leveson are
mentioned only once and in a far less precise manner, giving rise to
various speculations as to why they had become involved. Thomas
Savage was a wealthy goldsmith and Leveson a merchant adventurer,
deeply involved at one stage in the London Virginia Company. It is
possible that they were simply doing the sharers a favour, but, given
their business track record, there could well have been another reason.
In 1597, for instance, Leveson was said to have loaned 'some hundreds
of pounds' to the queen, and between 1605 and 1608 Heminges mortgaged to Savage at least two properties in Aldenmanbury parish.[107]
These 'friendly' transactions with the company sharers might therefore have involved the advancement of money to facilitate their
investment. When, later in 1599, William Kemp surrendered his Globe
share to three of his fellow housekeepers, Shakespeare, John Heminges,
and Augustine Phillipps, arrangements were made for this to pass to one

---

107. Hotson, *Shakespeare's Sonnets Dated*, pp. 126–7; Eccles, 'Elizabethan Actors, E–J',
    p. 458; Honigmann, *Shakespeare: the Lost Years*, pp. 84–9; Corrigan, *Playhouse Law in
    Shakespeare's World*, p. 66 (though Corrigan does not believe that money was raised
    on the Globe theatre lease). We might also note that Thomas Savage appointed as
    overseer of his will John Jackson, who later acted as a trustee for Shakespeare on
    his purchase of the Blackfriars Gatehouse (Hotson, *Shakespeare's Sonnets Dated*,
    pp. 132–4).

Thomas Cressey (as yet waiting further identification) before being granted back to Shakespeare, Heminges, and Phillipps. Some legal niceties might have been involved, but here again Cressey, like Savage and Leveson earlier in the year, could also have been oiling the financial wheels.[108] In 1635, Cuthbert Burbage, the only surviving party to the 1599 lease, claimed that the Globe had been built with 'summes of money taken up at interest, which lay heavy upon us [the Burbage family] many yeeres.'[109] No doubt this was an exaggeration, but that fellow sharers had had to do something similar is not unlikely. As described above (p. 84), Shakespeare in the spring of 1597, had raised some £120 for the purchase of New Place at exactly the time when the lease of the Theatre was due to expire. Though this might suggest that Shakespeare had no immediate fears for the future, the Burbages' dramatic solution to their need for a new permanent home, requiring the sharers to raise something in the region of £100 apiece, may have stretched Shakespeare's credit to the point that other investments had to be put off for a while.

As with the estimated income enjoyed by the company 'sharers', patchy evidence makes precision impossible when considering the additional income they would now derive from their enhanced role as 'housekeepers'. However, on the basis of such evidence as has survived, it has been estimated that Shakespeare's annual income as a housekeeper, in a year not affected by the plague, would have grown to around £80 by 1605.[110] It would thus have taken a year or two before his investment in the Globe project in February was yielding a profit, long enough to delay any immediate land purchases. It was only in May 1602, some nine months after his father's death, that he reached an agreement with John Combe, a leading member of Stratford's town gentry, for the sale by him of 107 acres of land for the sum of £320.[111] Also named as a vendor was John Combe's uncle, William Combe, a lawyer living in Warwick, who had earlier been involved in his nephew's acquisition of the land in question but probably acting only in a legal capacity.[112]

108. Chambers, *William Shakespeare*, ii, p. 54.
109. Gurr, *Shakespeare Company*, p. 278.
110. Gurr, *Shakespeare Company*, p. 108.
111. SCLA, ER 27/1, transcribed in full in Halliwell, *Outlines*, ii, pp. 17–19.
112. Below, p. 107.

The deed by which this land was conveyed describes it as comprising 107 acres lying in the fields of Old Stratford, then in the tenure of Thomas and Lewis Hiccox. Such imprecision may seem surprising, but a detailed description would have been equally unsatisfactory. For these 107 acres did not comprise a series of neatly enclosed fields but were made up of strips, or 'lands', dotted around in the old unenclosed fields which bordered Stratford on the north and east. When these fields were eventually enclosed in the 1770s, there were four of them, then styled quarters (Guild Pitts Quarter, Rowley Quarter, Bishopton Quarter, and Windmill Hill Quarter); earlier there may have only been three, Bishopton, Old Stratford, and Welcombe. These were subdivided into furlongs, each one made up of a batch of strips, or 'lands'. It was a collection of such 'lands' which made up Shakespeare's purchase. Thanks to a lucky discovery by Mairi Macdonald, we know the names of the eighteen furlongs in which these strips lay.[113] Together they made up all but ten of the 107 acres, the final ten being the equivalent amount of grazing land (or 'common of pasture') to which Shakespeare was entitled in the water meadows by virtue of his 'open-field' holdings. It is not certain exactly where these furlongs were located, but surviving evidence suggests that most of them lay between the present-day Birmingham Road (and its extension Guild Street) on the south-west, Clopton Park to the north (already enclosed by that date) and Warwick Road to the east. Two acres, for example, lay in Nether Gill Pit Furlong and another two in Over Gill Pitt Furlong, both clearly lying close to Guild Street, or Gill Pits as it was then known. Eight acres lay in furlongs 'uppon the topp of Rowley' and 'under Rowley', rising land to the north-east of the town after which the present-day Rowley House and Rowley Crescent are named. Twelve acres lay in Clopton Nether Furlong and a further ten in Clopton Over Furlong, whilst four acres were in Base Thorn Furlong 'shooting into Clopton Hedge'—all three furlongs by implication bordering on the enclosed Clopton estate. The four acres in Nether Furlong must have been close by as they were 'shooting into the Base thorne ffurlong.' A further four acres were in Stony Furlong which at the time of the late eighteenth-century enclosure was located in Rowley Quarter. Shakespeare's four acres in Long Furlong, 'at the upper end of Stoney ffurlong', must therefore also have been close by as must his four acres

113. Macdonald, 'A new discovery about Shakespeare's estate in Old Stratford'.

'shooting and lying into ffordes Greene', a furlong also placed in Rowley Quarter in the late eighteenth century.[114]

Shakespeare's 'estate', then, was not an identifiable block of land which can in any real sense be recreated today but a collection of strips, or 'lands', already let to, and thus farmed by, tenants, Lewis Hiccox, and his father, Thomas Hiccox, named in the deed of conveyance, whose rents would have been a return on Shakespeare's investment, and a first step in securing an independent income.[115] It was during the drawing up of the deed of conveyance of this property that Shakespeare's 'official' title—'William Shakespeare of Stratford-upon-Avon, gentleman'—was first used in its extended form, signifying to his contemporaries not necessarily where he may have been living at the time but where lay his landed possessions which gave him a right to claim gentry status.

As with the acquisition of New Place, we may legitimately enquire as to the circumstances leading up to this particular purchase. The previous history of the descent of this land has been established with some certainty.[116] Originally part of the holdings of Richard Catesby of Bishopton, it had been given to William Clopton, it was said, in 1542

---

114. Further clues as to the location of these 'lands' can be obtained from later surveys of other landholders' estates in these open fields, whose 'lands' were often located by giving the names of those who owned the neighbouring strips. These included the names of Shakespeare's successors in title to his Stratford estate, namely, Thomas Nash (the first husband of Shakespeare's granddaughter) until 1647, John Barnard (her second husband) until 1674, John Clopton until 1719, and Frances Partheriche, the last of the Cloptons, who died in 1792. When William Combe's estate was surveyed in 1677 (SCLA, ER 3/4115), Shakespeare's successor was John Clopton, whose name occurs four times as the owner of abutting land in Upper and Lower Rowley Furlongs. The furlong in the 1677 survey described as 'betweene Maidenhead way and Church Way', where John Clopton's name appears nine times, is almost certainly the furlong described in 1602 as 'the Buttes between Welcombe Church way and Bryneclose way', where four of Shakespeare's acres lay. Today, this furlong would have been between the present Maidenhead Road and the Welcombe Road and its footpath extension. Shakespeare's holding of six acres in 'lime ffurlong' probably lay in the Brick Kiln Furlong, a name which first occurs in a survey of 1763 (SCLA, DR 165/385b) as lying in Guild Pitts Quarter and in which, in a slightly later survey, Frances Partheriche is also named as a landholder. The only other furlongs where John Clopton is known to have held land in 1677 were Black Ground, a furlong shooting into Clopton Way (presumably today's Clopton Road), Windmill Hill Furlong, Slow Hill Furlong, and Greenhill Furlong: of these, all except Windmill Hill Furlong, were later known to have been in Guild Pitts Quarter or Rowley Quarter.

115. These are not specified though a calculation is proposed below.

116. Macdonald, 'A new discovery about Shakespeare's estate in Old Stratford', pp. 87–8; Chambers, *William Shakespeare*, ii, p. 110.

as part of an exchange. Not subject to any entail, it was sold by Clopton's son in December 1570 to Rice Griffin in part fulfilment, it seems, of an arrangement by Rice's father, Edward Griffin, that land should be bought for Rice's benefit for life, with remainder to his elder brother, Edward. In 1593, however, Rice apparently sold the land on to John Combe and thus to his brother's disadvantage.[117] This was the estate which John Combe, with his lawyer uncle William Combe acting with him, sold to William Shakespeare.

However, the story may be even more complicated than that. The Stratford Combes had been first represented by John Combe, an entrepreneur from Worcestershire, who, taking advantage of the fluid property market following the dissolution of the monasteries, had built up for himself a substantial estate in Stratford and in and around Crowle in Worcestershire.[118] On his death in 1550 he was succeeded in his estates by his son John who for many years lived in the College, in Old Town, Stratford's finest house, further increasing the family estates on the purchase of the manor of Rhyn Clifford in 1569.[119] When he died in 1588, most of the family's freehold estates passed to his eldest son, Edward.[120] His second son, Thomas, took over the tenancy of the College, still clearly a man of substance and more so, first, on inheriting his brother Edward's lands in 1597 and then after making several significant purchases of his own.[121] But it was a third brother, John Combe, who was to sell the 107 acres in Old Stratford to William Shakespeare. From the evidence of his will, he never appears to have built up much of a freehold estate in the town, but, from early days, perhaps using money he had inherited from his father and taking advantage of his father's extensive contacts, he appears to have made a substantial fortune in the local money markets. From the year of his father's death he was constantly seeking redress in the local court of record for money

117. On the evidence of the only surviving document concerning this sale—a foot of fine—the purchaser was William Combe, the Warwick lawyer, but later evidence confirms that he was in fact acting for his nephew, John Combe. Significantly, warranty was given against any subsequent claim to the land by Edward Griffin.

118. Taplin, *Shakespeare's Country Families*, pp. 57–9; Bearman, 'The early Reformation experience in a Warwickshire market town', pp. 75–80. For John Combe's inquisition post mortem, see TNA, C 142/94/98.

119. Chambers, *William Shakespeare*, ii, pp. 131–2, 135; SCLA, DR 140/4.

120. For his inquisition post mortem, see TNA, C 142/219/79.

121. For Edward Combe's inquisition post mortem, see TNA, C 142/252/54; C 142/259/43. There were complications following Edward's death but, as he left only daughters, his entailed estates were eventually inherited by his brother Thomas.

owing to him: one such case, the pursuit of William Walford and John Lupton for the repayment of £20 'on a writing of obligation' in 1604, indicates the way in which many of these debts must have been incurred.[122] In his will, he remitted one pound in every twenty from debts of £20 or more owing to him, further suggesting a substantial business portfolio.[123] In January 1598 it seems that he was even holding the Corporation plate in pawn when it was seeking to raise money following the town fires of 1594/95.[124] Such arrangements appear to be the explanation for other transactions in which he is known to have been involved. In addition to the purchase of the land which he later sold to Shakespeare there are fines, for example, of Easter Term 1593, Easter 1594, Hilary Term 1603, and Hilary Term 1604, to indicate trans-actions in connection with land in Stratford-upon-Avon, Old Stratford, Ingon, Hampton Lucy, Alveston, and Tiddington.[125] Nevertheless, his freehold estate, judging from bequests in his will, consisted at the time of his death of little more than a house in Warwick and five closes in Ingon and Hampton Lucy. These may be represented by one or two of the transactions recorded by the above fines, but clearly not all of them: one, for instance, was reputedly of some sixty acres. The implication, then, is that these estates, like the 107 acres purchased from Griffin, were subsequently sold on. Alternatively, they may in effect have sim-ply represented mortgages: given our knowledge of Combe's other operations, these fines may merely have served the purpose of securing loans by the pledging of land which could either be redeemed by the freeholder on repayment or sold off by Combe if the mortgagor failed to do so.

When, in 1593, John Combe acquired from Rice Griffin the 107 acres of land subsequently sold to Shakespeare, he ensured that it came with a warranty against any claim which Rice's brother, Edward Griffin, might make as Rice's heir. He took the same precaution when a year later he acquired a further sixty acres from Rice, suggesting that both transactions were mortgages rather than outright sales and that Combe, on Griffin's failure to repay money advanced on these securities, had foreclosed on at least one of them before selling the land on to Shakespeare. This accords well with what is known more generally

122. SCLA, BRU 12/6/178.
123. TNA, PROB 11/126, ff. 419–21.
124. Fripp, *Master Richard Quyny*, pp. 122–3.
125. Yeatman, *The Gentle Shakespere*, p. 237.

about Griffin's circumstances, characterized from the early 1590s by a shortage of money and the consequent sale of lands.[126]

If this were the case, it would imply some negotiation with John Combe; maybe Shakespeare was even seeking his advice on an investment. The two men certainly already knew one another. As we have seen, five years earlier, when the Shakespeares were pressing their case against John Lambert for the recovery of the Wilmcote estate, John Combe was one of the commissioners appointed to take evidence from witnesses on their behalf.[127] That the relationship between the two men was more than a business one is also clear from the bequest, albeit modest, which Combe later made to Shakespeare of £5; and there is further evidence, discussed below, of Shakespeare's continuing friendship with other members of his family.[128] At the very least, it is clear that Shakespeare's increasing financial success had allowed him to enter into negotiations with one of the town's most well-to-do men, which, as with the purchase of New Place, perhaps allowed him to strike an advantageous deal.

The deed of conveyance, by a process known as bargain and sale, also identifies those who by now we might regard as Shakespeare's active local friends and contacts. The man to whom, before witnesses, the deed, duly sealed and signed, was delivered 'to the use of... William Shakespeare' was his younger brother, Gilbert. Gilbert Shakespeare, born in 1566, remains a shadowy figure. A Gilbert Shakespeare of St Bride's in London, haberdasher, stood surety for one William Sampson, a Stratford clockmaker, in 1597 and this is more than likely to have been Shakespeare's brother, who had followed him to London in the hope of earning a living.[129] But of his years in Stratford, at least from 1602, the year he took delivery of the Combe conveyance, there is more certainty. He witnessed, in his own neat hand, a Stratford document of 1610, and the year before he had been involved in Stratford litigation which had reached the Court of Requests.[130] But he died in Stratford unmarried in February 1612, without, as far as can be established,

126. *Victoria History of the County of Warwick*, iii, p. 53; Yeatman, *The Gentle Shakespere*, pp. 278–9.

127. Above, p. 89.

128. Below, p. 142.

129. Eccles, *Shakespeare in Warwickshire*, p. 108; Hotson, *Shakespeare's Sonnets Dated*, pp. 230–1. Hotson described Sampson as a cloakmaker, but Eccles has corrected this.

130. Eccles, *Shakespeare in Warwickshire*, pp. 108–9.

making a will or leaving possessions which required administration. This was also the case with his other bachelor brother, Richard, who, apart from his baptism in March 1574, a citation in Stratford's church court for an unspecified offence in 1608, and his burial in February 1613, has gone completely unrecorded.[131] That neither is known ever to have maintained his own establishment further suggests that their father John's straitened circumstances had had its effect on the brothers' prospects and that William may therefore have been willing to provide them with a home at New Place. Arguing from absence of evidence is not usually to be recommended and it might still be proposed that both men had carved out niches for themselves of which we are simply unaware. However, for men of business, in Stratford's tightly knit community, to have left no trail at all would have been almost impossible. Far more likely would be a simple lack of means, when they were boys, to place them in suitable apprenticeships. Their youngest sibling Edmund's decision to try his hand as an actor in London suggests a similar lack of a structured childhood. On the other hand, Shakespeare's recruitment of Gilbert as his representative in 1602 certainly suggests his willingness to offer this otherwise shadowy figure some degree of support.

Of more significance is the name of the principal witness, Anthony Nash. His father, probably Thomas Nash of Bicester, had achieved minor gentry status through service in the ranks of greater families, particularly after the marriage of his elder brother Michael Nash of Woodstock to a sister of John Hubaud of Ipsley, a man who achieved eminence as steward both to Robert earl of Leicester, from 1572, and to his brother, Ambrose earl of Warwick, lord of the manor of Stratford.[132] Thomas Nash settled in Stratford in the early 1570s[133] mainly, it would seem, as local agent for Sir John, presiding over the town's court leet on the earl's behalf, a position he had obtained through his brother Michael's connections.[134] Hubaud purchased the lease of Stratford's tithes in January 1575, and from 1577 Nash, as his agent, was regularly held to account for the portion of the rent due

---

131. Eccles, *Shakespeare in Warwickshire*, p. 107; Brinkworth, *Shakespeare and the Bawdy Court*, pp. 110, 141.

132. Eccles, *Shakespeare in Warwickshire*, pp. 121–2; Taplin, *Shakespeare's Country Families*, pp. 101–6.

133. His son George was baptised in the parish church on 18 October 1573.

134. John Hubaud's will of April 1583 included a bequest to 'my servant Thomas Nash'.

from these to the Stratford Corporation.[135] He died suddenly at Aylesbury on his way back to Stratford from London in the summer of 1587 and was buried there on 2 June.[136] His eldest son, Anthony, born before his father came to Stratford, arrived in the town, by his own recollection, in the year of his father's death or the year after.[137] The family lived at Welcombe, in a house belonging to the earl of Warwick, the lord of the manor, and later to William Combe. He was reportedly maintaining a household there of twelve in 1595, with a very substantial stock of fifty-three quarters of corn and malt recorded by commissioners investigating the alleged hoarding at a time of national shortage.[138] Of freehold property he had little, though around 1604 he became owner of the Bear Inn at the bottom of Bridge Street, which he left to his son Thomas.[139] But there is good evidence that, as with John Combe, he boosted his income by lending money. Throughout his years in Stratford, until his death in 1622, he sought frequent redress in the local court of record for the repayment of debts, some specifically said to have been due on bonds of obligation.[140] In 1616 it was claimed that on his death the late Sir William Somerville owed him £105[141] and, like John Combe, he may also have profited from holding land as security for loans; in 1595, he secured from the impecunious Rice Griffin land in Hampton Lucy and Ingon which, when sold on in 1616, was secured by warranty against any claims that Griffin might subsequently make.[142] His will also included money bequests of some £1200.[143] Given that he witnessed two further documents involving Shakespeare's Stratford interests, that, from the accounting year 1606, he regularly answered for the payment of

135. Fripp and others, eds., *Minutes and Accounts*, iii, p. 12. The accounts for the previous two years are incomplete.
136. Halliwell, *Outlines*, ii, p. 324.
137. In 1617, he declared that he had been resident in Stratford for some forty years (SCLA, BRU 15/8/175).
138. Fripp and others, eds., *Minutes and Accounts*, v, p. 66.
139. TNA, PROB 11/140, f. 397. His younger brother John occurs as licensee from 1604 (Fripp and others, eds., *Minutes and Accounts*, vi, p. 284).
140. E.g., SCLA, BRU 15/3/102 (Richard Freeman attached to repay a debt, 1603); BRU 12/6/182 (Mary Green summoned to answer Anthony Nash, on a bill of obligation, 1603); BRU 15/5/90 (George Shackleton attached to answer to Anthony Nash, for a debt due from one Edward Sweetinge, 1604).
141. Stopes, *Shakespeare's Warwickshire Contemporaries*, pp. 85–6.
142. SCLA, BRU 15/9/15; ER 2/40.
143. Below, p. 162.

Shakespeare's tithe rent to the Corporation[144] (of which more below, pp. 119–21) and that he received a bequest from Shakespeare of 26s. 8d. to buy a mourning ring, he must be regarded as one of Shakespeare's principal local gentry contacts; indeed, another witness to the 1602 conveyance was Anthony's brother John, who, though not found in immediate contact with Shakespeare on later occasions, also received a bequest for the purchase of a mourning ring.[145] This is of some interest as, later in 1602, John Nash was bound over to appear before the royal justices on a charge of felony, and two years later was accused of using his 'fystes and with a spade & other weapons' in an assault on one of the local constables.[146] That he was of a quarrelsome disposition is further indicated by his involvement in legal proceedings as early as 1588 and, with his second wife Dorothy, he was also repeatedly in trouble over the management of the Bear.[147] These failings led, on one occasion—the baptism of his daughter Alice in 1604—to an apparent downgrading of his status in local eyes when, in the parish register, he was described as a yeoman instead of the more usual gentleman. However, that Shakespeare did not sever links with him confirms the impression that, by the time he came to make his purchase in 1602, he had graduated into the much smaller gentry circle in his native town, represented by the Combe and Nash families, and with whom he remained in alliance thereafter.

John Combe and Anthony Nash were not representatives of the old landed elite. They owed their position instead to shrewd service in the households of bishops and aristocracy, accumulating sufficient capital to invest in modest landholding or lend to the impecunious. Shakespeare, working his family out of a more humble (and in his case financially embarrassed) situation into one with gentry associations, would have been more easily assimilated into such a group both socially and as a party to mutually beneficial projects. In the process,

---

144. Fripp and others, eds., *Minutes and Accounts*, vi, p. 400; SCLA, BRU 4/2, p. 262.
145. For John, see Eccles, *Shakespeare in Warwickshire*, pp. 122–3; Taplin, *Shakespeare's Country Families*, p. 109.
146. Fripp and others, eds., *Minutes and Accounts*, vi, pp. 206, 287.
147. Eccles, *Shakespeare in Warwickshire*, p. 122; Fripp and others, eds., *Minutes and Accounts*, vi, pp. 284, 350, 369, 382, 418, 448. Dorothy was a relative of the previous licensee, Francis Bellers, cited in 1606, before her marriage to Nash, for not administering Francis Bellers' estate (Brinkworth, *Shakespeare and the Bawdy Court*, pp. 130, 133). However, she was not Bellers' widow; she was Elizabeth who had died in August 1604. For John's tenancy of the Bear in 1617–20, see BL, Add. MS 74241–2.

the Quiney and Sturley families, still associated with town politics and mercantile interests, appear to have fallen into the background.

Of the other witnesses to the 1602 conveyance—William Sheldon, Humphrey Mainwaring, and Richard Mason—only Mason appears to have been a local man, who, on the evidence of his signature, was the yeoman of that name who in 1596 became a lessee of a Corporation tenement in Church Street.[148] Sheldon was probably of the Broadway branch of the family, descended from Baldwin Sheldon whose widow Jane had become the third wife of John Combe's grandfather.[149] Humphrey Mainwaring must be of a branch of the Mainwaring family settled in Nantwich, in Cheshire, part of a clan descended from the Mainwarings of Peover. This also included the Mainwarings of Ightfield, in Shropshire, and thus Arthur Mainwaring who was later to play an important part in the attempted enclosure of Welcombe involving both the Combes and Shakespeare.[150] Whether Humphrey was called on as a witness by Combe or by Shakespeare, or both, is not clear, but this earlier link with the Mainwaring family certainly suggests that the Combes' later recruitment of Arthur Mainwaring as a front man in the Welcombe enclosure project was the result of a longer association between the two families than is normally acknowledged.

There remains to consider the rental income which Shakespeare would have derived from this purchase. In his day the sum negotiated for a purchase was based on the annual value of the land in rental income multiplied by the number of years sufficient to generate a return of around 5 per cent on the sum invested, namely twenty years.[151] In the case of Shakespeare's purchase of 107 acres for £320, an

148. SCLA, BRU 8/5/8. He died in May 1615.
149. Barnard, *The Sheldons*, pp. 97–104; Taplin, *Shakespeare's Country Families*, p. 61. Baldwin Sheldon had a grandson William who died in 1613. Jane Sheldon's marriage to Thomas Combe produced one child, William Combe, the lawyer, John Combe's uncle, who left his 'cousin' William Sheldon of Broadway £20. The Sheldons of Broadway were also related to the Hubaud family, with whom Shakespeare was later to have dealings (below, pp. 120–1).
150. For pedigrees of all the related branches, see *Visitation of Cheshire, 1580*, pp. 163–7; *Pedigrees Made at the Visitation of Cheshire, 1613*, pp. 156–62; *Visitation of Shropshire, 1623*, ii, pp. 348–9. The unusual baptismal name Humphrey occurs mainly in the Nantwich branch: *Visitation of Cheshire, 1580*, pp. 127, 163; *Pedigrees, Visitation of Cheshire, 1613*, pp. 98, 159.
151. Habbakuk, 'The long term rate of interest and the price of land in the seventeenth century'; Allen, 'The price of freehold land and the interest rate in the seventeenth and eighteenth centuries'.

annual return as low as £16 and not more than £20 (i.e. 5 per cent or
6 per cent of the purchase price) might therefore have been the annual
return estimated at the time. This might need an upward (or downward) adjustment as other considerations may have been taken into
account in negotiating the price. Indeed, there is evidence that unenclosed arable land in the midlands might be rented out at that time for
about 5 shillings an acre,[152] giving a measurably higher figure of around
£25 for Shakespeare's 107 acres, £5 more than the annual salary of the
local schoolmaster. This was not, then, an inconsiderable sum, but on
the other hand was in no way sufficient to elevate him into the ranks
of the independent gentry.

Further investment, 1602–1605

Later in 1602 Shakespeare made an addition to his Stratford property
holdings by securing possession of a copyhold cottage with a quar-
ter-acre garden on the south side of Chapel Lane, opposite the gardens
running back behind his main residence, New Place, in Chapel Street.
We do not know whether he acquired it with a particular purpose in
mind or merely snapped it up when it became available. It has been
plausibly suggested that it might have been acquired as service quarters, with the quarter acre of land serving as a kitchen garden.[153]

The cottage, together with another small property in Church Street,
still formed part of the manor of Rowington, some eight miles north
of Stratford.[154] When the tenancy of such a piece of land changed
hands it was usual for the outgoing tenant, or his legal representative,
to appear in the manor court to surrender his holding into the lord's
hands and for the new tenant, usually at the same court, to receive it
back. This transaction would be duly recorded on the manor rolls as
part of that court's proceedings and a copy made of the relevant passage, which was then handed to the new tenant. His title was thus
secured by copy of court roll, hence the term 'copyhold'.

152. Bowden, 'Agricultural prices, farm profits, and rents', p. 653; Allen, 'Price of freehold
      land', pp. 34, 43.
153. Contrary to popular belief, not more than half, and possibly less, of the Great Garden
      now attached to New Place was ever owned by Shakespeare.
154. Much of the evidence is conveniently summarized in Chambers, *William Shakespeare*,
      ii, pp. 111–13.

By 1602 the lordship of the manor of Rowington had passed to Ann widow of Ambrose earl of Warwick and the copyholder of the Chapel Lane property was Walter Getley, an otherwise elusive character.[155] Shakespeare had evidently negotiated for a transfer of the property in question and on 28 September Getley's attorney appeared at the manor court and surrendered the cottage into the lord's hands to Shakespeare's use. If the transaction had followed its normal course, Shakespeare, or his attorney, would then have appeared and have been granted possession. In fact, this did not happen. Shakespeare, probably in London, failed to make arrangements for anyone to act for him and the court roll merely recorded that the land would be held by the lord of the manor until Shakespeare came to take possession. A copy of this transaction, though incomplete, was still made and duly became Shakespeare's title deed. It survives to this day and, because the original manor rolls are no longer extant, provides us with our only knowledge of the deal.[156]

There is no doubt that Shakespeare's title to this property was regarded as valid, even though there is no evidence that he ever formally appeared at the manor court to receive the land out of the lord's hands and thus complete the formalities. For instance, in 1604, a survey records him as holding the property at an annual rent of 2s. 6d. and it is also one of the properties mentioned in his will.[157] Nevertheless, when in 1606 another major survey of the manor was carried out, the compiler was aware of an irregularity. For although he duly entered Shakespeare as the tenant, he was unable to find the date of the court at which Shakespeare was admitted and so left a blank space.[158]

Shakespeare thus became one of seventy-one copyhold tenants of Rowington manor, some paying to the lord as much £4 4s. 4d. for extensive holdings of farmland but John Baylies only a penny for what must have been a tiny cottage.[159] Shakespeare's cottage, held under an annual rent of 2s. 6d., was still on the low side, with only sixteen of the seventy-one copyholders paying less than that. This has been described

155. There were three Getley brothers active in Stratford at this time, Henry, Richard, and Thomas (probably sons of Humphrey), the first of whom died in 1604 (Jones, ed., *Stratford Inventories*, i, p. 232).
156. SCLA, ER 28/1. For transcript, see Chambers, *William Shakespeare*, ii, p. 112.
157. Ryland, *Records of Rowington*, i, p. 184; below, p. 128.
158. For the complete survey, see TNA, LR 2/228, ff. 149–208. The incomplete entry, however (f. 199), seems to imply that the rent was only 2 shillings.
159. Ryland, *Records of Rowington*, i, pp. 180–4.

as nominal and was indeed less than that paid for a tenancy under a straightforward lease. Few, if any, Corporation town properties were let for less than 5 shillings a year and, as proposed above (pp. 86–7), Shakespeare could have been deriving eight times that from his tenant of the Maidenhead. To have acquired a cottage and a quarter acre of land subject to a modest annual outlay of 2s. 6d. could therefore be seen as an opportunistic move. In theory, the freehold remained with the lord of the manor, but it was customary for the tenancy to descend in the family on the payment of the appropriate fee. This varied according to the size of the holding and was in the order of 2 shillings for a cottage to ensure long-term occupation, although in 1617, following Shakespeare's death, John Hall paid 2s. 6d. for admittance to the Chapel Lane cottage.[160]

What the surviving documentation does not tell us, however, is how much Shakespeare might have had to pay Getley to arrange for these favourable terms to be transferred to him. Contemporary freehold purchase prices have been discussed above (pp. 83, 95n). Over the period 1571–1630, the purchase price of £20 or less has been traced for seven freehold properties. Given that copyhold tenure, being subject to a rent charge, was less attractive, Shakespeare could hardly have paid more than £10 for his Chapel Lane cottage, and probably much less. However, although it is usually assumed that Shakespeare bought the cottage for his own use, the manorial customs of the day did allow for subletting, on the payment of a fee of 21 pence, giving the nominal tenant the opportunity of making a profit.[161] Whether or not Shakespeare took advantage of this, we do not know.

We might note at this stage, however, that there were apparent limits to Shakespeare's willingness to make disbursements, at least until after due consideration. In March 1601, Thomas Whittington, a shepherd then living with John Pace of Shottery, left to the poor of Stratford, under the terms of his will dated 25 March, '40ˢ that is in the hand of Anne Shaxspere, wife unto Mʳ Wyllyam Shaxspere, and is due debt

---

160. TNA, LR 11/50/720. This is a list of fines imposed at the manor court, on which occasion Shakespeare, though by then deceased, also appears to have been fined 6d., with three other absentees, for non-attendance. See also Chambers, *William Shakespeare*, ii, p. 112.

161. For the Rowington customs in Shakespeare's day, see Ryland, *Records of Rowington*, i, pp. 178–9. See also p. 192 for a series of payments of 21d. made in 1632 for permission to sublet. This same sum also occurs in 1617 (TNA, LR 11/50/720).

unto me, beyng payd to myne Executor by the sayd Wyllyam Shaxspere.'[162] Various attempts have been made to explain this somewhat puzzling bequest, but it may simply have been that this modest sum became Shakespeare's responsibility on his marriage to Ann Hathaway. Whittingdon had once been in the service of Ann's father, Richard Hathaway, who in his will of September 1581, acknowledged that he owed Whittington £4 6s. 8d.[163] Richard's widow, Joan, who was buried in 1599, apparently left him a further £2 17s. 0d. (or possibly the remaining unpaid part of Richard's debt), a sum still owing from her executors, John and William Hathaway, when Whittingdon came to make his own will in 1601.[164] At the foot of his will this debt is listed alongside a further £2 15s. 7d. owed by John and William Hathaway jointly, and additional sums of 4s. 4d. and 3 shillings owed by the two brothers respectively, a total debt, then of £5 19s. 11d., some of which may have originated under the obligation which their father Richard had acknowledged in his will. Significantly, Whittington, in his inventory, includes these latter Hathaway debts as 'desperate', that is, ones he had given up on, implying that he had fallen out with the family with whom he had once lodged.[165] It is therefore more than likely that the 40 shillings owed by Ann Shakespeare also represents part of the Hathaway debt to the family's former shepherd, but with this significant difference: namely, that it was not listed as 'desperate' but incorporated into the wording of the will, indicating that in this case there was some hope of its recovery by his executor. On the other hand, it does not suggest an automatic willingness on Shakespeare's part to discharge debts which were not of his own family's making, even for the benefit of the poor.

It was another three years before Shakespeare made a further investment. For his company, reconstituted as the King's Men soon after James I's accession, this may not have been as profitable a period, when compared with the previous eight, as the result of the closure of the

---

162. Worcestershire County Record Office, 008.7 1601/16, reproduced in facsimile in Schoenbaum, *Documentary Life* (1975 ed.), p. 68. For extracts, see Chambers, *William Shakespeare*, ii, pp. 42–3.

163. Halliwell, *Outlines*, ii, pp. 195–6.

164. Whittington claimed that this money was due from Jane's two sons as executors of her will, though such a will has not been traced.

165. Jones, ed., *Stratford-upon-Avon Inven*tories, i, pp. 186–7. Set against the debts listed at the foot of his will is an unspecified sum for 'an yeares bord' which he owed to the Hathaways.

London theatres due to outbreaks of plague. A 'worst-case' scenario, based largely on statistical returns of plague deaths, would have it that the theatres were closed for all but two or three months in 1603, with only a slight improvement in 1604 followed by a better (but still disrupted) year in 1605.[166] Some commentators have taken a less drastic view, arguing that in 1603 closures were confined to less than two months in the spring though accepting widespread closure after May 1604 until April the following year with further closure towards the end of 1605.[167] On the positive side, we can also set regular court performances by the King's Men (only two in 1602/3 but seven in 1603/4 and ten in 1604/5[168]), a payment of £30 to the company for performances at Wilton in early December 1603 and a one-off payment of £30 by James I in February 1604 to his company, 'being prohibited to present plays publicly in or near London' by reason of the plague.[169] The company is also known to have gone on tour in each of the years 1603, 1604, and 1605, not perhaps as profitable an exercise as daily performances in a purpose-built and spacious playing space but equally clearly not a loss-making enterprise or such tours would not have been regularly undertaken. Whether Shakespeare accompanied his fellow actors on these expeditions is uncertain, but this would not have affected his income as a sharer and he may still have been fulfilling commissions for the writing of new plays. In any event, though the company finances might have been dented during these years, it did little to undermine Shakespeare's creditworthiness, no doubt buttressed by the modest lifestyle of a man who by around 1602, though at the height of his literary career, is found lodging in a quiet and economical manner in the house of Christopher Mountjoy, a well-established man of business (a maker of jewelled headdresses for ladies) who lived in Silver Street, Cripplegate.[170] In the summer of 1605, he was therefore able to raise the very considerable sum of £440 to purchase a half-share in a lease of a portion of the Stratford tithes.[171] As a

166. Barroll, *Politics, Plague and Shakespeare's Theater*, p. 173.
167. Gurr, *Shakespearian Playing Companies*, pp. 91–2.
168. Astington, *English Court Theatre*, pp. 237–9; Gurr, *The Shakespeare Company*, pp. 302–3.
169. Barroll, *Politics, Plague and Shakespeare's Theater*, pp. 112–14.
170. According, that is, to evidence given in the Bellott/Mountjoy case in 1612 (Chambers, *William Shakespeare*, ii, pp. 90–5).
171. SCLA, ER 27/2, illustrated in facsimile in Schoenbaum, *Documentary Life* (1975 edn), p. 193, transcribed in full in Halliwell, *Outlines*, ii, pp. 19–24.

form of property, this differed from his purchase of land three years previously, but the purpose was the same: to provide himself and his family with a reliable source of income not dependent on his ability to continue to work.

Tithes originated as a payment to the rector of a parish by his parishioners of a tenth part of agricultural produce. Over the years the right to the tithes of many parishes passed into the hands of religious houses which appointed a vicar and paid him out of the proceeds. When these foundations were suppressed during the reigns of Henry VIII and Edward VI the title to such tithes passed, with their other possessions, to the Crown, and were then liable to be sold off in the same way as any other piece of property. In Stratford's case, the advowson and tithes had been granted in the fourteenth century to the warden and priests of a chantry established in Holy Trinity Church, later housed in an adjacent College. When, at the Reformation, this College was suppressed, its property, including the tithes, passed into royal ownership. Then, in 1553, when Stratford was granted its charter of incorporation, part of these tithes (those of grain and hay for Old Stratford, Bishopton, and Welcombe, and the lesser tithes of the whole parish) valued at £34, were conveyed to the Corporation, the income from which was to be used to pay the vicar and curate annual salaries of £20 and £10, and to find a house for the vicar.[172]

The owners of tithes at this period rarely collected them themselves. Instead, for a fixed sum, they let the right to collect them to a tenant who was free to make what profit he could. Unluckily for the Corporation, the last warden of the College, Anthony Barker, no doubt sensing the imminent dissolution of his establishment, had in 1544 leased nearly all its property, including the tithes, for ninety-two years to a relative, William Barker, for an annual rent of just over £120. This lease was allowed to stand at the Dissolution, with the rent initially paid to the Crown and then, when the ownership of the tithes was broken up, divided between the new owners. As already explained, the Corporation was allotted £34 as the rent to which it was entitled for the portion of the tithes it had been given. This may have been a realistic sum in 1553 but, as the lease to Barker still had around eighty years to run, it became a matter of increasing annoyance to the Corporation that well into the seventeenth century, it was still

172. Fripp and others, eds., *Minutes and Accounts*, i, pp. 14–17.

receiving only £34 a year in rent from its tithe leaseholders who in fact were gathering in larger and larger sums. In 1580, John Barker, to whom the original lease had descended, assigned his interest in it to Sir John Hubaud, subject to an annuity of £27 13s. 4d. Under the terms of Hubaud's will, the situation became yet more confused, with the portion of the lease relating to the Corporation's tithes further divided, half going to his brother Ralph Hubaud and half to his 'cousin', George Digby, each paying £17 annually to the Corporation (and £5 apiece to the Barkers as their share of the annuity) for the remainder of the ninety-two-year term.[173] It was the lease of the half that went to Ralph Hubaud which Shakespeare contracted to buy in 1605, subject to the same rental payments to the Corporation and the Barkers. A few years later these tithes were said to be worth £60 a year, which, after deductions to the Corporation and the Barkers, would have left Shakespeare with an annual surplus in the region of £40.[174] In ten years or so he would therefore have made good the £440 he had had to raise to pay Hubaud, and for the remaining twenty-one years of the 1544 lease the £40 surplus would have been clear profit. In fact, £60 is a conservative figure: as late as 1609, Thomas Greene was prepared to pay £360 to purchase a reversionary interest in the other half of the Corporation's tithes, with a mere twenty years to run from 1613; and when he sold this interest in 1617, it netted him some £400.[175] Even later, in 1625, when Shakespeare's son-in-law, John Hall, surrendered Shakespeare's former lease of the other half of the Corporation tithes, he was paid £400,[176] only £40 less than Shakespeare had paid almost twenty years earlier even though by that time the lease had less than ten years to run. When Greene's share of the tithes was re-let, the annual rent was set at £90, over five times more than Greene had been paying.[177]

Shakespeare's investment may have been a very shrewd one, typical of a local gentleman seeking to establish a broader base for an independent

173. Hubaud was son of one of the daughters of Sir John Danvers and Digby the grand-son of another daughter (and thus Hubaud's first cousin once removed). I would like to thank John Taplin for help on this point.
174. The figure of £60 was cited in a legal case of c. 1611 (below, pp. 135–7).
175. Bearman, 'Thomas Greene: Stratford's town clerk and Shakespeare's lodger', p. 297. He valued the remaining years of the lease at £550: '20 Cropps to Come ... worth 100 markes per Annum' (SCLA, BRU 15/7/125) but had to settle for less.
176. SCLA, BRU 2/2, pp. 455, 467, 469.
177. SCLA, BRU 2/2, p. 337. After this process of buying out, the tithes were leased out for a total of at least £184: SCLA, BRU 4/2, f. 45.

income, but it was also an action unlikely to endear him to the Corporation, whose members, drawn almost exclusively from the business community, believed that the loss of tithe income resulting from these long running leases was an obstacle to effective civic government.

The witnesses to Ralph Hubaud's sale to Shakespeare in 1605 confirm the circle in which he was now moving. As in 1602, the principal witness was Anthony Nash. Not only were the Hubaud and Nash families linked by marriage but Anthony's father, and then Anthony himself, were, as previously explained, also clearly dependent on the Hubauds for their position in Stratford.[178] It would therefore not be unreasonable to propose that Nash, known both to the Hubauds and to Shakespeare, acted as a local go-between in the negotiations leading up to Shakespeare's purchase. In fact, Hubaud was then elderly; he died within six months of the sale, at which time it seems that Shakespeare still owed him £20, probably part of the purchase price.[179] This is in itself of interest, evidence of Shakespeare's creditworthiness amongst the local gentry, Hubaud willing to allow some latitude over the terms of payment.

Of the other witnesses, William Hubaud was clearly a relative of the vendor, but of more interest is the lawyer, Francis Collins. He was acting for Shakespeare on this occasion, as a draft of the tithe conveyance is in his hand.[180] He was later the writer and overseer of Shakespeare's will and the man who, outside the family, was to receive the biggest personal bequest, implying a long-standing business relationship, if not friendship, reaching back to at least this time.[181] Of relevance here too is Collins' close involvement in the affairs of the Combe family with whom Shakespeare was also on friendly terms. Collins witnessed Thomas Combe's will, originally made in December 1608, and then a

178. Above, pp. 110–11.
179. Barnard, *New Links with Shakespeare*, pp. 60–1. This debt is noted in Hubaud's brief inventory in which it is recorded that Hubaud owed a sum of £20 to William Sheldon of Broadway, probably the same man who had witnessed John Combe's sale to Shakespeare of land in Old Stratford (above, p. 113). Ralph Hubaud was linked to the Sheldon family in two ways: his mother-in-law was the daughter of an earlier William Sheldon of Beoley whilst his sister Mary had married Ralph Sheldon of Broadway (Taplin, *Shakespeare's County Families*, p. 61; Whitfield, 'Anthony and John Nash, Shakespeare's Legatees').
180. SCLA, BRU 15/2/2.
181. Below, p. 158.

codicil added to it.[182] John Combe, when he came to make his will in January 1613, left £10 to Francis Collins (who drafted the will), ten marks to his wife Susanna, and £10 to their son John to whom Combe had stood godfather back in November 1604.[183] When he made his own will in 1617, Collins refers to a further sum of £20 which Thomas Combe had promised to give to his children.[184]

Shakespeare the gentleman?

The year 1605 marks something of a turning point in Shakespeare's financial dealings. Over a period of eight years he had had the means to purchase one of the town's most substantial properties, New Place, together with 107 acres of land on the edge of the town acquired in 1602, and a share in the parish tithes in 1605. The two latest purchases had cost him £760, and New Place in the region of £120—in all, then, around £900. To this we can add the £100 Shakespeare invested in a share of the Globe theatre lease and whatever was required to buy the Getley copyhold in Chapel Lane. Thereafter, he made only one further, and rather odd addition to his portfolio—the Blackfriars Gatehouse—to which we will return, which he bought in 1613, some eight years later.[185] To explain this change of direction, it could be argued that Shakespeare continued to accumulate capital at the former rate but then spent it in a different fashion—or indeed merely saved it. However, there is no evidence to bear this out. This argument also overlooks the fact that Shakespeare had probably only been able to raise the necessary capital to make his purchases because his credit was good, that is, that he could be trusted to repay any money that he had had to borrow. If this proved difficult, due, for instance, to the closure of the theatres during plague years (discussed below, p. 147) any future investment would have to be put off. Certainly his will, also discussed below (pp. 162–4), does not reveal a man with large sums of ready money at his disposal; and, from 1605, what evidence we have points to a wish, if not a need, to safeguard his sources of income. With the benefit of hindsight, we might be tempted into the belief that

182. TNA, PROB 11/113, ff. 93v–94.
183. TNA, PROB 11/126, f. 420.
184. TNA, PROB 11/130, ff. 294–294v.
185. Below, pp. 166–71.

Shakespeare had begun to think of 'retirement' and that the apparent reduction in the flow of funds was the result of a conscious decision on his part to scale down operations. But can it convincingly be argued that Shakespeare, still only in his mid-forties, made such a decision? To speak of retirement at such a period would, in any case, be anachronistic. He may have acquired property which to some extent would yield an income sufficient to maintain himself and his family in some comfort but the idea that he thought the process of rebuilding the family fortunes should simply be left at that level would, at the very least, indicate a new approach when compared with the clear pattern which had emerged from the moment that he began to achieve success: the steady investment in income-yielding assets funded by money raised on his creditworthiness.

However, if, in purely business terms, we are to regard the years 1605–7 as the high point of his fortunes, we must also ask ourselves to what level in contemporary society he had managed to raise his family; and, in that context, whether he could now be regarded as wealthy. One of Shakespeare's misfortunes was the death of his only son, Hamnet, in 1596, by which time his wife was forty-one and unlikely to bear a further child. Short of Ann's death and his subsequent remarriage, the prospect of his handing on his estate to a male heir was therefore remote. On the other hand, at that time there was no estate worthy of the name and it is therefore difficult to link his subsequent acquisitions with any ambition to found a family dynasty: instead, they more closely fit the role of investments from which he could simply draw an income for himself and his family. But Hamnet's death did at least give his daughters, Susanna and Judith, then aged thirteen and eleven, the status of co-heirs. This would not immediately have been of great significance, but by 1605, when Shakespeare's estate, if that is not too grand a name for it, had reached what was to be its fullest extent, the two girls might have been thought worthy of mates of gentlemanly status. But any such hopes were not realized. In June 1607 the twenty-three-year-old Susanna married a physician, John Hall, nine years her senior. Hall was a university graduate and his chosen profession might have conferred gentlemanly status, but there is no indication that Hall was a man of any real means. His father, William Hall of Acton—also a physician, though he may have dabbled in alchemy and astrology—was in any case still alive at the time of the marriage and John also had an elder brother Dive. When William Hall came to make his will in the December following John's marriage, Dive was effectively cut out, receiving only 40 shillings in view of the fact that he had long ago been granted his portion and that he had since treated his father unkindly; but at the time of John's marriage, this could not necessarily have been safely anticipated and would therefore not have improved his prospects as a marriage partner.[186] In any event, Hall brought virtually nothing with him at the time of his marriage, nor a great deal after his father's death. He was made residuary legatee of his father's estate and we know from later evidence that this included a house, possibly copyhold, at Acton.[187] But even this would not have made him anything but a very minor catch for the elder daughter of an aspiring gentleman; and, despite a later statement which implies that Shakespeare settled his estate on his daughter at the time of the marriage, there is no contemporary evidence to substantiate this.[188] On the contrary, Shakespeare's settlement of his estate exclusively on his elder daughter, under his will of 1616, implies that no prior arrangement had been made. Nor is there evidence that Hall was ever able to live in true gentlemanly style. He and his wife were eventually destined to become heirs to Shakespeare's real estate but this did not transform Hall's life. As if to emphasize this point, John Hall did not submit any evidence to support a claim to gentry status at the heralds' visitation of the county in 1619. Whereas the Combes, the Reynolds, the Lanes, and the Nashes proudly produced pedigrees to substantiate their status, as did Thomas Greene when the heralds visited Gloucestershire, John Hall made no such appearance.[189] Instead, he continued to work as a physician and never accumulated sufficient funds to invest in significant purchases of property. In 1630, like many fellow gentry, his total possessions were valued at £40 a year whereupon,

186. William's will is transcribed in Marcham, *William Shakespeare and his Daughter Susannah*, pp. 20–3. In it, he implies that he has given all his 'bookes of phisicke' to John as part of his residuary bequest, whereas his 'bookes of Astonomye and Astrologie' were given to his 'man, Mathewe Morris' on the understanding that he would instruct John 'in the sayed Arte' if he chose to take it up.

187. But this copyhold house, later said to be held 'by Discent from his Auncestors' may have passed to his elder brother Dive first: Marcham, *William Shakespeare and his Daughter Susannah*, p. 66.

188. Macdonald, 'A new discovery about Shakespeare's estate in Old Stratford'.

189. *Visitation of the County of Warwick*, pp. 147, 242–3, 290–1, 306–7; *Visitation of the County of Gloucester*, p. 69. However, until the death of his elder brother, Dive, in 1626, Hall was not technically head of the family. The Hall coat of arms was subsequently quartered on John's gravestone.

under the terms of an obsolete custom, he was deemed liable to have attended Charles I's coronation in 1626 as a knight of the realm, which he had failed to do. He was therefore allowed to compound for this transgression on payment of £10.[190] This is sometimes interpreted as a positive decision on Hall's part to decline knighthood, though in fact no such offer had ever been made. Instead, like many others, he had merely become the hapless victim of a very unpopular and much contested measure, introduced by Charles I as a means of raising money without parliamentary consent. In the spring of 1635, some six months before Hall died, Baldwin Brooks, a Stratford mercer, obtained a judgment against him for the payment of a very substantial debt of £77 13s. 4d. Undeterred by his debtor's demise, Brooks pressed on with his suit and in August 1636, following the family's reluctance to pay, was alleged, with a body of associates, to have broken into New Place to seize chattels in lieu.[191] Figures of up to £2000 were bandied about in an attempt to value Hall's estate but, judging from his brief nuncupative (orally declared) will, he owned very little in his own right.[192] The Acton house, possibly a copyhold, which he must have received under his father's will, and a 'meadow', probably the close adjoining Evesham Way which he appears to have bought from Abraham Sturley in 1611 or 1612 (allegedly yielding only 10 shillings a year[193]) were left to his daughter, Elizabeth, wife of Thomas Nash. He also bequeathed a house in London to his wife which may, in fact, have been the Blackfriars gatehouse, entailed under Shakespeare's will.

Shakespeare's grand-daughter Elizabeth's marriage in 1626 to Thomas Nash does, however, raise another interesting issue. Nash was his wealthy father's principal legatee. The status of Anthony Nash in local gentry circles and his role in Shakespeare's affairs has already been discussed and the provisions of his will are described below.[194] Thomas's marriage to Elizabeth Hall in 1626 was a natural development arising out of this relationship but with one important difference when compared with the marriage of her mother to John Hall back in

190. Fripp, *Shakespeare Man and Artist*, ii, p. 884.
191. The litigation is published in Marcham, *William Shakespeare and his Daughter Susannah*, pp. 57–76.
192. Marcham, *William Shakespeare and his Daughter Susannah*, p. 25.
193. SCLA, BRU 4/1, pp. 218, 230; Marcham, *William Shakespeare and his Daughter Susannah*, p. 67.
194. Above, pp. 110–12; below, p. 162.

1607, namely, that she could now be safely regarded as the sole heiress to the Shakespeare estate.[195] On the Shakespeares' side, the marriage could be seen as equally advantageous as Nash was, under his father's will, a man of considerable wealth. Admitted to Lincoln's Inn in 1616 and called to the bar in 1623, he had begun buying property in the town even before his father's death in November 1622.[196] However, on inheriting the bulk of his father's estate, there is no indication that he felt a need to put his legal training to practical use, able instead to live on a private income. Due caution is required when analysing contemporary tax returns, but it is still worth noting that, even in 1625, the year before his marriage to Elizabeth, his goods were assessed at a higher value (£4) than those of his future father-in-law, John Hall (£3) and this remained the case in later years.[197] Nash's father had also not been slow to certify his claim to gentry status at the heralds' visitation of 1619,[198] enabling Thomas to exhibit the family arms, quartered with those into whose families the Nashes had married.[199] It is not entirely clear whether, on his marriage, Nash moved into New Place, but the fact that he was assessed, for tax purposes, within the borough and that he is not known to have lived elsewhere before Hall's death, strongly suggests that he did.[200] His wealth and status is also confirmed on the eve of the Civil War. By then John Hall was dead, but the ancestral estates were still vested in his widow, Susanna. Even so Nash, on 24 September 1642, made an astonishingly generous loan to Parliament in cash and plate of £100, twice that contributed by the Corporation, and ten times the greatest sum offered by any other single individual.[201] Later he was supportive of the parliamentary cause and on several occasions provided accommodation for leading parliamentary commanders.[202] Such support was probably what led to Royalist reprisals in 1645, casting some doubt on the tradition, albeit on

195. By then her mother was forty-three and therefore unlikely to bear a further child.
196. Mairi Macdonald, 'Thomas Nash' in *ODNB*, xl, pp. 233–4; SCLA, TR 46/6/4.
197. TNA, E 179/193/302.
198. *Visitation of the County of Warwick*, p. 147.
199. These are prominently displayed on his gravestone, comprising Nash quartered with Bulstrode (through his grandmother, Ann Bulstrode, who had married Thomas Nash the elder), and Hall quartered with Shakespeare through his wife.
200. His father, who lived at Welcombe, was always assessed under Old Stratford.
201. Tennant, *The Civil War in Stratford-upon-Avon*, pp. 23–6. He later, in 1644, made another grant of £110, far outstripping any other contributions (pp. 92–3).
202. Tennant, *Civil War in Stratford-upon-Avon*, pp. 41, 84–5, 126.

record as early as 1733, that in 1643 Nash and his mother-in-law had entertained Queen Henrietta during her two-day visit to the town.[203] Be that as it may, there can be little doubt that Nash cut a finer figure in Stratford than his father-in-law. Attention is often drawn to Hall's involvement in civic affairs, as church sidesman and then church-warden, and as a reluctant capital burgess. On the evidence of tax assessments, he was also one of the more well-to-do of the town's civic leaders. However, that he was thought suitable for appointment to such offices serves to confirm that he was not regarded as, nor did he think himself, too grand for such positions. And the reason that he gave for his neglect of his civic duties, and his ultimate resignation from the Corporation—that it was interfering with his professional practice as a physician—is in itself an indication of the fact that he was not a man of independent means.

Shakespeare's younger daughter, Judith, fared even less well than Susanna in the marriage stakes. At the age of thirty-one she was even-tually married off to Thomas Quiney, four years her junior, certainly a member of a very well-to-do family but only a third son and still in trade as a vintner. The marriage took place on 10 February 1616 between the day on which Shakespeare apparently first drafted his will (5 January) and the date that he revised it (25 March). It would seem that even in January Shakespeare had decided to make over the bulk of his freehold estate to Susanna, leaving Judith with a money legacy only charged on his estate. When he came to revise the will in March, he set this at £300 but with strings attached.[204] The reason for Shakespeare's apparent distrust of Quiney was almost certainly the result of the disclosure, made public in the church court on 26 March but doubtless known about earlier, that he had fathered an illegiti-mate child by Margaret Wheeler, both of whom had been buried on 15 March.[205] Judith was to receive £100 as a marriage portion, to be

203. Tennant, *Civil War in Stratford-upon-Avon*, pp. 72–3, 106, 183–4.
204. For a transcript and facsimile of the will see Chambers, *William Shakespeare*, ii, pp. 170–4. When Shakespeare revised his will, the first page was rewritten but the second and third pages merely revised. One of the main revisions on p. 2 was the deletion of three lines originally at the top comprising the closing clause of a bequest to Judith of a money legacy only, although the actual sum must have been on the replaced page 1.
205. Brinkworth, *Shakespeare and the Bawdy Court*, pp. 78–81, 143. For a transcript and translation of the proceedings, see Hanley, 'Shakespeare's family in the Stratford records'.

paid within twelve months of her father's decease, plus a further £50 if she gave up any claim to the copyhold cottage in Chapel Lane.[206] Quite what her interest would have been is not entirely clear. The customs of the manor, as recorded in 1605, imply that, unless other arrangements were made, properties would descend by primogeniture to sons or in default to daughters.[207] Judith, a younger daughter, would therefore have had to give way to Susanna anyway. Perhaps Shakespeare simply wished to ensure that there would be no argument over the issue. As to the remaining £150, Judith was to enjoy the interest from this (at the rate of 2 shillings in the pound) for three years, after which it would continue to be held in trust for her and her issue if Quiney (or, as Shakespeare chillingly put it, 'such husbond as she shall...be married unto') within those three years had not settled on her and her children land of equal value to her original marriage portion. Only if he had done so, would the money go to him. Another alteration in the will appears to substitute his grand-daughter Elizabeth, for Judith, as the recipient of 'All my plate', leaving Judith with only 'my broad silver gilt bole'. Underlying this whole provision, then, is Shakespeare's clear distrust of his prospective son-in-law who had brought nothing tangible into the marriage on which his daughter's future security would depend. If he failed to make such provision, then the remaining £150 settled on her would continue to be held in trust with the interest paid directly to her. Later events were to justify Shakespeare's misgivings. The first instalment—Judith's marriage portion—certainly enabled Quiney, within months, to exchange a lease of a modest property in High Street which he held of the Corporation for a much more prominent one on the opposite corner of the street.[208] For a while he cut something of a figure in the town, securing election as one of the Corporation's capital burgesses in August of the following year, and serving as constable for the following two years, before going on to act as chamberlain in the early 1620s.[209] Judith also

---

206. She was also to receive interest on this bequest, at the rate of 2 shillings in the pound, depending on how long it took his executors, i.e. John Hall and Susanna, to make payment, suggesting some friction between the sisters.

207. Ryland, *Records of Rowington*, i, pp. 178–9, although the manuscript is damaged. By making this arrangement he was, under the same customs, preventing his wife from claiming 'free bench' in the property for life.

208. SCLA, BRU 2/2, p. 312. His new property was held for double the rent of the former one.

209. SCLA, BRU 2/2, pp. 332, 334, 362; BRU 4/2, ff. 5–9.

evidently surrendered her claim to the Chapel Lane cottage, so a further £50 would have found its way into his coffers. But it seems
unlikely that Quiney ever settled land on his wife, a precondition for
receiving the further £150. He never made it onto the aldermanic
bench and following a series of misdemeanours, resulting in fines in
1630 for swearing and 'suffering townsmen to tipple in his house', he
was pressured into surrendering his seat on the Corporation.[210]
Furthermore, when in 1633 he sought to renew the lease of his High
Street property, relatives stepped in to ensure that he could not sell the
lease on but that it should instead be vested in trustees for the benefit
of his wife and two surviving children, clearly pointing to his failure to
have provided for them independently.[211] By 1655, he may even have
left Stratford to live with, or near, his wealthy brother Richard, a prosperous London merchant: for the latter, in his will of 1655, charged his
Shottery estate with an annuity of £12 payable to Thomas for life,
together with a one-off payment of £5 to cover Thomas's burial
expenses, both indications of his brother's straitened circumstances.[212]
Whether he died there soon afterwards has not been established:
indeed, when Judith was buried in Stratford, on 9 February 1662, she
was described simply as the wife of Thomas Quincy, gentleman, leaving open the question of whether or not he was still alive.

We might also note in passing Shakespeare's reluctance in his will to
give his other son-in-law, John Hall, any significant mention. In fact,
he was not named at all until the very end of the will, when he and his
wife Susanna were made residuary legatees and executors, with only
Susanna named as the beneficiary in respect of the family's freehold
estate. In Susanna's case there is also the rather odd episode of the slan-
derous remarks made against her in July 1613 that she had committed
adultery with Ralf Smith and had 'the runninge of the reins', that is, a
venereal infection.[213] The words had been spoken by the young John
Lane, nephew of Richard Lane, the man with whom Shakespeare had
recently gone to law over the Stratford tithes.[214] Steps were immediately taken, through complaint to the bishop's court, to clear her name

210. Halliwell, *Outlines*, ii, p. 306.
211. SCLA, BRU 8/9/33.
212. TNA, PROB 11/261, ff. 41–42v.
213. Facsimile in Schoenbaum, *Documentary Life* (1975 edn), p. 237; transcript, Lewis,
     Shakespeare Documents, ii, p. 450.
214. Below, p. 136.

and this succeeded to the extent that Lane, on his failure to attend the court, was excommunicated. Almost certainly there was no truth in the accusation, but the interesting feature here is that one of Shakespeare's daughters had been made the target of common gossip. Cases of abuse, scandal, and defamation were not amongst those commonly brought to the attention of Stratford's church court: in fact, in the period 1590–1625 only eight are recorded.[215] Such instances were largely confined to those from a lower level of Stratford townspeople, implying that the Shakespeare family name did not command universal respect within the town.

On the evidence of his daughters' marriages, then, there is little to suggest that the family's status had risen to a level which guaranteed it a secure place amongst the minor gentry. Neither daughter had married into such families—the marriage arrangements of these families are discussed later—let alone found husbands who already enjoyed a private income, and this may reflect the fact that Shakespeare had not yet succeeded in cutting out for himself a recognized niche in the local landed hierarchy. In short his daughters' fortunes do not reflect lives of ease arising out of inherited wealth.

---

215. Brinkworth, *Shakespeare and the Bawdy Court*, pp. 69–71. There is a gap in the record from 1617–21.

5

Retrenchment

Shakespeare the maltster

Evidence from 1605—that is, after this proposed high point in
Shakespeare's financial fortunes—points to measures to protect this
hard-won investment income. One local source from which
Shakespeare had been deriving some income, though how much it is
difficult to say, was the sale of malt. He alleged in Stratford's court of
record that between March and June 1604, in a series of six transactions, he had sold to Philip Rogers of Stratford, a local apothecary,
twenty bushels of malt for a total sum of 39s. 10d.[1] He had also lent him
2 shillings bringing the total debt to 41s. 10d. At some later stage
Rogers had repaid 6 shillings but, despite frequent requests, he had
refused to pay the balance for which Shakespeare then claimed an
additional 10 shillings in damages, bringing the total claimed back up to
45s. 10d. It is usual to date Shakespeare's attempt to recover this money
to the year 1604, given that this was the year the sales and loans were
said to have been made. However, the court register for this period has
not survived, only multifarious loose papers relating to some of the
cases which came before it. In this particular instance, only the undated
formal complaint, made by Shakespeare's attorney, William Tetherton,
is extant. In the period up to 1601, for which the court register survives, it is clear that the date a case came to court could be at least a
year after a debt had been incurred. Indeed, from the pleadings in this
case we know that frequent, but unsuccessful, applications for repayment were said to have already been made. So the case may well not
have reached the court until early 1605, perhaps at the time when

1. Chambers, *William Shakespeare*, ii, pp. 113–14. For a facsimile, see Schoenbaum,
   Documentary Life (1975 edn), p. 182.

calling in any debts would have helped Shakespeare fund his purchase
of the tithes. This was also the time, of course, that Shakespeare would
have become aware of any slackening off of his theatre income as the
result of the plague closure which had begun in May 1604, to last for
almost twelve months.

This is not the first occasion on which Shakespeare is known to
have been in possession of significant quantities of malt. As we have
seen, in February 1598, less than a year after his purchase of New Place,
he was known to have been storing ten quarters (eighty bushels) of
malt there.[2] Malt was made from barley and the area around Stratford
was noted by contemporaries as a prime region for the growing of this
crop. Drying the barley to produce malt was widespread in the town
and was often carried on as a supplementary business activity. In
November 1595, in order to preserve the grain as a foodstuff at a time
of high corn prices, forty-four Stratford townsfolk were bound over to
cease making malt.[3] Yet few, if any, of them occur in other documents
as maltsters. Many were innkeepers and victuallers, who needed the
malt to make beer, but some were butchers, and even the schoolmaster,
Alexander Aspinall, was numbered amongst them. Some, then, particularly those who used malt in beer production, were simply purchasing
quantities of barley to produce sufficient malt to run their businesses
successfully. Others might prepare a certain quantity for domestic use,
but for the better off there was clearly scope for laying in larger quantities of barley for the production of malt which could then be resold.
At times of food shortages, such men were likely to attract criticism,
being suspected of hoarding and subsequent sales at inflated prices.
Even the government had strong words for some offenders, recogniz-
ing that amongst their number were 'men which are of good lyvely-
hoode and in estymacion of worshipp.'[4] Whether or not Shakespeare,
in 1598, was indulging in deliberate speculation, he had clearly become
involved in a trade by which many of the town's elite sought to boost
their revenues. Eighty bushels would have been way above the amount
required for Shakespeare's immediate domestic use implying that he,
or his family or agent, had soon entered into what was a profitable
business.

2. Above, pp. 98–101.
3. Fripp and others, eds., *Minutes and Accounts*, v, pp. 47–8.
4. This, and similar complaints, are conveniently listed by Chambers, *William Shakespeare*,
    ii, p. 100.

We cannot be certain to what extent and over what period Shakespeare remained involved in the malting trade, but the Rogers case of 1604–5 suggests that it remained a feature of his business interests. This may be the only known instance of such involvement, but nevertheless, on the assumption that other customers and clients would have made due payment and thereby not have been brought to book, it is unlikely to have been the only one. Moreover, as the records after 1601 are incomplete, cases which got no further than an initial complaint are not known to us either. That only this one case reached a more advanced stage cannot therefore be taken to establish that Shakespeare, or agents acting on his behalf, were not engaged in the malting business during these years. Indeed, the opposite is more likely. Philip Rogers has been persistently identified simply as an apothecary and this was indeed one of the ways in which he made a living. But he was also a victualler, and it was in this capacity that he also frequently occurs in the Stratford records. Married, in October 1597, to Eleanor Saunders of Wroxall, he was sued in the local court of record in an isolated case in July 1597,[5] but occurs more regularly from about 1602, first occurring as a victualler in January 1603.[6] There is little doubt, then, that Shakespeare was supplying Rogers with malt in 1604 in order for him to carry on his victualler's business: in other words, not a transaction of a personal nature on either side but a business deal of which this was almost certainly not the only one.

The Addenbrooke case

A later case, of 1609, also indicates a keen interest in recovering a debt, this time a more substantial one of £6, plus 4 shillings in damages, from John Addenbrooke, a local man of some substance. Again the evidence comes from the proceedings of Stratford's court of record. As already explained, the court register for this period does not survive, but seven loose documents concerning this case are extant, dated between 17 December 1608 and 7 June 1609.[7] In the first of these

---

5. SCLA, BRU 12/1 (iv), f. 30; BRU 15/4/63.
6. Fripp and others, eds., *Minutes and Accounts*, vi, p. 222; and see pp. 240, 291, 328, 347, 390 (when he is also styled apothecary).
7. Halliwell, *Outlines*, ii, pp. 78–80. For a facsimile of one of these, see Schoenbaum, *Documentary Life* (1975 edn), p. 183.

Addenbrooke is described as a gentleman (*generosus*), but his place of residence is not specified, nor is it in the other six. However, the fact that, as the case proceeded, Shakespeare's claim was frustrated because Addenbrooke was not to be found within the borough is a sure indication that he lived elsewhere. In fact, he can almost certainly be identified as the John Addenbrooke of Tanworth-in-Arden and nearby Beoley, in Worcestershire. Married in Tanworth in June 1574, he is described as a yeoman both in 1579, when he bought the vicarage and advowson of Tanworth, and in 1585 when he sold them.[8] In 1594 he sued John Armstrong in Stratford's court of record for the recovery of a debt of 40 shillings and is described as a gentleman in 1597 when witnessing a court declaration.[9] He can probably also be identified with one 'Addenbrooke' who, around 1600, was involved in the selling of licences in Warwickshire for the production of starch, which had been curtailed in the 1590s during a period of bad harvests.[10] By the time the dispute with Shakespeare reached the courts, he may well have been ill, a sufficient explanation for the difficulties in settling the claim. He was buried at Tanworth on 19 June 1609: in his inventory drawn up in 1610, he had reverted to the status of yeoman, though his goods were valued at a very respectable £32 19s. 8d.[11]

How or why he had become indebted to Shakespeare in this considerable sum is not apparent from surviving records. The most informative of the surviving documents is the final one, dated 7 June 1609.[12] From this we learn that Shakespeare's claim had previously been upheld, probably in February, but that the court serjeants had been unable to secure Addenbrooke's appearance at the next court sitting to make payment because he could not be found within the town. This did not mean that he had fled, merely that the court officials had no power to act outside the borough—in Addenbrooke's case, in Tanworth or Beoley. Serious illness might also have been a complicating factor. Shakespeare therefore requested that he be allowed instead to seek redress from Addenbrooke's unlucky surety, Thomas Hornby, a Stratford

---

8. SCLA, DR 37/1/1414, 1476.
9. SCLA, BRU 12/1 (iii), f. 73; (iv), f. 26v.
10. Chambers, *William Shakespeare*, ii, p. 118.
11. Fry, ed., *Calendar of Wills, Worcester*, ii, p. 39. Unfortunately, any debts he owed are not listed.
12. SCLA, ER 27/7; Chambers, *William Shakespeare*, ii, pp. 115–16.

blacksmith, whose appearance at the next court was made the subject of a court order. The documentation then fails us and the outcome is unknown. At no point is it explained how the debt was contracted: for example, did it merely represent a straight cash loan or was it a debt incurred through non-payment for goods or materials supplied? However, we may still note that it provides evidence of Shakespeare's local dealings with a man of some standing and on a matter not obviously related to an ordinary mercantile transaction. Of equal interest is Shakespeare's apparent determination to secure payment by transferring his attention to Addenbrooke's surety, Thomas Hornby, on Addenbrooke's refusal, or inability, to meet his obligations. We do not know whether such determination was intended to have the effect of persuading Addenbrooke to come to terms: if so, then his death within a fortnight would clearly have made this impossible. One can, of course, interpret this sequence of events as a somewhat heartless pursuit of, first, a sick man and then of his unfortunate surety, although it could equally well be argued that the documents fail us because that was as far as the case went, Shakespeare forgoing repayment in view of the debtor's circumstances. But Shakespeare's initial determination could still have a bearing on his own means at the time. The fact that, due to plague, the theatres were closed from July 1608 to December 1609 (the longest continuous period in an already disrupted decade, 1603–13), thus curtailing Shakespeare's income, may well have been a consideration, and this is further discussed later.[13]

The Stratford tithes

Shakespeare's determination to safeguard his investment income is best demonstrated in his determination to protect his interest in a lease of a half part of the Stratford Corporation's share of the tithes. As we have seen, this, at £440, was his biggest investment and one that was bringing in a net sum of at least £40 a year, probably more.[14] Under the terms by which this lease was assigned to him, he was to pay a straightforward rent of £17 a year to the Stratford Corporation, together with

---

13. Below, p. 147.
14. Above, p. 120.

£5 as part of an annuity of £27 13s. 4d. awarded back in 1580 to the Barker family to whom the whole tithes of the parish had originally been leased.[15] Other holders of shares in the original lease ought also to have been paying a proportion of this annuity to the Barkers, but, due, it was alleged, to imprecision in the documentation when these shares were acquired, only two were legally obliged to do so, namely Shakespeare paying his specified £5 for half the Corporation tithes, and Mary Combe, and her sons, William and Thomas, who at that time held the other half, also paying £5.[16] To make up the shortfall, Henry Barker, it was further alleged, to whom the right to the annuity had descended, was threatening Shakespeare, Richard Lane (who currently held the tithes of Clopton and Shottery, worth £80, and a reversion in the Bridgetown tithes), and 'some fewe others' with the prospect of paying the balance, on threat of dispossession. Around 1611, Lane and Shakespeare, anxious to settle the issue, petitioned in Chancery that the other holders of tithes forming part of the original lease to the Barkers should be made to agree to a payment of a reasonable part of this annuity so that they (Lane and Shakespeare) were no longer faced with the prospect of bearing the whole cost. In drawing up their case, they were joined by Thomas Greene, who had recently purchased the reversion of the lease of the half share of the Corporation tithes then held by the Combes and who would thus be anxious to establish exactly what proportion of the rent he would be called on to pay. His involvement may even have saved Lane and Shakespeare money as their draft bill of complaint bears several of Greene's interlineations and alterations.[17] Their principal targets were Sir Edward Conway who held the tithes of Luddington, worth £30, under the same ninety-two-year lease, and George Carew, Baron Clopton, who held the tithes of Bridgetown, worth £20. Little apparently came of this, except for the Combes' acknowledgement that they were already paying £5 for their moiety of the Corporation tithes, to which, with the plaintiff's agreement, they were prepared to add 6s. 8d. annually to account for a lease of the tithes of Rhyn Clifford, valued at £10, which they also held, as long as the other men alleged to be withholding their fair share of the rent did the same.[18]

15. For a copy, made in 1611, of the 1580 agreement, see SCLA, BRU 15/9/11.
16. Halliwell, *Outlines*, ii, pp. 25–31.
17. SCLA, BRU 15/2/11.
18. SCLA, BRU 15/10/9 summarized in Chambers, *William Shakespeare*, ii, pp. 124–5.

Shakespeare's willingness to be a fellow petitioner in Chancery is a sure indication of his wish to derive full benefit from his investment in the tithes. If, as he alleged, he were indeed being pressurized into paying more than £5 to Barker then his tithe income would have suffered. By how much is uncertain: as the Combes claimed to have been paying £5, and Richard Lane an unspecified amount, the shortfall could not have exceeded much more than £15, for which Shakespeare is unlikely to have been dunned for more than half. However, if, as indicated above (p. 120), his net tithe income was not much more than £40 a year, then it would be cut by nearly 20 per cent if a further £7 10s. od. became a regular feature of his outgoings. In any case, the fact that Shakespeare was willing to go to law over the issue must surely be taken as an indication that it was a matter of concern to him, either because he was in immediate need of the money or, more likely, because the uncertainty represented a threat to the family's future income. We do, though, need to consider the context. The status of this £27 13s. 4d. rent, and of the original ninety-two-year lease, had been questioned in the years leading up to Shakespeare's involvement. In July 1608 the Stratford Corporation had begun negotiations with the Barkers to buy out their interests at the very significant cost of £276 13s. 4d., which apparently got as far as the drafting of the relevant deeds but which were later abandoned when the difficulties of assigning the fragmented lease became clear.[19] Lane and Shakespeare, aware of these failing negotiations, might therefore have had a particular reason for ensuring that they were not going to lose out. Nevertheless, Shakespeare's willingness to become involved remains a significant indicator of his concerns and priorities, at a time, as discussed later, of declining income from theatrical sources. A readiness to act alongside Lane, a landed gentleman who back in 1596 had been chosen to take evidence on the Shakespeares' behalf over disputed Wilmcote property,[20] is also a further indication of the circle whose financial interests now coincided with Shakespeare's own.

---

19. Fripp and others, eds., *Minutes and Accounts*, vi, pp. 471, 473, 475; SCLA, BRU 2/2, pp. 184, 234. For the draft deeds, dated 1 and 3 May 1610, but with adverse legal opinion, see SCLA, BRU 15/10/8, 10. For a letter of 1609 from John Nash, who had an interest in the Drayton tithes, offering support to the Corporation if it took action over the rent, see BRU 15/12/102.
20. Above, p. 89.

The Welcombe enclosures

Shakespeare's involvement in the 1611 Chancery case proved but a prelude to a more dramatic turn of events which began in 1614 and continued until well after his death two years later, centring on an attempt to enclose some of the old open fields at Welcombe lying to the north-east of the town. At this date enclosure of any sort was likely to arouse great passions, associated in the popular mind, reaching back to the late fifteenth and early sixteenth centuries, with the depopulation of many local villages. As a result of agitation the government had taken steps to limit further enclosure, but any hint of a renewal of the process would still inevitably arouse the fears not only of the common folk who stood to lose most but also of those who would have to deal with, or feel the effects of, any outbreak of civil disorder. Of particular concern were the threats posed by the enclosure of arable land and its conversion to sheep pasture. Sheep husbandry required far less labour than arable farming and, not surprisingly, was almost universally associated in the popular imagination with unemployment, hardship, and depopulation.

The Stratford-upon-Avon Corporation also immediately took against this particular scheme. Under its 1553 foundation charter it had become one of the principal tithe owners within the parish and naturally feared that enclosure, by taking arable land out of production, would threaten its tithe income and thus make more difficult the performance of the statutory duties placed upon it. Times were also hard. In the course of the dispute, it was alleged that 700 townsfolk, out of a population of some 2000, were in receipt of poor relief[21] and a town fire in 1614 had caused additional general suffering. There were also fears of the kind of breakdown in law and order that often accompanied attempted enclosure.

The controversy, though well documented, is tantalizingly imprecise in some of its detail. The instigators of the scheme were said to be Arthur Mainwaring of Shropshire and his agent, William Replingham of Great Harborough, a relation by marriage. However, these men were almost certainly fronting the scheme on behalf of William

---

21. Below, p. 143. This was no doubt an exaggeration but a figure of 400 had been given in 1598 (Fripp and others, eds., *Minutes and Accounts*, v, p. 133).

Combe, the principal landowner in the area proposed for enclosure, who soon emerges as its single protagonist. Early in 1610 he had succeeded his father Thomas in most of his estates and in the same year was made joint residuary legatee of the estate of his great-uncle, William Combe of Warwick.[22] At the very end of 1611, he had bought a substantial freehold in the common fields of Stratford and in the summer of 1614 had inherited from his uncle John four enclosed fields in the neighbouring parish of Hampton Lucy.[23] It was therefore surely the case that the enclosure was his idea from the start and that Mainwaring, in the early stages and for a reason yet to be established, had simply agreed to screen him from immediate censure.

Freeholders' arable lands generally lay scattered in strips across the open fields, which meant that any attempt to enclose them, for example as sheep pasture, could only take place by mutual consent. Though we may assume that Combe owned most of the strips in the area proposed for enclosure, he still needed the agreement of other freeholders whose lands might be affected. The Corporation therefore quickly set about identifying those who might be recruited as opponents of the scheme. On 5 September 1614 Thomas Greene, the Corporation's steward, looked out a survey of the manor of Old Stratford made early in 1603, brought it up to date with his own annotations, and then appended to it a list of the current freeholders on the manor. Shakespeare topped this list with the 107 acres (or four yardlands) that he had bought from the Combes in 1602, with no one else holding more than about fifteen acres.[24] These, then, were the freeholders on whom the Corporation could then exert pressure in its efforts to thwart the scheme. Shakespeare, according to Greene's note, held 'noe common nor ground beyond gospell bushe', one of the limits, it was later said, of the proposed enclosure, and was therefore not regarded as a key player in this respect.[25] But, given the Corporation's overriding wish to protect its tithe income, it was clearly hoped that its lessees of the two halves into which it had been divided, namely William

22. For their wills, see TNA, PROB 11/113, ff. 98–100; 117, ff. 413–413v.
23. SCLA, ER 3/321; TNA, PROB 11/126, ff. 419–21v.
24. Chambers, *William Shakespeare*, ii, p. 141, transcribes the Shakespeare entry only from SCLA, BRU 15/1/94.
25. The exact location of Gospel Bush is uncertain though the references to it imply that it marked one of the western limits of the proposed enclosure and that only land 'beyond' it (i.e. to the east) would be affected.

Shakespeare, and its own steward, Thomas Greene (who had recently acquired from the Combes the other half), would nevertheless join in the protest.[26] However, any prospect that they might side with the Corporation was quickly undermined, though this may not have been obvious at the time. On 28 October Shakespeare concluded an agreement with William Replingham, acting on behalf of the enclosure party, that he would be guaranteed against any losses that he might suffer 'by reason of anie inclosure or decaye of tyllage', the losses to be estimated by 'foure indifferent persons.'[27] In other words, whatever Shakespeare may have felt about the ethics of enclosure, he had within two months, no doubt after some discussion, ensured that his own income would not be adversely affected by any enclosure scheme. Thomas Greene, the lessee of the other half of the tithes, was also written into the agreement, either at the last moment or in a subsequent amendment,[28] though it is quite likely that the affair was kept secret, not least because Greene as the town's steward had been entrusted by the Corporation to take all possible steps to frustrate Combe's plans.

The nature of the documentation concerning this agreement also needs to be taken into account. What survives today is not the original agreement but a near contemporary copy, drawn up, it seems, for Thomas Greene's benefit, and comprising only the one clause affecting Greene's (alongside Shakespeare's) interests (Figure 6).[29] The wording of the other clauses (whose inclusion is proved by the marginal note 'inter alia', or 'amongst other things', against the one surviving clause) is therefore unknown. The known guarantee offered to Shakespeare is therefore only 'a bottom line'. The remaining clauses

26. For Greene's interest in the tithes, see Bearman, 'Thomas Greene, Stratford's town clerk and Shakespeare's lodger', pp. 297–301.

27. SCLA, ER 27/3 (Figure 6). For transcript, see Chambers, *William Shakespeare*, ii, pp. 141–2.

28. The insertion of Greene's name is established by a note in his diary: 'Mr Replyngham 28 Oct[o]bris articled w[i]th Mr Shakspeare & then I was putt in by T. Lucas'. This entry occurs near notes recording events on 9 January 1615 but may just have been written into a blank space. On 11 January he further noted that Replingham had assured him he would 'be well dealt w[i]thal... confessyng former promisses... by himself, Mr Manneryng & his agreement for me w[i]th my Cosen Shakspeare' (Ingleby, ed., *Shakespeare and the Enclosure*, p. 6).

29. As this is a copy, the late insertion of Greene's name is not immediately apparent. For a fuller discussion of this, see Bearman, *Shakespeare in the Stratford Records*, pp. 54–5.

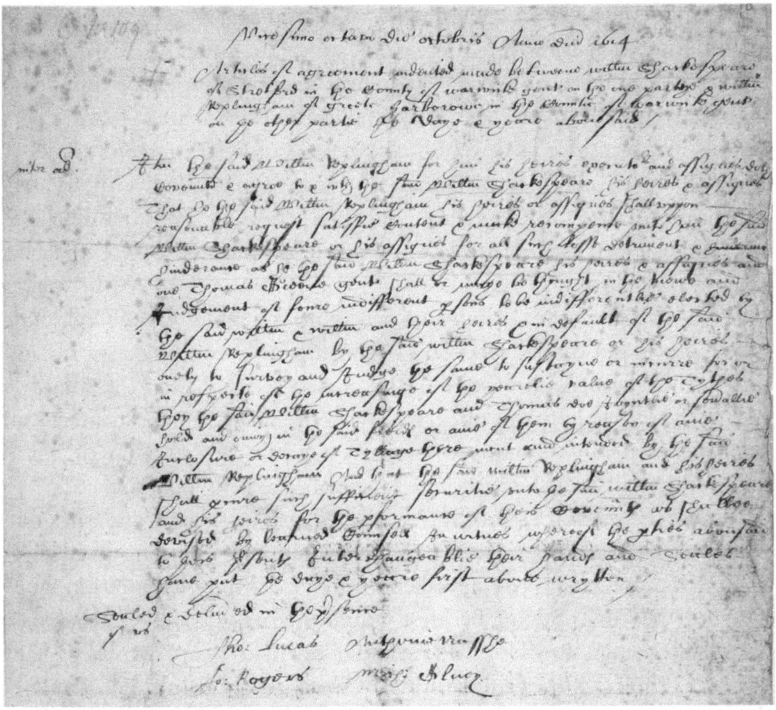

Figure 6. Agreement between William Replingham (acting on William Combe's behalf) and William Shakespeare that Shakespeare would be recompensed for any losses he might suffer as a tithe-holder 'by reason of anie Inclosure or decaye of Tyllage' at Welcombe, 5 September 1614

Source: The note in the left margin, 'inter alia' ('amongst other things') indicates that this is a copy of only one clause of the agreement. The copy was probably made for Thomas Greene, the other major tithe-holder, whose name ('and one Thomas Greene') was clearly inserted afterwards. This is confirmed in his 'diary' but is not obvious here as the result of the copying process.

Shakespeare Centre Library and Archive, ER 27/3

may have dealt with other areas of cooperation, perhaps extending to some of his freehold interests which might also have been affected, but more likely to the common pasture rights associated with his freehold, defined somewhat vaguely in the 1602 conveyance to him as 'all the common pasture...in the feildes of Olde Stretford aforesaide, to the said fowre yarde lande belonginge or in any wise apperteyninge', but in the more detailed survey of his property as 'in the hame 10 acres of leez ground...w[i]th all the leez lying in the dyngyllis and about

Welcombe hilles down to Millway.'[30] The witnesses to the agreement are of interest, suggesting they were privy to its terms, namely the lawyer, Thomas Lucas (whom Greene credited for getting his name included) and his 'man', Michael Olney, but also Anthony Nash, making his reappearance as one of Shakespeare's closest Stratford contacts, and 'Jo: Rogers', presumably the vicar, recently provided with a vicarage alongside the Guild Chapel (and thus a near neighbour) who was later appealed to as a man able to persuade William Combe to halt his proposed enclosure plans.[31]

Such an agreement should come as no surprise. Other evidence substantiates good relations, even friendship, between Shakespeare and the Combe family. John Combe (the encloser's uncle and the member of the family principally concerned with the sale to Shakespeare of his freehold estate in the common fields) left him £5 in his will,[32] and Shakespeare himself bequeathed his sword (a very personal item) to Thomas (the encloser's brother) in the course of the dispute, the man who on 12 December 1614, when the dispute was entering its liveliest phase, was reported as having called members of the Corporation 'dogges' and 'Curres.'[33] Such a bequest would normally have been made to the testator's son and heir and, in default, Shakespeare would at least have had the option of substituting his son-in-law, John Hall. The fact that he chose not to, preferring a member of a local land-holding family in open dispute with the Corporation, suggests both that he had no great love for the man who had married his elder daughter and also that he was sufficiently close to the Combes, as fellow gentry, to lead him into alliances to protect mutual interests.

From 15 October the steward, Thomas Greene, kept notes (often referred to as a diary) of the attempted enclosure, allowing us to follow the progress of the dispute in some detail, including several references to Shakespeare's involvement.[34] In mid-November 1614, when in

---

30. Chambers, *William Shakespeare*, ii, p. 107; Macdonald, 'New discovery about Shakespeare's estate', p. 88. It was the threat to common pasture which formed one of the principal objections, for which see, for instance, SCLA, BRU 15/7/8; BRU 15/8/175.
31. Ingleby, ed., *Shakespeare and the Enclosure*, p. 6; Eccles, *Shakespeare in Warwickshire*, pp. 133–4; Fripp, *Shakespeare Man and Artist*, ii, pp. 735, 786, 903.
32. Above, p. 109; Halliwell, *Life of William Shakespeare*, p. 238, with facsimile in Schoenbaum, *Documentary life* (1975 edn), p. 187.
33. Ingleby, *Shakespeare and the Enclosure*, p. 3.
34. Reproduced in facsimile and transcript in Ingleby, *Shakespeare and the Enclosure*, but users should be aware that the final two pages are transposed.

London to present the Corporation's petition against the scheme, he records the only known conversation with Shakespeare, he 'commyng yesterday to towne', in which Shakespeare showed himself fully informed about the enclosure plans, detailing the area affected, stating that the land would be surveyed the following spring, but giving his opinion that 'there will be nothyng done at all.' (Figure 7).[35] Greene's note that 'he told me they assured him they ment to inclose noe further then to gospel bushe . . . and that they meane in Aprill to servey the Land' clearly implies direct contact between Shakespeare and the promoters of the scheme and on 10 December, back in Stratford, Greene notes that he called at Shakespeare's home, New Place, in an unsuccessful attempt to see Replingham, Combe's agent, again implying Shakespeare's willingness to negotiate with the enclosure party.[36] Following a council meeting on 23 December, at which the Corporation agreed further measures to halt the plans, Greene was instructed to draft letters both to Combe's front man, Arthur Mainwaring, and to Shakespeare 'with almost all the comp[any's] hands [i.e. signatures of the members of the Corporation] to eyther', but he adds that he also sent a personal note to Shakespeare with 'Coppyes of all our oathes m[a]de then alsoe a note of the Inconvenyences wold g[row] by the Inclosure.'[37] We have a copy of the appeal to Mainwaring pleading with him not to proceed, and entreating him to 'call to mynde the manifold greate and often miseries this borough hath sustayned by casualties of fires Fresh in Memorie . . . wherein lyve aboue seaven hundred poore wch receave Almes, whose curses and clamours Wilbee daylie powred out to god against the interprisors of such a thinge.'[38] We do not have a copy of the letters that went to Shakespeare nor his personal note, but the latter would presumably have made reference to the agreement of the previous October which Shakespeare had reached with the enclosure party, and to which Greene was by then a party, whereby they had sought to safeguard their personal interests. In fact, Greene may well have felt constrained to write privately to Shakespeare in order to explain why he had had to write to him in stronger terms on the Corporation's behalf.

35. Ingleby, ed., *Shakespeare and the Welcombe Enclosure*, p. 1.
36. Ingleby, ed., *Shakespeare and the Welcombe Enclosure*, p. 3.
37. Ingleby, ed., *Shakespeare and the Welcombe Enclosure*, p. 4.
38. Ingleby, ed., *Shakespeare and the Welcombe Enclosure*, pp. 15–16.

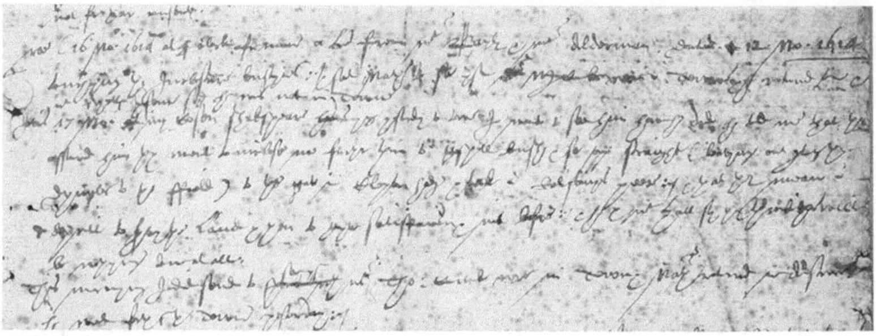

Figure 7. An extract from Thomas Greene's 'diary' recording a conversation in London with William Shakespeare, 'commyng yesterday to towne', about the proposed enclosure at Welcombe, 17 November 1614

Source: Thomas Greene's handwriting, challenging at the best of times, becomes even more difficult when he was making notes for his own use, but here he records the only known direct conversation with Shakespeare, after 'I went to see him howe he did.' The information Shakespeare supplied about the enclosure plans was clearly the result of his direct contact with the promoters of the scheme.

Shakespeare Centre Library and Archive, BRU 15/13/26a

Shakespeare is mentioned on one further occasion in Greene's diary, in September 1615: 'W. Shakespeares tellyng J. Greene [Thomas's brother] that I [or possibly "J"] was not able to beare the encloseing of Welcombe.'[39] It has been suggested that the phrase beginning, 'I was...', represents direct speech and that it was therefore Shakespeare who could not 'bear' the enclosure. However, Greene does not report any other conversations over the enclosure in this way, which in any case would have been unlikely in the context of hasty notes. To read the 'I' as 'J' (that it was John who could not 'bear' the enclosure) also makes little sense, given that John had no financial involvement.[40] A more likely interpretation is that it was Shakespeare who told John that it was Thomas ('I') who could not 'bear' the enclosure. Thomas's reason for jotting this down, presumably after chatting with his brother, is not entirely clear though, if Shakespeare, in talking to John Greene, had implied that Thomas could not in some way support the enclosure then this would have been at odds with what we now know, namely that Thomas, despite his official role as the Corporation's spokesman against the scheme, had, with Shakespeare, already reached an agreement to

39. Ingleby, ed., Shakespeare and the Welcombe Enclosures, p. 6.
40. Additionally he is surely more likely to have written 'he' if John were intended.

ensure that he would not suffer financially.[41] Shakespeare's alleged remark, implying something different, may therefore have puzzled Thomas, leading him to make his cryptic comment. Furthermore, this would imply that John did not know of the steps which his brother Thomas and Shakespeare had already taken to protect their position. In any event, what emerges from overall consideration of the enclosure documentation is Shakespeare's careful concern, whatever he may have felt about the general issue of enclosure, that his income would not be undermined.

41. Attaching a different meaning to the word bear—to promote or sustain—is also prob-lematical in that Greene himself was never in the position of championing the scheme.

6

The final count

Shakespeare's income

On the face of it, there would seem, from around 1605, to be a clear
falling away of Shakespeare's ability to raise capital for further investments, coupled with evidence of measures taken to protect his existing
income arising out of those already made. Whereas, from 1597, when
he bought New Place, until his purchase of an interest in the Stratford
tithes in 1605, he had been able at regular intervals to invest increasingly large sums—£120, £320, and then £440—in the purchase of
property, the second two producing an investment income, these were
not followed by further acquisitions. There were other means of using
surplus capital: some of his fellow town gentry, as we have seen, lent
money at interest, though for Shakespeare there is no evidence of this.
The buying and selling of goods could also be profitable, of course, and
was pursued to great advantage by the merchant adventurers of the big
cities. Reference has been made to Shakespeare's local dealings in malt,
but there is no evidence that he was engaged in any large-scale business of this sort, either in Stratford or London, nor would such a
'hands-on' activity have had much appeal for a man earning his living
in the London theatre. The purchase of land was much the preferred
option for the investment of surplus capital by men aspiring to enter
the ranks of the local gentry, enabling them to claim the status of men
of independent means. Even if Shakespeare had not shared this ultimate ambition, investment in property would still have remained the
simplest way of using money beyond his immediate needs in order to
generate further income both for his own benefit and also his dependants. That Shakespeare did not do this after 1605, with the odd exception of the Blackfriars gatehouse to which we will return, implies that

he was in a less secure position as far as raising capital was concerned. We should therefore turn to a closer examination of the sort of income he might have been enjoying from his work in the theatre in an effort to establish whether the apparent slackening off of his rate of investment might be a reflection of a falling professional income.

Shakespeare's income from his theatrical interests comprised two elements: firstly, from at least 1594, his share of the company profits, perhaps as much as £120 a year by 1605, and, secondly, from 1599, his share as a 'housekeeper' of the Globe, calculated by 1605 to have been in the region of £80.[1] His income in a good year could thus have been some £200. There is good reason to regard this as an upper limit and one not normally achieved in the years following 1605. Indeed, during the eleven months, May 1604 to April 1605, when the playhouses in London were closed as the result of plague, it is particularly difficult to believe that this figure was reached.[2] By way of contrast, there had been no closures since October 1596, the precise period during which evidence of Shakespeare's improving financial situation is most obvious. The closures of 1604/5 may not have had an immediate effect as far as raising money was concerned—for the purchase of a share in the Stratford tithes, for example—but over the following years further closures would have had a cumulative impact. In 1606 and 1607 the theatres may have been open for around six months of the year, but from July 1608 until the end of 1609 they were closed and there may also have been closures in 1610. At such times, the company could, of course, go on tour and during this period there is also no evidence of any falling away in the number of times the company was summoned to perform at court. Nevertheless, it is very doubtful that the theoretical income of £200 was regularly realized during these years; or, at the very least that the steady income he had enjoyed for the years 1596 to 1603/4 was thereafter maintained.

In August 1608, when the King's Men at last secured control of the Blackfriars Theatre as a second venue, Shakespeare was granted a seventh share as housekeeper here too.[3] Following the Burbages' failure in

1. In the absence of any detailed accounts, these figures must remain uncertain but see Gurr, *The Shakespeare Company*, pp. 108–15.
2. Gurr, *Shakespearian Playing Companies*, pp. 87–92; Barroll, *Politics, Plague and Shakespeare's Theater*, p. 173; Wilson, *Plague in Shakespeare's London*, pp. 124–5.
3. Chambers, *William Shakespeare*, ii, pp. 62–4; Wickham, Berry and Ingram, eds., *English Professional Theatre*, pp. 501–3, 514–22. The original documentation does not survive, but

1598/9 to open a theatre here, they had leased the premises to Henry Evans for use by the Children of the Queen's Revels. The premises may not have required major refurbishment when the Burbages negotiated with Evans for the surrender of this lease, but he still had to be bought out 'for a competent consideracion' and this may have been reflected in the amount of rent the sharers were now asked to pay under a set of identical leases dated 9 August 1608 in order to take up the management of their new premises.[4] Whereas Shakespeare's share of the ground rent for the Globe was only £1 9s. 0d., for the Blackfriars he was expected to pay £5 14s. 4d. No doubt this was calculated in expectation that the profits would be greater, but whether this became a reality is unclear. The higher seat prices charged at the Blackfriars may have boosted takings, but this needs to be offset against the theatre's smaller capacity and the fact that the total number of company performances during the year (that is, in both the Globe and Blackfriars) would have remained much the same. Nor is it certain that Shakespeare retained this share for more than a few years. In February 1610, Robert Keysar, owner of a share in the original lease granted to Henry Evans, brought an action for compensation on its surrender against four named Blackfriars shareholders, Richard and Cuthbert Burbage and John Heminges and Henry Condell. At one point Keysar refers to 'and others', one of whom could have been Shakespeare. One of the original seven shareholders, William Sly, had died almost immediately after the arrangements of August 1608 and was not replaced, by William Ostler, until 25 March 1611, leaving only Shakespeare and one Thomas Evans, an outside financier but included as an original sharer, to comprise 'the others'. This is hardly proof one way or the other of Shakespeare's continuing involvement, though, when Ostler was recruited the following year, it was to a seventh share, suggesting that Shakespeare still had interests in the Blackfriars.[5]

Besides his income as a sharer/housekeeper Shakespeare would presumably also have received payment for new plays which he added to the company's repertory. However highly the company valued this

identical leases, dated 9 August 1608, to the five sharers—two shares were reserved to the Burbages—are cited in a legal case of May 1611.

4. Cuthbert Burbage rather overlooked this when he later claimed that Hemings and Condell (and by implication the other sharers) had received their shares 'of the blackfriers of us for nothing' (Gurr, *Shakespeare Company*, p. 279).

5. Chambers, *William Shakespeare*, ii, pp. 62–5.

additional service, this may well have been reflected simply in his 'author's fee' and would not necessarily have relieved him of the basic duty of an actor/sharer, that is, of performing roles on stage. On three occasions, between 1598 and 1603, he is recorded as appearing in company productions[6] and his role as actor in his own works is recorded on the title page of the First Folio. Some have argued that 1603 was, in fact, the last occasion that he took to the stage, mainly on the shaky ground that his name does not reoccur in the few surviving 'cast-lists' subsequent to that date. Whilst this may be overstating the case, it is still possible, given Shakespeare's long service, that his fellow sharers might have expected less of him in later years in an acting capacity. However, this would not have affected the general expectation that he would continue to produce new work for the company's repertory. The frequent closure of the theatres during this period might be thought to have reduced the need for this but, in fact, in more general terms, the knowledge that over the winter months the court would still expect to be provided with a succession of new plays was sufficient incentive to make sure this happened. In any case, at the rate of £10 a performance, the company stood to benefit very considerably in a winter season which during these years could involve between fifteen and twenty appearances.[7]

Against this background, Shakespeare's output could therefore be regarded as a valuable asset. The extent to which James I's direct patronage of Shakespeare's company affected its finances, and general standing, is a matter of debate. Whilst it has been argued that the king's personal commitment to the company that bore his name was not as great as might be inferred, and that this patronage was only of indirect financial benefit, the contrary view has been put that the court positively nurtured the company in order to secure a string of high-class plays for the winter season, even to the extent of direct liaison between the company and the Master of the Revels.[8] Whichever scenario is preferred, there is, however, no getting away from the popularity of Shakespeare's plays as far the court's winter season was concerned. The titles of those performed were not always recorded but, following

6. Chambers, *William Shakespeare*, ii, pp. 71–2.
7. Knutson, *The Repertory of Shakespeare's Company, 1594–1613*, pp. 179–209; Gurr, *The Shakespeare Company, 1594–1642*, pp. 281–8, 303–4.
8. Barroll, *Politics, Plague and Shakespeare's Theater*, pp. 23–69; Dutton, 'The Court, the Master of the Revels, and the Players', pp. 362–79.

James I's accession, we know that at least one Shakespeare play was performed in 1603/4, seven in 1604/5, one in 1606/7 and two in 1611/12.[9] Moreover, 1604/5 apart, these are very much minimum figures. Over a period of four years, 1607/8–1610/11, for instance, we know that the King's Men gave fifty-three performances at court (some half of the total) though none of the plays was named, and in other years the naming of plays was also generally patchy. Only in 1604/5, when we know that Shakespeare was the author of seven of the ten plays offered by the King's Men (almost a third of the total that year), do we have reliable data on which to gauge the likely number of those performed in other years. In any event, at £10 a performance, Shakespeare's plays would have netted £60 for the company in 1604/5 and, even if we regard this as exceptional in a single year, the company must have been aware that it was reliant on Shakespeare's ability to produce a series of plays likely to be thought suitable for presentation at court. However, whether this would have affected to any significant degree his 'author's fee' is less certain. If the calculations of the company's theoretical annual income derived from public performances are thought reasonable—£1650 in the years 1603–8[10]—then £50 to £60, though welcome, especially during the plague years, may not have been sufficient to justify the payment of more than the standard author's fee.[11]

There is, in any case, incontrovertible evidence that Shakespeare's own output began to fall away during this same period. Although the chronology of the writing of the plays cannot be determined in all respects, there is sufficient agreement to establish that Shakespeare wrote over twenty-five plays in the period 1590–1605, whereas in the final nine years he produced not more than twelve, the last three of which (*Cardenio*, now lost, *All is True* (*Henry VIII*), and *The Two Noble Kinsman*), dating from 1612–14, were written in collaboration with the up-and-coming John Fletcher. *Timon of Athens*, from c.1604/5, is also now generally accepted to have been written in collaboration with Thomas Middleton, and George Wilkins is believed by many to have contributed significantly to *Pericles* (by

9. For this, and what follows, see Astington, *English Court Theatre, 1558–1642*, pp. 237–47.
10. Gurr, *Shakespeare Company*, p. 108.
11. At an earlier date (above, pp. 38–9) this fee was frequently set at £7, though by the time of Shakespeare's death, judging from dealings between Henlsowe and Robert Daborne, this could have almost trebled (Ioppolo, *Dramatists and their Manuscripts*, pp. 20–3).

May 1608).[12] As a result, any income he might have enjoyed from his privileged position as what might be described as 'resident playwright' would also have fallen.

Alongside this evidence of a dwindling output is Shakespeare's surprising decision to part with his shares in both the company and its playhouses. There is some uncertainty here as no documentation exists to establish exactly if, and when, he decided on this course of action. But as the shares are not mentioned specifically in his will, and as his family is not subsequently known to have had any interest in what would have been valuable assets, it is more than likely that they were disposed of during his lifetime. If this were the case, then the burning down of the Globe in June 1613 might have been the catalyst, although it is proposed below (p. 170) that he might have surrendered his shares earlier that year.[13] According to later evidence, the 'housekeepers' were called on to subscribe £50 or £60 to the rebuilding costs, which Shakespeare would have been able to avoid if he had disposed of his shares at that point. As things turned out, the sharers ended up paying at least twice this sum.[14]

The question inevitably arises as to whether this surrender of his shares was an entirely voluntary decision or whether Shakespeare's fellow sharers, aware of his lower profile, did not press him to remain fully within the company. The latter seems unlikely, if Shakespeare was still a sharer when the Globe burnt down. The housekeepers, according to the terms on which they held their shares in the ground lease, were liable for the maintenance of buildings on the site and it is therefore hardly likely, given the urgent need of immediate funds, that they would have chosen such a moment to accept Shakespeare's resignation. With the benefit of hindsight (namely that Shakespeare was destined to live for less than three years) it is tempting instead to argue that Shakespeare had simply decided to wind down, freeing himself from any obligation to act on stage by surrendering his shares but retaining

12. The Fletcher collaborations were omitted from the First Folio and *Pericles* also.
13. Shakespeare is last recorded as a shareholder in the Globe in February 1612 (Chambers, *William Shakespeare*, ii, p. 58) and in the Blackfriars only in the record of its original lease to the Company in August 1608 (Gurr, *Shakespeare Company*, p. 255).
14. Wickham, Berry, and Ingram, eds., *English Professional Theatre*, pp. 607, 611–12. As with the expenditure on building the Globe in 1599, the costs of rebuilding after the fire are only known from later evidence. This was argued about until a total figure of £1600 was agreed (Berry, *Shakespeare's Playhouses*, pp. 182–3, 237), divided into fourteen shares.

some contact with his company (and some income) by collaborating with others in the writing of new work. However, the concept of a man in his mid-to-late forties voluntarily opting for semi-retirement on the grounds that his work was done is not convincing. In 1610 Shakespeare was as capable as we are today of living for another twenty-five productive years provided he avoided the life-threatening diseases and conditions the effects of which we are now able to mitigate. Voluntary retirement, in any case, was not a concept that Tudor and Stuart society would have recognized. Those who had inherited, or invested in, sufficient land to produce a substantial income, could indeed lead a life of independent means. But outside this select band, care within the family was the only realistic option for those no longer able to earn their keep; and even if creeping incapacity might threaten to undermine a man's business interests or earning capacity, there is little evidence to support the idea that he would have released these interests to other family members. In Shakespeare's case, as has already been shown, these later years were characterized by a determination to protect the income from his investments even though they were yielding much less than the income derived from his shares but on which he and his family would be dependent if he surrendered them. These, at around £70, were not inconsiderable but on their own clearly insufficient to guarantee for himself and his family over the next ten or twenty years the income to which they had become accustomed. One may legitimately speculate about ill-health, exhaustion, or even disaffection to account for Shakespeare's withdrawal from the front line, though, with the possible exception, from 1612, of his six ill-written signatures,[15] no material evidence survives to substantiate any such diagnosis. But whatever the reason, there is little to suggest that, in terms of his and his family's financial security, his retirement, or semi-retirement, is something that he could simply afford to do. At the same time, his fellow sharers, however indebted they may have thought themselves as the result of Shakespeare's prodigious labours, may not have pressed him to stay if, for whatever reason, he was increasingly reluctant to play his full part as a sharer, safe in the knowledge that they would still be able to choose to buy whatever

15. Five of the six are conveniently illustrated in Thomas, *Shakespeare in the Public Records*, p. 33, though it is hardly surprising that the three on the will reflect a man in ill-health. There is also disagreement over whether or not all six are really in his hand.

new work he offered them. The central issue here, then, is whether Shakespeare, in his late forties, would have voluntarily given up his income of, at best, some £200 a year when, as far as can be ascertained, his remaining income was limited to around £70 made up of £40 from his share in the tithes, £25 from his freehold estate of 107 acres, and £3 for the Henley Street property. Though not an insignificant sum, it was clearly far less important to him than the £200 or so he would have expected from his theatre shares. Looked at in this way, Shakespeare's business dealings during these later years are entirely consistent with such considerations.

During this later period in Shakespeare's career we also find him earning money in ways hitherto unrecorded. In 1613 he was paid 44 shillings 'in gold' to help make an *impresa*, or elaborate emblem with a motto, for the eighth earl of Rutland, Francis Manners, to display as part of the celebrations to commemorate the king's accession day in March 1613.[16] His theatrical colleague, Richard Burbage, was paid the same for making and painting it, so Shakespeare's role was presumably to devise the words or motto to go on it. This commission is certainly of interest in establishing a link between these two members of the King's Men and a leading figure at James I's court. Manners had only recently—on 9 May 1612—succeeded his childless brother Roger as earl, but both men had a well-attested interest in the theatre. Roger, a close friend of the earl of Southampton, had been criticized, with Southampton, in 1599, for passing away 'the tyme in London merely in going to plais every day', a habit confirmed by surviving accounts recording his visits to playhouses 'sondry tymes' in September and November of that year and incurring expenditure in the region of 10 shillings.[17] The same accounts record several payments to troupes of travelling players performing before him, including the Lord Dudley's players in 1602 and the Queen's Men in 1607.[18] His brother Francis showed similar interests, inviting Lady Elizabeth's Men to his home in 1614, Lord Willoughby's Men in 1617, and the earl of Shrewsbury's in 1618.[19] Unlike his brother, who for many years had been in poor health, Francis was also a leading courtier and had no

16. Chambers, *William Shakespeare*, ii, p. 153.
17. Duncan Jones, *Ungentle Shakespeare*, p. 108; HMC, *Duke of Rutland Manuscripts*, iv, pp. 419–20.
18. HMC, *Rutland*, iv, pp. 452, 461, 464.
19. HMC, *Rutland*, iv, pp. 498, 514.

doubt turned to Shakespeare and Burbage for help with his *impresa*, having come into contact with them during the King's Men's regular appearances at court. However, although these *imprese* were of special importance to the great families who carried them ceremonially into the tilts, the commission itself surely raises more mundane issues. Whilst confirming the benefits which Shakespeare derived from his contact with the court, it does not, for instance, suggest that Shakespeare was a man either resting on his laurels or likely to regard such modest commissions as beneath him, rather that he welcomed the opportunity to acquire ready cash. Arguing on the basis of absence of evidence has been warned against more than once and we cannot therefore be sure that at an earlier date he had not undertaken similar commissions. However, that they must all therefore have gone unrecorded would imply they were not numerous.

The frequent closure of the London theatres due to plague during this later period may also have induced Shakespeare to turn to publication as a source of additional income. The precise circumstances surrounding the publication in 1609 of the *Sonnets* is not entirely clear: it cannot even be established with certainty that Shakespeare agreed that they should be made public. However, it is not the general view that Shakespeare was not involved in the publication process at all, rather that, even if he had not initiated the process himself, he had been prepared to hand over a roughly worked manuscript to the publisher, Thomas Thorpe, in effect parting with his intellectual ownership of the work. Given the imperfections of the work as first published,[20] it is difficult to believe that he oversaw its production and therefore that he saw the project in terms of his securing public recognition as a poet. It does carry a dedication, to the unidentified 'Mr W.H.', although this is not Shakespeare's work but Thorpe's. This too suggests that Shakespeare was not overly concerned in the publication process once he had parted with the text. As Thorpe himself, however, was clearly hoping to make money out of the enterprise, Shakespeare's surrender of the manuscript would hardly have been on any other terms than that he would also benefit financially.

20. As indicated by Colin Burrow in his introduction to *William Shakespeare: Complete Sonnets*, pp. 91–8.

Shakespeare's status

Linked to the issue of Shakespeare's income, especially in the later years, is the position in society which he now occupied. It is often somewhat vaguely assumed that the genius of this great writer was reflected in the accumulation of considerable wealth and the accompanying respect of the community. This does, however, need to be seen in context. The personal circumstances of Shakespeare's family have already been discussed. His father is not known to have left a will, nor did his male siblings, who also remained unmarried. His sister, Joan, did not find a husband until the age of thirty or so and then he was in trade as hatter. All this suggests a general shortage of money within the wider family, and the marriages of Shakespeare's own daughters, as discussed above (pp. 123–30), to the second son of a doctor and the third son of a mercer, also indicate that Shakespeare himself, despite his considerable success, had not convincingly broken into the ranks of the gentry even of a local market town. They were, of course, known to him and, on the evidence of his will, the only document by which to gauge the value of his estate, some were counted amongst his friends. They were Thomas Combe, Anthony Nash and his brother John, William Reynolds, Francis Collins, Hamnet Sadler (substituted in the second draft for Richard Tyler), and Thomas Russell. Of these one of the most interesting is Thomas Combe, who received only a minor legacy, but a highly significant one, Shakespeare's sword, suggesting personal affection for the young twenty-seven-year-old. As we have seen, a connection of some years standing with Combe's family is clear, and particularly with Thomas's uncle, John Combe, from at least 1597, who in 1613 had left Shakespeare £5 in his will.[21] The two families had also colluded to protect Shakespeare's interests should a proposed enclosure at Welcombe go ahead.[22] Anthony Nash and his brother John, who both received 26s. 8d. (probably to buy mourning rings, although the wording is a little ambiguous), could also trace their connection with Shakespeare back to at least the 1602 purchase, as they both witnessed the deed of conveyance.[23]

21. Above, p. 109.
22. Above, pp. 140–2.
23. Above, pp. 110–12.

For William Reynolds, gentleman, another recipient of 26s. 8d. to buy himself a mourning ring, there is no other evidence to link him with Shakespeare even though such a bequest implies real friendship. He lived in a large house in Old Town, now known as the Dower House. He was third-generation minor gentry: his grandfather, Hugh, described himself as such in his will of 1556, though his inventory indicates that his wealth was derived from farming. At his death, his goods were valued at over £220—only two other Stratford inventories, out of nearly 160 dating from before 1620, boast a higher total.[24] His son, Thomas, consistently described as a gentleman, was said to be maintaining a household of twenty-two persons in 1595.[25] He married Margaret daughter and co-heiress of William Gower of Redmarley, a cousin of John Combe, and she and her children benefited considerably under Combe's will when he died in 1613.[26] Thomas Reynolds also died in 1613 though his will, if made, has not survived. But his widow Margaret, who died two years later, evidently had large sums of money at her disposal, leaving over £140 in bequests to relatives and servants.[27] Friendship with Shakespeare is also implied in the appointment of John Hall as one of the overseers of her will. William Reynolds died in February 1632 possessed of a considerable property in and around the town and leaving £100 apiece to his two daughters, although a Chancery case of 1624 implies that he had had difficulty in establishing his rights to property which had been entailed by his grandfather Hugh.[28]

One of the more intriguing beneficiaries was Shakespeare's godson, William Walker, who received 20 shillings. His name occurs in the middle of a list of local Stratford beneficiaries and he is therefore in all probability William, son of the mercer Henry Walker, baptised in Stratford on 16 October 1608; but why Shakespeare should have done Henry the favour of standing godfather to his son, we shall probably never know. Born in Alcester in 1564, the same year as Shakespeare, Walker seems to have moved his mercer's business to Stratford soon after his marriage in 1594. An early notice of him in Stratford is as a

24. Jones, ed., *Stratford-upon-Avon-Inventories*, i, pp. 9–12.
25. Fripp and others, eds., *Minutes and Accounts*, v, p. 69.
26. Halliwell, *Life of Shakespeare*, pp. 236–7; *Visitation of Warwickshire*, pp. 242–3.
27. Vine Hall, *Wills from Shakespeare's Town and Times*, i, pp. 21–2.
28. TNA, PROB 11/163, ff. 466–466v; TNA, C 3/323/43. He may also have lost a valuable tenancy of lands held under a lease of 1585 from the earl of Warwick but limited to the lives of William's mother and father and of their son Henry who had predeceased them (*MA*, iv, p. 114).

witness in 1597 to John Shakespeare's sale of land in Henley Street, and so it may be because of a former friendship with Shakespeare's father that William agreed to be godfather to Henry's son.[29] Walker was not drawn from quite the same background as the legatees so far mentioned. He was elected a capital burgess in 1598, an alderman in 1606, and served as bailiff three times, in 1607/8, 1624/25, and 1635/36. Though, like many of his contemporaries, he began to adopt the style of gentleman from the year he was first bailiff, he never made a point of distancing himself from his business roots. There is another link, though, with Shakespeare's circle of acquaintance: in 1613, he received a bequest of 20 shillings from John Combe.[30]

A man from a similar background was Hamnet Sadler, who received 26s. 8d. for a mourning ring, albeit as a substitute for Richard Tyler named in the first draft. He also witnessed the will, so was fairly close to Shakespeare at this point. A link between the two families can probably be traced back to 1585 and the baptism of Shakespeare's twin children, Hamnet and Judith. Hamnet Sadler's wife was also named Judith, a coincidence sufficient to indicate a connection between the two families, and even that the Sadlers had acted as godparents to the twins. Sadler was a baker by trade and owed his position in the town to his 'cousin' Roger Sadler, also a baker, who in 1579 left him most of his property in the town and also made him executor of his will.[31] His parentage is unknown, but he was Shakespeare's senior by quite some years: by 1580 we know that he had made a surprisingly advantageous marriage to Judith, daughter of the gentleman, Thomas Staunton of Longbridge.[32] But why William or Ann turned to him and his wife to fill the roles of godparents (if they did) is not easily explained; nor why his name was inserted in the will between January and March in preference to Richard Tyler's, the first intended recipient of the money for the ring. The two men, though, were of similar status, Richard being the son of William Tyler, a Stratford butcher and alderman. It might have come to Shakespeare's notice that Tyler, appointed one of the collectors for charitable relief following the town fire of

29. Wellstood, *Catalogue of the Books... Exhibited in Shakespeare's Birthplace*, p. 28. Walker lived in High Street (Fripp and others, eds., *Minutes and Accounts*, v, p. 138) so he was not simply witnessing as a near neighbour.
30. Halliwell, *Life of Shakespeare*, p. 239.
31. Vine Hall, *Wills from Shakespeare's Town and Times*, ii, pp. 10–14.
32. TNA, PROB 11/115/516.

1614, was currently under suspicion for the inefficient, if not fraudulent, discharge of his duties.[33] Another witness to Shakespeare's will was July Shawe, a Stratford alderman, a near neighbour, and a prosperous yeoman and wool merchant.

Francis Collins was to receive £13 6s. 8d. under Shakespeare's will, the largest non-family bequest. This generosity certainly reflects confidence in—perhaps even affection for—a man who had acted as Shakespeare's attorney since at least 1605[34] and who was also made overseer of the will; but it is possible that the bequest represented a form of retrospective payment for services rendered. The other overseer was Thomas Russell, who also received a less generous but still significant bequest of £5. Russell was by far the wealthiest of those named in Shakespeare's will, holding extensive estates in Warwickshire, Worcestershire, and Gloucestershire, giving him the right to style himself esquire. A measure of his wealth was his proposed purchase in 1601 of the Clopton House estate, just outside Stratford, for £3700—over eight times as much as Shakespeare was able to lay out for his most ambitious purchase.[35] This bequest apart, there is no evidence which links Shakespeare and Russell, who indeed only occasionally occurs in Stratford records. He is better known for his exploits in London, particularly his pursuit of the wealthy widow, Ann Digges, whom he eventually married in 1603, and Shakespeare had probably first come into contact with him there. But despite this lack of other evidence, Russell's appearance in the will certainly implies that the two men were close, at least by that date. In confirmation of this, Russell's stepson, Leonard Digges, later wrote two poems in praise of Shakespeare, confirming his local status, which were included in the First Folio.

These, then, were the men with whom Shakespeare might be said to be on good personal terms. To them, we can probably add the name of Richard Lane of Bridgetown, whom, as we have seen, the Shakespeares named in 1599 as one of their arbitrators in their suit against John Lambert, and together with whom Shakespeare went to law in 1610 or 1611 to protect his tithe income.[36] Russell apart, these men were drawn either from local minor gentry families—the Combes, the Nashes, the Reynolds, the Lanes—or the upper reaches of the commercial elite of

33. SCLA, BRU 15/7/106a; BRU 15/16/14.
34. Above, pp. 121–2.
35. Eccles, *Shakespeare in Warwickshire*, pp. 116–18.
36. Above, pp. 136–7.

the town, the Sadlers, the Walkers, and the Shaws. And even Russell, before his marriage to Ann Digges, was of middling status. It would therefore not be unreasonable to propose that Shakespeare now enjoyed a similar social standing. The evidence we have for their financial resources will be discussed later, but there was another common thread which linked these families. Though they all generally styled themselves gentry by the early seventeenth century, this was a status which they, like Shakespeare, had achieved in the relatively recent past. The Combes, for instance, owed their advance into the ranks of the gentry to John Combe, from Astley, in Worcestershire, who had enriched himself when the monasteries were dissolved in the 1530s and through loyal service in the retinue of Bishop Hugh Latimer. The Nashes from Woodstock secured similar advancement in the service of Sir John Hubaud. Richard Lane's grandfather, another Richard, was a yeoman farmer who managed to make good: his son Nicholas's goods were valued at over £72 when he died in 1595—far in excess of most Stratford residents during this period—and his son Richard, who lived in what is now Alveston Manor, maintained a household of twelve and was able to pay for the erection of a handsome effigy in his father's memory in Alveston church.[37] William Reynolds's grandfather, Hugh, is similarly described in some documents simply as a yeoman and only in his will as a gentleman. By and large, then, these men owed their position to shrewd service in the households of bishops and members of the aristocracy, or to efficient management of their estates, accumulating sufficient capital to invest in, or increase, their modest landholdings, or to lend to the improvident. Such men may well have been the natural associates of a man in Shakespeare's position, himself having worked his family out of a more humble (and in his case financially embarrassed) situation into one with claims to gentry status, leading on naturally to a willingness to collaborate with them in mutually beneficial projects. Some links with business families were retained, with the Walkers and Sadlers for instance, but earlier contacts with such families as the Quineys and the Sturleys, still associated with purely mercantile interests, seem to have fallen away.

National subsidy records, assessed on the basis of the value of land or moveable goods, provide very poor evidence of actual wealth, due

37. *Victoria History of the County of Warwick*, iii, pp. 286–7; Fripp and others, eds., *Minutes and Accounts*, v, p. 51; Fripp, *Shakespeare's Stratford*, pp. 30–1.

to the determination of taxpayers to downplay their liability, or to
arrange for themselves to be excluded altogether. But the names of
those deemed liable are still of interest as representing the local elite.
Thus in 1609, and again in 1610, out of five assessed on their landholdings in Old Stratford, William Combe came out highest (at £4), followed by Anthony Nash and Thomas Greene (not the town's steward
but a Bishopton yeoman of the same man) at £2, and the remaining
two, Francis Ainge and William Ainge, at £1.[38] Richard Lane's estates,
listed under Alveston as he lived at Bridgetown, were valued at £7. In
1625, William Combe appears to have been succeeded by Thomas
Combe (rated at £4, increased in 1628 to £5), now one of only five
taxpayers, with Anthony Nash replaced by William Reynolds (at £2).[39]
Within the borough, both in 1609 and 1610 seven burgesses were
assessed (on goods rather than lands) at £3, including, from Shakespeare's
associates, Henry Walker and Julius Shawe.[40] Shakespeare himself does
not feature in any of these returns, almost certainly due to his absence
in London rather than a reflection of limited means, but when, in 1625,
his son-in-law, John Hall, first appears, his goods were assessed at £3, a
rate shared by six others, with his own son-in-law, Thomas Nash, who
had married his daughter Susanna, assessed at £4.[41] With due account
taken of the unreliability of such records in assessing the true situation,
they would not, at the very least, establish that the Shakespeare family
was wealthier than the other civic elite of a moderately sized market
town. Some men in this position, as if to emphasize their gentry status,
had distanced themselves from service in the Stratford Corporation,
traditionally dominated by the business elite, but it would be misleading to describe them as very rich. It may have been possible for merchants in Coventry and London to amass fortunes to invest in the
purchase of large landed estates. Robert Lee, alderman of London,
bought the manor of Billesley for £5000 in 1604.[42] Baptist Hicks, a
London mercer, purchased the manor of Chipping Campden in about

38. TNA, E 179/193/260a, 275. In 1609, Thomas Burman's goods were assessed at £3. The
    Stratford returns were unsatisfactorily published by Halliwell in 1864 in one of his
    very limited editions: *Extracts from the Ancient Subsidy Rolls . . . in Respect of the Inhabitants
    of Stratford-on-Avon.*
39. TNA, E 179/193/302, 312, 317. But see a return of 1621 (SCLA, BRU 21/4) which
    values William Combe's estate at an unprecedented £20.
40. TNA, E 179/93/260a, 275.
41. TNA, E 179/193/302.
42. *Victoria History of the County of Warwick*, iii, p. 60.

1609, spent colossal sums building and furnishing a mansion there and was credited with settling £100,000 on each of his two daughters.[43] The Skinner family of London, who, following the dissolution of the monasteries, had bought the manor of Kinwarton, sold it for £2500 in 1624. John Hales, a merchant of Coventry, was able to buy the manor of Snitterfield in 1545.[44] Of the capital's 140 aldermen holding office during the years 1600–24, more than a third (fifty-five) had their goods alone valued at over £20,000 (and some were worth very much more) with almost all of the remainder with personal estates of £10,000–£20,000.[45] But such wealth, and the investment this made possible, was way beyond the resources of Stratford's local gentry. Influential though they may have been in the context of a local market town, they did not rival either the representatives of great merchant adventurers from the big cities or the owners of ancient landed estates in the Stratford area; the Cloptons of Clopton, the Lucys of Charlecote, or the Verneys of Compton Verney. Stratford lay in Barlichway hundred, an ancient administrative subdivision of the county. Next to it, to the south and east lay Kineton hundred. Subsidy rolls (1609 for Barlichway and 1611 for Kineton[46]) list fifty-eight gentry with lands valued at £4 (the top rate in Stratford) or above. Heading the list, for their Warwickshire estates only, were Edward Greville at Milcote and Fulk Greville at Alcester, both rated at £66 13s. 4d. Thomas Lucy (at £30) and Richard Verney (at £26 13s. 4d.) were amongst the other fifteen (£20 or over) elite. Bartholomew Hales, Robert Lee, and Anthony Skinner, representatives of the mercantile families mentioned above, came in at £20, £15, and £8 respectively. As already explained, these figures, due to gross under-assessment, reveal only comparative standing within the local community. Actual wealth derived by the landed classes is thought to have been as much as fifty times what was admitted to.[47] Thomas Puckering, who came of age in 1612, put his total receipts in 1620 at slightly under £2600[48] whereas his mother Jane's estates had been assessed in 1611 at only £20. Against this background, the likes

43. Lang, 'Social origins and social aspirations of Jacobean London merchants', p. 30; Kingsley, *Country Houses of Gloucestershire*, pp. 68–9.
44. *Victoria History of the County of Warwick*, iii, pp. 127, 168.
45. Lang, 'Social origins and social aspirations of Jacobean London merchants', p. 30.
46. TNA, E 179/193/260a, 280.
47. Hughes, *Politics, Society and Civil War in Warwickshire*, p. 30.
48. Merry and Richardson, eds., *Household Account Book of Sir Thomas Puckering*, p. 291.

of William Combe (at £4) emerge as of very lowly status amongst the gentry, even though the Combes, from the evidence of sales of their estates Old Stratford later in the later seventeenth century, had holdings in the region of 350 acres.[49] William Shakespeare, with an income, as suggested above (pp. 147, 152–3), of around £270 at most, and a holding of not much more than a hundred acres and a leasehold interest in a share of the parish tithes, clearly occupied a place a rung or two lower.

To investigate further the wealth of Stratford's local gentry, and thus exactly how Shakespeare fits into the picture, is no easy matter. We have no estate or household accounts for any of these men, nor inventories of their goods. But we can at least turn to their wills. These, of course, are far from definitive. A testator, for instance, might make no personal bequests, merely leaving his entire estate, of unspecified value, to his widow or son and heir; but this would not necessarily mean that his or her estate was worth less than that of a testator who made specific bequests, both large and small. Nevertheless, certain observations can be made. John Combe, for example, in his will of 1612, left £200 to his cousin, Sir Henry Clare, £300 to his brother's children, and to his cousin, Margaret Reynolds, and her son, Thomas Reynolds, £100 apiece. Together with numerous other bequests to family members and servants, we can account for over £1500. On top of this he left £60 to pay for the erection of a monument in the church and over £130 for charitable purposes.[50] His brother Thomas, who had died in 1608, had the resources to arrange for an annuity of £30 to be paid to his son, Thomas, and annuities of £15 apiece to two daughters, until marriage, when they were to receive marriage portions of £400 apiece; on top of this, his daughter-in-law was to receive £250 and his wife £100.[51] Anthony Nash, when he died in 1622, charged his estate with payments of £600 to his wife, £500 to his eldest son, £40 to his daughter, and £10 to a servant, that is, well over £1000.[52] Richard Lane left to his daughter Mary an annuity of £30 whilst she remained single, with £830 as her marriage portion, and also made arrangements for the disposition of a debt of £1000 owed to him by Sir Edward Greville on its repayment in 1616.[53] The pecuniary bequests in the will of Richard

49. SCLA, ER 3/321, 4115; DR 38/1203, 1206.
50. Halliwell, *Life of Shakespeare*, pp. 234–40.
51. TNA, PROB 11/113, ff. 98–100.
52. TNA, PROB 11/140, ff. 397–397v.
53. TNA, PROB 11/122, ff. 299–300.

Woodward of Shottery, dating from 1600, totalled nearly £700, including £600 between his three daughters; and even William Walford, described as a woollen-draper in his will of 1624, charged his estate, consisting of numerous properties in the town, with payments of over £610.[54] By way of contrast, the pecuniary bequests in Shakespeare's will do not indicate a man with more resources to hand. His younger daughter, Judith, was provided with £300, his sister with £20, and her three children (that is, his nephews) with £5 apiece. Francis Collins, as we have seen, was to receive a legacy of over £13, but Shakespeare's godson only received £1, and seven others just sufficient (£1 6s. 8d.) to buy mourning rings. We do not know, of course, what might have passed to his daughter, Susanna, and her husband John Hall under the final catch-all phrase of 'All the Rest of my goodes, Chattel[s], Leases, plate, Jewels & household stuffe', but it has already been shown that they did not inherit an estate from which they could draw sufficient income to live as members of the land-owning gentry. In terms of specific pecuniary provision, Shakespeare's will (with such bequests totalling not much more than £350, placing him sixth in this somewhat arbitrary league table) is overall far less impressive than those of his fellow Stratford gentry, and that of the bequests that were made, the modest sums of £5 apiece to his nephews could hardly be described as generous. Though only an approximate method of measuring wealth, this analysis, at the very least, does not allow us automatically to regard Shakespeare as a man with more means at his disposal than his local contemporaries of minor gentry status, or possessed of an estate which could be charged with substantial legacies: the opposite, in fact. And this is to some extent confirmed by the eligibility of his daughters, whose partners, as we have seen, stand in marked contrast to the alliances forged by these other families. Richard Lane married Joan daughter of Henry Whitney, lord of the manor of Biggin and Tamworth in Mitcham, in Surrey, and their son Edward married a daughter of Thomas Combe. Richard's younger brother John Lane married Frances, a daughter of Thomas Nash.[55] Margaret Reynolds, husband of Thomas and father of William, was a cousin of John Combe's and a substantial beneficiary under his will.[56] Anthony Nash married Mary, daughter of

---

54. TNA, PROB 11/99, ff. 338v–341; 11/143, ff. 380–381v.
55. *Visitation of the County of Warwick*, p. 147.
56. Above, p. 156.

the well-to-do Roland Baugh of Twyning, near Tewkesbury, and Thomas Combe married the widowed daughter of Anthony Savage of Elmley Castle and Broadway.[57] Though Shakespeare clearly numbered such men as acquaintances, if not friends, the circumstances of his daughters' marriages do call into question whether he had broken convincingly into their ranks.

We must not overlook a final piece of evidence which could reflect on the state of Shakespeare's finances towards the end of his life. In 1609, Thomas Greene, then living at New Place, entered into contracts totalling £600 for the purchase of a house called St Mary's and a share of the Stratford tithes. £300 of this was due to be paid over in 1613.[58] However, when in 1617 Greene sold up and left the town, he used £300 of the sale price of his property to pay off substantial debts, implying that he had had to borrow heavily to complete his purchase. One of the debts was of £40, due to John Hall. As Shakespeare had died barely twelve months previously, this very substantial sum may well have represented money advanced, or secured, through Shakespeare's cooperation rather than his son-in-law's. There is much uncertainty here, of course, but it would seem unlikely that Shakespeare could have advanced such a large cash sum, even at interest, thus representing a form of investment. A more likely scenario, if the money was indeed due to Shakespeare, is that he (and Greene's fellow creditors) had been persuaded to stand surety for loans which Greene had been unable to repay which in turn would have affected Shakespeare's own credit.

We can also consider Shakespeare's status in the context of his fellow sharers in theatrical companies, thanks mainly to Ernst Honigmann's and Susan Brock's invaluable *Playhouse Wills*. Here again, due caution is required in reaching any firm conclusions. Only rarely is a will accompanied by a surviving inventory to provide us with a more reliable indication of personal wealth. For actors who made no wills, grants of administration almost invariably fail to give the value of the estate. Nevertheless, certain trends do again emerge. Firstly, real wealth

---

57. For the Baugh pedigree, see *Visitation of the County of Gloucester*, p. 11, and *Visitation of the County of Worcester*, p. 9. For Combe, see *Visitation of the County of Warwick*, pp. 290–1.
58. Bearman, 'Thomas Greene, Stratford's Town clerk and Shakespeare's lodger', esp. pp. 296–302. Greene may have been Shakespeare's tenant from his appointment as steward in 1603 until the purchase of St Mary's.

is most obviously apparent in the wills of the very select band of theatre owners and managers. Philip Henslowe, who died in 1616, owner/manager of four theatres, divided his very extensive property portfolio between family members but only after the death of his widow Agnes, to whom he also left almost all his personal estate.[59] His son-in-law, Edward Alleyn (d.1626), who began his career as an actor, became a man of great wealth following his marriage to Henslowe's daughter and his deep involvement in his father-in-law's theatrical enterprises. With pecuniary bequests alone totalling £1870, and with further money provided for the building of twenty almshouses, his will reveals a level of wealth at death far greater than any of his theatrical contemporaries—and this even after his founding and endowment of what became known as Dulwich College.[60] Richard Burbage, in effect the owner of a moiety of the Globe Theatre, made only a brief nuncupative will leaving his entire estate to his widow but was nevertheless said to have left 'better than 300li land.'[61] But these are very much exceptions. The wills of actors who simply held shares in theatrical companies reflect less substantial means. Of these, one would have expected sharers in the King's Men, and also therefore its joint 'house-keepers', to have left evidence of comfortable circumstances, and this was certainly true in Thomas Pope's case (d.1603) who, amongst pecuniary bequests totalling £308, left £20 for the erection of a monument in his name and who died with an interest in three leasehold properties in St Saviour's parish.[62] His fellow sharer, Augustine Phillips (d.1605), who died in possession of a freehold house in Mortlake, made personal bequests totalling some £100 (including £5 to William Shakespeare).[63] Henry Condell (d.1627) left slightly more in personal bequests and also owned three freehold properties.[64] Alexander Cook, also of the King's Men (d.1614), makes no mention of any freehold or leasehold property but left £50 apiece ('bothe in one purse in my Cuberd') to his son and daughter, and the value of his theatre share, put at £50, to the child his wife was expecting.[65] Outside the King's Men,

59. Honigmann and Brock, *Playhouse Wills, 1558–1642*, pp. 101–3.
60. Honigmann and Brock, *Playhouse Wills, 1558–1642*, pp. 150–3.
61. Honigmann and Brock, *Playhouse Wills, 1558–1642*, pp. 113–14.
62. Honigmann and Brock, *Playhouse Wills, 1558–1642*, pp. 68–71.
63. Honigmann and Brock, *Playhouse Wills, 1558–1642*, pp. 72–5.
64. Honigmann and Brock, *Playhouse Wills, 1558–1642*, pp. 156–60.
65. Honigmann and Brock, *Playhouse Wills, 1558–1642*, pp. 94–5.

Thomas Greene of Queen Anne's Men emerges as possibly the most well-to-do with personal bequests amounting to nearly £300 although he may have owed some of his good fortune to his marriage to the widow of Robert Browne through whom he acquired a leasehold interest in the Boar's Head playhouse.[66] Against this background, Shakespeare's will, with its pecuniary bequests of some £350, takes on a new perspective. Although it may still reflect the fact that Shakespeare did not enjoy a local reputation beyond that afforded to minor gentry, it does imply that as a professional actor/playwright he appears, in financial terms, to have done better than his fellow sharers. This could be attributed in part to the additional income to which he would have been entitled as the author of a succession of popular plays. On the other hand, given that spread over more than twenty years, this would not have amounted to anything like the amount he would have drawn as a sharer/housekeeper, his comparative success can be more simply attributed to a more prudent exploitation of his creditworthiness in the 1590s and early 1600s.

The Blackfriars Gatehouse

It remains to fit into the picture one of the most puzzling features of Shakespeare's later career, namely his purchase from Henry Walker of the so-called Blackfriars Gatehouse on 10 March 1613. This formerly gave access to the prior's lodging house and was described in the purchase deed as 'All that dwelling house... within the precinct, circuit and compasse of the late Black Fryers... part of which said tenement is erected over a great gate leading to a capitall messuage.'[67] On the face of it, this would seem to run contrary to the argument presented above, that Shakespeare's property purchases peaked in 1605 and that thereafter his dwindling literary output was paralleled by evidence of a static, if not declining, income. However, there are peculiarities associated with this purchase which, although difficult to explain, point towards a compromise arrangement between Shakespeare and his theatrical colleagues, perhaps dating from the time of the sale of his company

---

66. Honigmann and Brock, *Playhouse Wills, 1558–1642*, pp. 90–1.
67. Both the vendor's and purchaser's copies of the conveyance survive. For facsimiles of both, see Lewis, *Shakespeare Documents*, ii, between pp. 438 and 439. Lewis (ii, pp. 440–3) also transcribes the purchaser's copy, signed by Walker.

shares at about that time. Unlike his earlier purchases, Shakespeare does not appear to have been in the position of a cash buyer. In 1602, he had raised over £320 when he bought his 107 acres of land at Stratford. In 1605 he was able to come up with the larger sum of £440 to invest in a share of Stratford's tithes. But in 1613 he was £60 short of the much smaller sum of £140 needed for the purchase of the Blackfriars Gatehouse. As a result, on the following day the property was mortgaged back to the vendor subject to the payment of the outstanding sum by the following September.[68] Another distinguishing feature of the purchase was the inclusion of trustees, namely three of his London contacts, William Johnson, John Jackson, and John Heminges, to whom, with Shakespeare, the property was conveyed, and for their use, although only Shakespeare paid any money. Finally, Shakespeare, or his trustees, were concerned about vacant possession. The conveyance survives in two indented copies, the vendor's, signed by Shakespeare and his trustees, and the purchaser's, signed by the vendor, Henry Walker.[69] The first of these had included a clause to the effect that a lease of the premises to one William Ireland, granted in December 1604 for twenty-five years, should be allowed to stand until it expired in 1629. But this clause was then manually struck through and omitted completely from the purchaser's copy;[70] and when Shakespeare made his will in 1616, he named one John Robinson as tenant. Furthermore in 1618 when, after Shakespeare's death, his trustees assigned the property to two other trustees, Robinson's tenure of the premises was protected by virtue of a 'lease...heretofore made by the said William Shakespeare...unto one John Robinson, now tennant of the said premisses, for the terme of certen yeres yet to come and unexpired.'[71] A John Robinson, perhaps the same man, witnessed Shakespeare's will.[72]

---

68. For facsimile, see Schoenbaum, *Documentary Life* (1975 edn), facing p. 224; for complete transcript, Halliwell, *Outlines*, ii, pp. 34–6.
69. See note 68.
70. Halliwell, *Outlines*, ii, pp. 31–4. The deletion is clearly visible in the facsimile of the vendor's copy (above, n. 68) and, for confirmation that this was done more or less at the time of sealing, see the enrolled copy which does not contain the clause (TNA, C 54/2184/45). Chambers, who provides a partial transcript of this copy (*William Shakespeare*, ii, pp. 154–7) only summarizes the deleted clause.
71. Halliwell, *Outlines*, ii, pp. 36–41.
72. However, see Eccles, *Shakespeare in Warwickshire*, p. 142, citing evidence for an exactly contemporary man of this name living in Stratford.

This arrangement strongly suggests that the purchase was linked in some way to Shakespeare's theatrical interests. Not only did the gatehouse stand close by the Blackfriars Theatre, but also one of his trustees was the actor, John Heminges, a fellow partner in the King's Men. Another, William Johnson, 'citizein and vintener of London', was the prosperous landlord of the Mermaid Tavern.[73] The third trustee was John Jackson, described simply as a gentleman. Leslie Hotson has identified him as the wealthy John Jackson, originally from Kingston-upon-Hull, who died in London in 1624/25, and who in 1611 had been appointed overseer of the will of Thomas Savage, the man with whom, back in 1599, Shakespeare had had dealings during the purchase of the Globe Theatre.[74] Hotson also proposed, less convincingly, that he could be identified with the John Jackson who was persuaded by Thomas Coryate to contribute a poem, in the form of an egg, to *Coryate's Crudities*, published in 1611. Later evidence (1616), in *Thomas Coriate Traveller for the English Wits*, that Coryate was a member of a drinking society associated with the Mermaid Tavern thus provided a convenient link with Johnson.[75] Heminges' involvement is, of course, easily understood, but in a sense more interesting is the recruitment on this occasion of men of real substance to act with him. Was Shakespeare, even if he had recently surrendered his shares in both the Globe and Blackfriars, purchasing a nearby house so that he could remain in contact? But why, by bringing in trustees, was he in effect also ensuring that on his death the management of the property would remain with his trustees and not revert to his family as owners of the freehold? And why did he make the purchase in an apparently hurried manner, without the necessary money immediately to hand but at the same time apparently pressing for vacant possession so that the premises could then be let to Robinson? To these questions there are no certain answers, yet at the very least it is difficult to interpret this final example of Shakespeare's property purchases as a continuation of a policy of straightforward investment. Robinson's lease, in particular, which in

---

73. Hotson, *Shakespeare's Sonnets Dated*, pp. 77–88.
74. Hotson, *Shakespeare's Sonnets Dated*, pp. 132–40; above, p. 103. Jackson had also been appointed Heminges' deputy as a London Sea Coal Meter, or Measurer (Eccles, 'Elizabethan Actors E–J', p. 458). Savage was also a Sea Coal Meter.
75. But for a balanced assessment of this possibility, see Michelle O'Callaghan, 'Patrons of the Mermaid tavern (act. 1611)', *ODNB*, October 2006, online edn [http://www.oxforddnb.com/view/theme/95279, accessed 9 June 2015].

normal circumstances might have been expected to have yielded a rent
to Shakespeare and his trustees, has more the air of a protected tenancy.
Robinson may have been the son of an earlier John Robinson, steward
to Sir John Fortescue, who had been living in the Blackfriars vicinity
since at least 1596. He was dead by 1613, but he is known to have had
two sons, one of whom (though unnamed) could perhaps have become
Shakespeare's tenant. The fact that the other brother, Edward, entered
the English College at Rome provides a link with the well-known
earlier history of the Blackfriars Gatehouse and its associations with
Catholic recusancy.[76] However, whether this had any connection with
Shakespeare's decision to buy the building remains highly speculative.
On the face of it, the close vicinity of the Blackfriars Theatre provides
a far more likely motive for the purchase, whilst the enlistment of
trustees implies some special purpose in which Robinson was to play
a role. Park Honan has suggested that the Gatehouse would have provided lodgings for Shakespeare during his continuing visits to London,
thus explaining the choice of site.[77] This in turn raises the issue of where
Shakespeare had lodged in London after his move from St Helen's,
Bishopsgate, to Southwark in the mid to late 1590s. During some of
this intervening period, though for precisely how long is uncertain,
we know he took up lodgings in a house in Silver Street, Cripplegate,
belonging to Christopher Mountjoy.[78] He was certainly there in 1604,
possibly as early as 1602, and no doubt for a year or two afterwards.
Mountjoy was a well-to-do skilled artisan and his house a substantial
one, but Shakespeare, in the style of many of his fellow playwrights,
lived there simply as a lodger, the only requirement being that he
was able to pay the rent. Edmond Malone claimed to have seen a
document, now untraced, establishing that by 1608, Shakespeare had
crossed the river again 'to reside in Southwark' nearer the Globe
Theatre.[79]

Such a move cannot now be substantiated, but it is linked to the
more intriguing issue of whether the purchase of the Gatehouse,
implying a further move on Shakespeare's part from Southwark to
Blackfriars, was the direct consequence of the surrender of his theatre
shares and whether the money raised thereby was invested, at least

76. Chambers, *William Shakespeare*, ii, pp. 165–7.
77. Honan, *Shakespeare; A Life*, p. 379.
78. Above, p. 168.
79. Above, p. 65.

in part, by arrangement with, and for the possible benefit of, his colleagues. As already explained, Shakespeare's surrender of his shares, though almost certainly finalized before his death, post-dated 20 February 1612.[80] The burning down of the Globe on 29 June 1613 has been suggested as a catalyst for this action, but just as persuasive a proposition would be that the purchase of the Blackfriars Gatehouse in March of the same year, tying Shakespeare as it did into an agreement with at least one of the King's Men, reflects a mutual understanding that, though Shakespeare would resign his full sharer/'housekeeper' status in return for a cash payment, this payment would be invested in such a way as to ensure that he would remain close at hand, perhaps to help in the general management of affairs but, more importantly, in the expectation that he would continue to supply new work for the company. Of course, there are other explanations. Shakespeare may simply have wished to provide a home for the elusive John Robinson or, indeed, Robinson may simply have become a straightforward rent-paying tenant. But the coincidence of date, the location of the property, and the involvement of trustees, one of whom was from the King's Men, certainly reflect more complicated arrangements. If Shakespeare's health were failing, a step back from full 'membership' of the King's Men, but accompanied by mutually advantageous measures to maintain links with the company, is what we would expect: in other words, far from retiring, he was simply keen to keep his options open. If we wish to speculate further, John Robinson, who in all probability was the man who, in a neat hand, witnessed Shakespeare's will, may have been acting in the role of a secretary for a man in failing health.

Finally, it is worth noting that Shakespeare thought it worthwhile going to law to secure the title to his Blackfriars purchase. Some two years later, in the spring of 1615, he joined with five other parties to ensure that Mathias Bacon, whose mother and grandmother had previously owned not just the Gatehouse but the former prior's lodging house and neighbouring property as well, should surrender into the court the title deeds still in his possession relating to the family's combined holding. The purchasers of the individual lots into which it had

---

80. Above, p. 151n; Chambers, *William Shakespeare*, ii, p. 67.

been broken up would then have the means of proving title.[81] As far as Shakespeare was concerned, these deeds would have established Mathias Bacon's right to the Gatehouse as granted to him in 1590 by his mother Ann and which, in 1604, he had sold to Henry Walker, the man from whom Shakespeare had later bought it.[82] This case, the subject of Chancery proceedings, has traditionally been described as 'friendly litigation', but this is hardly borne out by the plaintiffs' (or orators') complaint that Bacon 'doth...withhould, keepe and deteyne awaye from your oratours the foresaid letters patente and other deedes, evidences, charteres, munimentes and wrightings aforesaid and will not deliver the same unto your oratours, wherby your oratours be in great danger for to loose and be disinherited of the messuages, tenementes and premisses aforesaid.' Pushed in this way, Bacon replied to the effect that he was only holding on to the documents at issue 'untill such tyme as hee may be lawfully and orderlie discharged thereof upon his deliverie of the same.' The court therefore ordered him to produce them.

Suitors in Chancery were frequently prone to overstating their case, but there would seem little justification for arguing, in this instance, that their complaint was simply a fabrication. Going to law was an expensive business and the wording in this instance is typical of that used in cases where the title to property was under threat, either through a legal challenge or perhaps when the owner needed proof that it had been properly conveyed to him before negotiations began to sell it on. But, whatever the immediate reason, the owners of property formerly belonging to the Bacon family had clearly decided that clarification was required. Shakespeare, who had only recently acquired his portion, and only after it had passed through the hands of another freeholder, is unlikely to have initiated the proceedings. However, if any doubt had arisen during transactions involving other portions of the ex-Bacon Blackfriars estate, then it would have been typical of Shakespeare's other cautious steps taken at this time to make sure that his interests would not be adversely affected.

81. The three documents relating to the case are most conveniently transcribed in Chambers, *William Shakespeare*, ii, pp. 159–64.
82. The earlier history of the Blackfriars site, until 1590, when it was broken up and the Gatehouse settled on Mathew Bacon, is recorded in an abstract of title, together with details of the 1604 conveyance to Walker, in Folger Shakespeare Library ms, W.b.123. See also Lewis, *Shakespeare Documents*, ii, pp. 436–7.

Shakespeare's monument

There is one further consideration relevant to the issue of Shakespeare's status at the end of his life, namely the monument, erected in his memory soon after his death, in the chancel of Holy Trinity Church depicting him, as one might expect, as a man of gentlemanly status. One of the endearing features of Shakespeare's will is his request that his body simply be returned 'to the Earth whereof yt ys made' with no provision for any other memorial—unlike John Combe, for instance, who left the very considerable sum of £60 to erect a tomb, or the wealthy Margaret Reynolds, who asked to be buried in the chancel, near her husband Thomas. However, it is far from certain that members of Shakespeare's family, even if undeterred by his humble protestations, would have had sufficient funds to hand to allow them to erect William's impressive monument in the chancel. Given that Combe's tomb cost £60, it might well be that £20 would have been needed to erect Shakespeare's in its present form. But some years ago Diana Price made some acute observations as to the nature of this monument—in particular, the inappropriateness of one phrase of the inscription: 'Stay passenger, why goest thou by so fast?'[83] This has often been commented on, given that the location of the monument makes such a manoeuvre hardly possible, but there are other oddities in the inscription: the failure to include Shakespeare's baptismal forename, for instance, and the reference to Shakespeare having been 'plast with in this monument.' The wording, of course, is partly dictated by the fact that the inscription was written in verse, but it would still have been most unusual for the deceased's name not to have been given in its full form. This led Diana Price to suggest that the bust was separately commissioned in the expectation that, complete with its poetic inscription, it would be placed above a larger monument (of which several local examples survive) on which the necessary details would be conventionally recorded. However, as far as is known, not even a gravestone was inscribed with such details, leaving posterity to assume that the anonymous slab with its startling maledictory verse was placed there instead. It follows from this, Price argues, that the bust may well have been commissioned, not by the family but by those unaware of the position

83. Price, 'Reconsidering Shakespeare's monument'.

in which it would be placed within the church and on the assumption that the grave would be conventionally marked; and, given that it was later attributed to 'Gerard Johnson', or Gheerart Janssen the younger, whose father's workshop was sited at Southwark, near the Globe, it may well have been that it was Shakespeare's theatrical colleagues, who, in an effort to pay this belated tribute to the man who through his writings had so benefited the company, were responsible for the commission. A further memorial, of course, was the publication of the First Folio in 1623, although, as Heminges and Condell partly concede in their preface, the company had sound commercial reasons for establishing ownership of the plays which Shakespeare had written for them. As 1623 is also the year in which his monument in the church is first recorded (in one of the dedicatory poems included in the First Folio), and as it was in 1622 that the King's Men had visited Stratford (though they were paid 6 shillings for not performing in the Guild Hall),[84] it is again tempting to suggest that the King's Men, intent on honouring their former colleague, were willing to contribute towards commemorating Shakespeare in his native town in a manner that the family may not have been able to afford.[85]

84. SCLA, BRU 4/2, f. 3.
85. The King's Men were also recorded locally in Warwick in 1620 (Merry and Richardson, eds., *Household Account Book of Sir Thomas Puckering*, p. 145), perhaps to be identified with the unnamed players named in Stratford accounts for that year (SCLA, BRU 4/1, p. 177).

7

Conclusion

In one respect the life of William Shakespeare can be presented as a triumphal progress, a struggling jobbing actor from a financially embarrassed family who became the leading playwright of his day, and whose achievements were enshrined, albeit posthumously, in the publication of the equivalent of a 'collected works'. With the benefit of hindsight, this is particularly striking, but it does not follow, in the more mundane world of making a living, that Shakespeare's personal circumstances reflected a similar and uninterrupted path from poverty to affluence. It is undeniable, of course, that Shakespeare died a man of considerable means, but what evidence we have relating to his worldly affairs, though not of the stuff on which to base a meaningful biography, does suggest a more complicated picture, marked by an initial period of material improvement during which a man still in his thirties, from a very low point caused by his father's business failure and his own youthful indiscretions, struggled to create financial security both for himself and his family. Part of this process involved the acquisition of assets which would provide an income, for himself when no longer able to work and for his family after his death. But it is easy to exaggerate his success in this respect. His purchases came to a virtual end in 1605 even though, by themselves, they would not have been yielding an independent income. On the other hand, his theatre income, which was always more valuable to him, may well have come to a virtual end when, in or soon after 1612, he surrendered his company shares. This may have been a voluntary decision, though the idea of semi-retirement would not only be anachronistic but very unlikely in a man not yet fifty. His death in 1616, of course, makes the idea of retirement superficially plausible but, unless Shakespeare were physically ill, is not convincing. The 'less than successful' marriages of his two daughters only serve to emphasize that by then he barely merited inclusion in the ranks of the local gentry. It could therefore just as easily be argued that his stepping back from full-time theatrical work was something more or less forced upon him as the result of his prodigious labours over the previous fifteen years. That this may not have been something he welcomed is suggested by the careful husbanding of his resources which becomes a feature of his activities thereafter. In other words, whilst in receipt of his theatre income, he could cut a considerable figure locally, without it he was a less convincing candidate for gentlemanly status. The circumstances surrounding the purchase of the Blackfriars Gatehouse indicate that he had not cut his theatre ties completely. The motives behind this uncharacteristic move, if they can ever be satisfactorily resolved, might provide that much-needed explanation of how Shakespeare saw his future prospects, but for the moment, short of resorting to specula-tion, we can at least observe that these prospects appeared to include maintaining a link with his former colleagues. But with or without this, it is difficult to interpret his financial position as being as secure as it had been a decade before; and ultimately it is clear that any hope he might have had of establishing his family as one of independent means was not to be realized. Deservedly renowned though his career as a writer had, or would, become, in financial terms he achieved only modest success. More importantly, this fundamental issue in any assessment of his life is derived from those very documents which are barely considered as relevant by many Shakespeare biographers who prefer not to see their subject engaged in the more practical issue of making a living and providing for his family, concentrating instead on attempts to reach some understanding of his character through an analysis of his writings. Whereas it is, of course, self-evident that all writers' works will include references to features, circumstances, and situations which they have encountered, there is no guarantee that their response would have been that of the characters they have cre-ated. Where biographical information is more plentiful, writers' lives are routinely revealed as beset with crises and difficulties shared by their contemporaries. Their methods of dealing with them also reflect easily recognizable, and often disconcertingly mundane, character traits. Shakespeare may have been engaged in the creation of one of the greatest contributions to the country's literary heritage, but this does not mean he was exempt from the more immediate demands made on him as head of an early seventeenth-century family unit. What evidence we do have reflects a career in which, through dedication to the work in hand, he certainly built up his financial resources to a comfortable level. On the other hand, this was not an upward trajectory which was sustained. Exhaustion or ill-health would be possible explanations for this, far less likely the idea that he voluntarily decided to retire, or semi-retire, on the proceeds of any money he had made. Documentary evidence simply does not confirm that there was room for such complacency, the opposite in fact, as the careful husbanding of his resources in later life and the circumstances of his family descendants indicate. That the writer of *Hamlet* may have had money worries in later life may come as an unwelcome diversion for those of Shakespeare's admirers only concerned with his literary output. On the other hand, this might endear him to those who see nothing incongruous in the coexistence of great powers of imagination on the one hand and mundane day-to-day considerations arising out of the world he lived in on the other. For that is what those allegedly humdrum records indicate.

There is also the more general picture to consider. Elizabethan society, and indeed our own, depended on credit. As a matter of routine, most people of means at some time or another would need to borrow money, secured by bond, and their creditworthiness measured by their ability to repay at the stipulated time. Moreover, those in business might simultaneously be owed money by some for goods or services supplied and be indebted to others for a different range of purchases or services. Maintaining the necessary balance was therefore essential and the failure to do so, and the consequent loss of credit, a serious threat to a family's security. Such a fate, it has been argued above (pp. 10–23), befell Shakespeare's father in the 1580s, leading to the mortgaging and then forfeiture of freehold land and a clear falling away in his business dealings thereafter which placed him and his dependants at a serious disadvantage.

Shakespeare's business career could hardly have been more different. This does not mean that he never had to borrow money. On each occasion that he made an investment—the purchasing of a share in the Chamberlain's Men and then of the Globe, for example, or the purchase of real estate in the Stratford neighbourhood—he is very unlikely to have had to hand the very large sums of money involved and would therefore have had to borrow. On the purchase of the Blackfriars

Gatehouse, this is, in effect, what he did by delaying the payment of £60 (out of £140) for six months. But a clear difference, not just between him and his father, but many of his acquaintance too, is that this borrowing never seems to have resulted in financial difficulties— in other words, that he did not take on obligations which he was later unable to meet. Warnings have already been sounded that absence of documentary proof, at a time when so much has been lost, is hardly a reliable test. We also know that on one or two occasions he, or his family, did resort to the local Stratford court of record to recover debts. But this is very different from being pursued for debt oneself or making arrangements to extend credit. His failure, as a resident of St Helen's, Bishopsgate, to pay sums due under government subsidies apart—and even here this may simply be due to his having moved house—there is no record, despite exhaustive searches in central and local records, of any action taken against him as a debtor. Shakespeare could hardly have been unaware of James Burbage's fierce financial wrangles with John Brayne and then Giles Allen over the siting and building of the Theatre, or of his son Richard Burbage's dispute with earlier lease-holders of the Blackfriars Theatre. Francis Langley's financially inept attempts to develop the Swan Theatre and later the Boar's Head, ending in his death in 1602 as a virtual bankrupt, must also have been known to him. On another level, he would have been aware of Thomas Dekker's periods of imprisonment for debt and Henry Chettle's chronic insolvency. Yet, almost miraculously it now seems, Shakespeare appears to have steered his way through these troubled waters with no surviving evidence to indicate that he ever got into serious difficulties, albeit that problems of debt surface from time to time in his writings. This does not mean, especially in his early years, that he had not made some bold decisions. The very act of buying into a theatrical company so soon after the disruptions of the plague years in the early 1590s would indicate that he was prepared to put his credit at some risk. But thereafter there is no suggestion that, unlike his father, he went further than investing in purchases of land or other secure means of obtaining additional income. It was, of course, possible, as in the case of his neighbour John Combe, to lend money at interest, with the debtor's land as security, and then to make a considerable profit by foreclosure when the debtor failed to repay the loan. Shakespeare himself, as the Quiney letter makes clear, was well acquainted with the operations of London's money-men and usurers. Yet there is no reason to think that he was ever drawn into this world or that he was tempted to seek additional income in other ways—by means of a sinecure in government service, for example, or by investment in the purchase of monopolies or in the trading companies of the day. It may have been possible to make fortunes in this way, but there was also the unfortunate local example of Sir Edward Greville, Stratford's lord of the manor, who bankrupted himself in endeavours to seek government patronage before falling into the hands of more efficient adventurers, Arthur Ingram and Lionel Cranfield.[1] Shakespeare never showed any inclination to dabble in such matters, rather an adherence to a policy of steady and 'safe' investment and then of a determination to safeguard his income when threats to undermine it arose. It may be a matter of disappointment to the more romantically inclined that he left behind him neither a family of great wealth nor one threatened with bankruptcy. But a more likely assessment of his career, in financial terms, indicates that, as the result of steady endeavour and wary concern, he had managed to rescue his family from a position of some financial difficulty—in contrast, we might add, to his father who, after a period of rapid advancement, seems to have overreached himself at an important moment in the young Shakespeare's life. Whether, consciously or unconsciously, this misfortune influenced Shakespeare's own business dealings it is impossible to say, though it remains a more than plausible explanation for his advancement of his family to one of financial security—though not, it has been argued, to one of great wealth. By the time of his death, the Shakespeares were clearly of considerable standing in the context of a Warwickshire market town, but there is little to suggest that Shakespeare was driven by any desire simply to accumulate wealth—or indeed achieve public recognition. Instead an image emerges of a man able to provide, and safeguard, a sufficiency for himself and his family through an extraordinary exploitation of his talents. For fifteen years, the style by which he was known—William Shakespeare of Stratford-upon-Avon, gentleman—would have carried much weight with his contemporaries: it might also have given him quiet satisfaction too.

---

1. For more details, see Prestwich, *Cranfield: Politics and Profits under the Early Stuarts*, esp. pp. 401–3, 407–8, 533–5.

Works cited

Acts of the Privy Council of England...1575–77 (London: 1894).

Akrigg, G.P.V., *Shakespeare and the Earl of Southampton* (London: 1968).

Alcock, N.A., *Topography and Land in Early Wilmcote, Warwickshire* (privately published: 2000).

Allen, Robert C., 'The price of freehold land and the interest rate in the seventeenth and eighteenth centuries', *Economic History Review*, new series, 41 (1988), pp. 33–50.

Arber, E., *Transcript of the Registers of the Company of Stationers*, 5 vols (London: 1875–94).

Arkell, Tom, with Nat Alcock, eds., *Warwickshire Hearth Tax Returns: Michaelmas 1670* (Dugdale Society, vol. 43, 2010).

Astington, John H., *English Court Theatre 1558–1642* (Cambridge: 1999).

Baker, John, *The Oxford History of the Laws of England. Vol. 6, 1483–1558* (Oxford: 2003).

Barnard, E.A.B., *New Links with Shakespeare* (Cambridge: 1930).

Barnard, E.A.B., *The Sheldons: being some account of the Sheldon family of Worcestershire and Warwickshire* (Cambridge: 1936).

Barroll, Leeds, *Politics, Plague, and Shakespeare's Theater* (Ithaca, NY: 1991).

Barry, Jonathan, 'Civility and civic culture in early modern England: the meanings of urban freedom' in, *Civil Histories; Essays Presented to Sir Keith Thomas*, ed. Peter Burke and others (Oxford: 2000), pp. 181–96.

Bearman, Robert, *Shakespeare in the Stratford Records* (Stroud: 1994).

Bearman, Robert, 'Stratford's fires of 1594 and 1595 revisited', *Midland History* 25 (2000), pp. 180–90.

Bearman, Robert, '"Was William Shakespeare William Shakeshafte?" revisited', *Shakespeare Quarterly* 53, no. 1 (Spring 2002), pp. 83–94.

Bearman, Robert, 'John Shakespeare's "Spiritual Testament": a reappraisal', *Shakespeare Survey* 56 (2003), pp. 184–202.

Bearman, Robert, 'John Shakespeare: a Papist or just penniless?', *Shakespeare Quarterly* 56, no. 4 (Winter 2005), pp. 411–33.

Bearman, Robert, 'The early reformation experience in a Warwickshire market town: Stratford-upon-Avon, 1530–1580', *Midland History* 32 (2007), pp. 68–109.

Bearman, Robert, 'Thomas Greene: Stratford-upon-Avon's town clerk and Shakespeare's lodger', *Shakespeare Survey* 65 (2012), pp. 290–305.

Bearman, Robert, 'Shakespeare's purchase of New Place', *Shakespeare Quarterly* 63, no. 4 (Winter 2012/13), pp. 465–86.

Beaven, Alfred B., *The Aldermen of the City of London. Temp Henry III-1913*, 2 vols (London: 1908–13).

Bednarz, James P., *Shakespeare and the Truth of Love: the mystery of 'The phoenix and turtle'* (Basingstoke: 2012).

Bentley, G.E., *The Profession of Dramatist in Shakespeare's Time 1590–1642* (Princeton: 1971).

Bergeron, David M., *Textual Patronage in English Drama, 1570–1640* (Aldershot: 2006).

Berry, Herbert, *Shakespeare's Playhouses* (New York: 1987).

Berry, Herbert, 'The first public playhouses, especially the Red Lion', *Shakespeare Quarterly* 40, no. 2 (Summer 1989), pp. 133–48.

Blayney, Peter W.M., 'Publication of playbooks' in, *A New History of Early English Drama*, ed. John D. Cox and David Scott Kastan (New York: 1997), pp. 383–422.

Blomefield, Francis, *An Essay Towards a Topographical History of the County of Norfolk*, 11 vols (London: 1805–10).

Bowden, Peter J., *The Wool Trade in Tudor and Stuart England* (London: 1962).

Bowden, Peter J., 'Agricultural prices, farm profits, and rents' in, *The Agrarian History of England and Wales, Vol. 4, 1500–1640*, ed. Joan Thirsk (Cambridge: 1967), pp. 593–695.

Brinkworth, E.R.C., *Shakespeare and the Bawdy Court of Stratford* (Chichester: 1972).

Bruster, Douglas, 'Shakespeare the Stationer' in, *Shakespeare's Stationers: studies in cultural bibliography*, ed. Marta Straznicky (Philadelphia: 2013), pp. 112–31.

Burrow, Colin, ed., *William Shakespeare: the Complete Sonnets and Poems* (Oxford: 2002).

Calendar of State Papers, Domestic Series . . . 1547–1580 (London: 1856).

Chambers, E.K., *The Elizabethan Stage*, 4 vols (Oxford: 1923).

Chambers, E.K., *William Shakespeare: a study of facts and problems*, 2 vols (Oxford: 1930).

Corrigan, Brian Jay, *Playhouse Law in Shakespeare's World* (Cranbury NJ: 2004).

Dobson, Michael, and Stanley Wells, eds., *The Oxford Companion to Shakespeare* (Oxford: 2001).

Duncan-Jones, Katherine, *Ungentle Shakespeare; scenes from his life* (London: 2001).

Dutton, Richard, 'The court, the Master of the Revels, and the players' in, *The Oxford Handbook of the Early Modern Theatre*, ed. Richard Dutton (Oxford: 2009), pp. 362–79.

Eccles, Mark, *Shakespeare in Warwickshire* (Madison: 1961).

Eccles, Mark, 'Elizabethan Actors, E-J', *Notes and Queries* 34, no. 4 (December 1991), pp. 454–61.

Ellis, David, *The Truth about William Shakespeare* (Edinburgh: 2012).

Erne, Lukas, *Shakespeare and the Book Trade* (Cambridge: 2013).

Erne, Lukas, *Shakespeare as Literary Dramatist*, 2nd edn (Cambridge: 2013).

Everitt, Alan, 'The marketing of agricultural produce' in, *The Agrarian History of England and Wales, Vol. 4*, ed. Joan Thirsk (Cambridge: 1967), pp. 466–592.

Farmer, Alan, and Zachary Lesser, 'The popularity of playbooks revisited', *Shakespeare Quarterly* 56, no. 1 (Spring 2005), pp. 1–32.

Ferris, John P., and Andrew Thrush, eds., *History of Parliament, House of Commons, 1604–1629*, 6 vols (Cambridge: 2010).

Foakes, R.A., ed., *Henslowe's Diary*, 2nd edn (Cambridge: 2002).

Foster, Joseph, ed., *Register of Admissions to Gray's Inn, 1521–1889* (London: 1889).

Foster, Joseph, *Alumni Oxoniensis: the members of the University of Oxford, 1500–1714*, 4 vols (Oxford: 1891).

Fripp, Edgar I., *Master Richard Quyny* (Oxford: 1924).

Fripp, Edgar I., *Shakespeare's Stratford* (Oxford: 1928).

Fripp, Edgar I., *Shakespeare Studies* (Oxford: 1930).

Fripp, Edgar I., *Shakespeare Man and Artist*, 2 vols (Oxford: 1938).

Fripp, Edgar I., Richard Savage, Levi Fox, and Robert Bearman, eds., *Minutes and Accounts of the Corporation of Stratford-upon-Avon and Other Records*, 6 vols (Dugdale Society, vols 1, 3, 5, 10, 35, 44, 1921–2011).

Fry, E.A., ed., *Calendar of Wills and Administrations in the Consistory Court of Worcester, 1451–1652*, 2 vols (Index Library, vols 31, 39, 1904–10).

George, David, 'Shakespeare and Pembroke's Men', *Shakespeare Quarterly* 32, no. 3 (Autumn 1981), pp. 305–23.

Gray, Joseph William, *Shakespeare's Marriage* (London: 1905).

Green, Ian, '"More polite learning": humanism and the new grammar school' in, *The Guild and Guild Buildings of Shakespeare's Stratford*, ed. J.R. Mulryne (Farnham: 2012), pp. 73–95.

Guise-Berrow, E., and A.M. Hodgson, 'Return of Recusants in Kineton and Barlichway Hundreds, 1605–1606', *Worcestershire Recusant*, no. 17 (June 1971), pp. 5–18; no. 18 (Dec 1971), pp. 7–32.

Giuseppi, M.S., 'The Exchequer documents relative to Shakespeare's residence in Southwark', *Transactions of the London and Middlesex Archaeological Society*, new series 5 (1929), pp. 281–8.

Gurr, Andrew, *The Shakespearian Playing Companies* (Oxford: 1996).

Gurr, Andrew, *The Shakespeare Company, 1594–1642* (Cambridge: 2004).

Habbakuk, H.J., 'The long term rate of interest and the price of land in the seventeenth century', *Economic History Review*, new series 5 (1952), pp. 26–45.

Halliwell-Phillipps, James O., *The Life of William Shakespeare* (London: 1848).

Halliwell-Phillipps, James O., *Outlines of the Life of Shakespeare*, 7th edn, 2 vols (London: 1887).

Hamer, Douglas, 'Was William Shakespeare William Shakeshafte?', *Review of English Studies*, new series 21, no. 81 (1970), pp. 41–8.

Hanley, Hugh, 'Shakespeare's family in Stratford records', *Times Literary Supplement*, 21 May 1964, p. 441.

Hasler, P.W., ed., *History of Parliament, House of Commons, 1558–1603*, 3 vols (Cambridge: 1981).

Hirschfeld, Heather, '"For the Author's Credit": issues of authorship in English Renaissance Drama' in, *The Oxford Handbook of the Early Modern Theatre*, ed. Richard Dutton (Oxford: 2009), pp. 441–55.

Historical Manuscripts Commission, *The Manuscripts of his Grace the Duke of Rutland*, 4 vols (London: 1888–1905).

Hodgetts, Michael, 'A certificate of Warwickshire recusants, 1592', *Worcestershire Recusant*, no. 5 (May 1965), pp. 20–31; no. 6 (December 1965), pp. 7–20.

Honan, Park, *Shakespeare: A Life* (Oxford: 1999).

Honigmann, E.A.J., *Shakespeare: the 'lost years'*, 2nd edn (Manchester: 1985).

Honigmann, E.A.J., '"There is a world elsewhere": William Shakespeare, businessman' in, *Images of Shakespeare: Proceedings of the Third Congress of the International Shakespeare Association*, ed. Werner Habicht, D.J. Palmer, and Roger Pringle (Cranbury, NJ, and London: 1988), pp. 40–6.

Honigmann, E.A.J., and Susan Brock, eds., *Playhouse Wills, 1558–1642* (Manchester: 1993).

Hooks, Adam G., 'Wise Ventures: Shakespeare and Thomas Playfere at the Sign of the Angel' in, *Shakespeare's Stationers*, ed. Marta Straznicky (Philadelphia: 2013), pp. 47–62.

Hotson, Leslie, *Shakespeare versus Shallow* (London: 1931).

Hotson, Leslie, *Shakespeare's Sonnets Dated and Other Essays* (London: 1949).

Hughes, Ann, *Politics, Society and Civil War in Warwickshire, 1620–1660* (Cambridge: 1987).

Hughes, Paul L., and James F. Larkin, eds., *Tudor Royal Proclamations*, 3 vols (New Haven and London: 1969).

Ingleby, Clement, ed., *Shakespeare and the Enclosure of Common Fields at Welcombe* (Birmingham: 1885).

Ingram, William, '"Near the Playe Howse": the Swan Theater and community blight', *Renaissance Drama*, new series 4 (1971), pp. 53–68.

Ingram, William, *A London Life in the Brazen Age: Francis Langley, 1548–1602* (Cambridge, MA, and London: 1978).

Ingram, William, *The Business of Playing: the beginnings of the adult professional theater in Elizabethan London* (Ithaca, NY, and London: 1992).

Ioppolo, Grace, *Dramatists and their Manuscripts in the Age of Shakespeare, Jonson, Middleton and Heywood* (Abingdon and New York: 2006).

Jacob, Giles, *The Law Dictionary*, rev. T.E. Tomlins, 2nd edn, 2 vols (London: 1809).

Johnson, Nora, *The Actor as Playwright in Early Modern Drama* (Cambridge: 2003).

Jones, Jeanne, *Family Life in Shakespeare's England: Stratford-upon-Avon, 1570–1630* (Stroud: 1996).

Jones, Jeanne, ed., *Stratford-upon-Avon Inventories, 1538–1699*, 2 vols (Dugdale Society, vols 39, 40, 2002–3).

Jowett, John, ed., *Sir Thomas More* (Arden Shakespeare, London: 2011).

Jowett, John, 'A collaboration: Shakespeare and Hand C in *Sir Thomas More*', *Shakespeare Survey* 65 (2013), pp. 255–68.

Jowett, John, 'Shakespeare as Collaborator' in, *Shakespeare Beyond Doubt*, ed. Paul Edmondson and Stanley Wells (Cambridge: 2013), pp. 88–99.

Kathman, David, 'Six biographical records "rediscovered": some neglected contemporary references to Shakespeare', *Shakespeare Newsletter* 45, No. 4 (Winter 1995), pp. 73, 76, 78.

Kathman, David, 'Grocers, Goldsmiths and Drapers: freemen and apprenticeships in the Elizabethan Theatre', *Shakespeare Quarterly* 55, no. 1 (Spring 2004), pp. 1–49.

Kathman, David, 'Richard Tarlton and the haberdashers', *Notes and Queries* 53, no. 4 (December 2006), pp. 440–2.

Kathman, David, 'Players, livery companies, and apprentices' in, *The Oxford Handbook of the Early Modern Theatre*, ed. Richard Dutton (Oxford: 2009), pp. 413–28.

Kingsley, Nicholas, *The Country Houses of Gloucestershire, Volume 1, 1500–1660* (Cheltenham: 1989).

Knutson, Roslyn L., *The Repertory of Shakespeare's Company, 1594–1613* (Fayetteville: 1991).

Lang, R.G., 'Social origins and social aspirations of Jacobean London Merchants', *Economic History Review*, new series, 27 (1974), pp. 28–47.

Lee, Sidney, *A Life of William Shakespeare* (London: 1922).

Lewis, B. Roland, *The Shakespeare Documents: facsimiles, transliterations, translations & commentary*, 2 vols (Stanford and London: 1941).

Macdonald, Mairi, 'A new discovery about Shakespeare's estate in Old Stratford', *Shakespeare Quarterly* 45, no. 1 (Spring 1994), pp. 87–9.

Malone, Edmond, *An Inquiry into the Authenticity of Certain Miscellaneous Papers and Legal Instruments* (London: 1796).

Malone, Edmond, *The Plays and Poems of William Shakespeare*, 21 vols (London: 1821).

Manley, Lawrence, and Sally-Beth MacLean, *Lord Strange's Men and Their Plays* (New Haven, CT: 2014).

Marcham, Frank, *William Shakespeare and his Daughter Susannah* (London: 1931).

Martin, J.M., 'A Warwickshire town in adversity: Stratford-upon-Avon in the sixteenth and seventeenth Centuries', *Midland History* 7 (1982), pp. 26–41.

Matus, Irvin Leigh, *Shakespeare in Fact* (New York: 1994).

McCoog, Thomas M., and Peter Davidson, 'Edmund Campion and William Shakespeare: "Much Ado about Nothing?"' in, *The Reckoned Expense:*

Edmund Campion and the early English Jesuits, 2nd edn, ed. Thomas McCoog (Rome: 2007), pp. 165–85.

McMillin, Scott, and Sally-Beth MacLean, *The Queen's Men and their Plays, 1583–1603* (Cambridge: 1998).

Merry, Mark, and Catherine Richardson, eds., *The Household Account Book of Sir Thomas Puckering of Warwick, 1620* (Dugdale Society, vol. 40, 2012).

Mulryne, J.R, 'Professional Theatre in the Guildhall 1568–1620' in, *The Guild and Guild Buildings of Shakespeare's Stratford*, ed. J.R. Mulryne (Farnham: 2012), pp. 171–206.

Orlin, Lea Cowen, 'Anne by indirection', *Shakespeare Quarterly* 65, no. 4 (Winter 2014), pp. 421–53.

Oxford Dictionary of National Biography, 62 vols (Oxford: 2004–13).

Page, C. and R., 'The location of Richard Shakespeare's farm in Snitterfield', *Warwickshire History* 5, no. 3 (Summer 1982), pp. 95–102.

Parry, Glyn, 'The context of John Shakespeare's "recusancy" re-examined', *Shakespeare Yearbook*, new series, 16 (2007), pp. 1–38.

Parry, Glyn, 'New Evidence on William Shakeshafte, and Edmund Campion', *Shakespeare Yearbook*, new series, 17 (2009), pp. 1–27.

Pedigrees Made at the Visitation of Cheshire, 1613 (Harleian Society, vol. 59, 1909).

Poole, Eric, 'John and Mary Shakespeare and the Aston Cantlow Mortgage', *Cahiers Elisabéthains* 17 (April 1980), pp. 21–41.

Prestwich, Menna, *Cranfield: Politics and Profits under the Early Stuarts* (Oxford: 1966).

Price, Diana, 'Reconsidering Shakespeare's monument', *Review of English Studies*, new series, 48 (1997), pp. 168–82.

Rollett, John M., 'William Shackspere vs. John Clayton', *Notes and Queries* 59, no. 4 (December 2012), p. 559.

Ryan, Patrick, 'Diocesan returns of recusants for England and Wales, 1577' in, *Miscellanea XII* (Catholic Record Society, vol. 22, 1921).

Ryland, J.W., *Records of Rowington*, 2 vols (Birmingham: 1896, 1927).

Savage, Richard, ed., *The Registers of Stratford-on-Avon ... Baptisms, 1558–1652* (Parish Register Society, vol. 6, 1897).

Savage, Richard, ed., *The Registers of Stratford-on-Avon ... Burials, 1558–1652/3* (Parish Register Society, vol. 55, 1905).

Schoenbaum, S., *William Shakespeare: a Documentary Life* (Oxford: 1975).

Schoone-Jongen, Terence G., *Shakespeare's Companies: William Shakespeare's early career and the acting companies* (Ashgate: 2008).

Simpson, Frank, 'New Place: the only representation of Shakespeare's House from an unpublished manuscript', *Shakespeare Survey* 5 (1952), pp. 55–7.

Slater, T.R., 'Domesday village to medieval town: the topography of medieval Stratford-upon-Avon' in, *The History of an English Borough: Stratford-upon-Avon 1196–1996*, ed. Robert Bearman (Thrupp: 1997), pp. 30–42.

Somerset, Alan, 'Not just Sir Oliver Owlet: from patrons to "patronage" of early modern theatre' in, *The Oxford Handbook of the Early Modern Theatre*, ed. Richard Dutton (Oxford: 2009), pp. 413–28.

Stewart, Alan, *Shakespeare's Letters* (Oxford: 2008).

Stopes, C.C., *Shakespeare's Warwickshire Contemporaries* (Stratford-upon-Avon: 1907).

Stopes, C.C., *Shakespeare's Industry* (London: 1916).

Strype, John, *The Life and Acts of...John Whitgift...Archbishop of Canterbury*, 3 vols (Oxford: 1822).

Survey of London, Vol. 22. Bankside: the parishes of St Saviour and Christchurch, Southwark (New York: 1950).

Syme, Holger Schott, 'Thomas Creede, William Barley, and the venture of printing plays' in, *Shakespeare's Stationers*, ed. Marta Straznicky (Philadelphia: 2013), pp. 28–46.

Taplin, John, *Shakespeare's Country Families: a documentary guide to Shakespeare's country society* (Warwick: 2011).

Tennant, Philip, *The Civil War in Stratford-upon-Avon: conflict and community in south Warwickshire, 1642–1646* (Stroud: 1996).

Thomas, D.L., and N.E. Evans, 'John Shakespeare in the Exchequer', *Shakespeare Quarterly* 25, no. 3 (Autumn 1984), pp. 314–18.

Thomas, David, *Shakespeare in the Public Records* (London: 1985).

Tobias, John, 'New light on recusancy in Warwickshire, 1592', *Worcestershire Recusant*, no. 36 (December 1980), pp. 8–27.

Venn, John, and J.A., *Alumni Cantabrigienses, Part 1*, 4 vols (Cambridge: 1922–6).

Victoria History of the County of Warwick, 8 vols (London: 1904–69).

Vine Hall, E., *Testamentary Papers I: Wills from Shakespeare's Town and Time* (London: [1932]).

Vine Hall, E., *Testamentary Papers II: Wills from Shakespeare's Town and Time* (London: [1933]).

The Visitation of Cheshire in the Year 1580 (Harleian Society, vol. 18, 1882).

The Visitation of the County of Gloucester, Taken in the Year 1623 (Harleian Society, vol. 21, 1885).

The Visitation of the County of Warwick in the Year 1619 (Harleian Society, vol. 12, 1877).

The Visitation of Shropshire, Taken in the Year 1623, 2 vols (Harleian Society, vols 28, 29, 1889).

The Visitation of Worcestershire 1634 (Harleian Society, vol. 90, 1938).

Wanklyn, Malcom, ed., *Inventories of Worcestershire Landed Gentry, 1537–1786* (Worcestershire Historical Society, new series, vol. 16, 1998).

Wellstood, Frederick C., *Catalogue of the Books, Manuscripts, Works of Art, Antiquities and Relics Exhibited in Shakespeare's Birthplace* (Stratford-upon-Avon: 1944).

Whitfield, Christopher, 'Anthony and John Nash, Shakespeare's Legatees', *Notes and Queries* 14, no. 4 (1967), pp. 123–30.

Wickham, Glynne, Herbert Berry, and William Ingram, eds., *English Professional Theatre, 1530–1660* (Cambridge: 2000).

Wiggins, Martin, *British Drama, 1533–1642: A Catalogue* (Oxford 2011–in progress).

Wilson, F.P., *The Plague in Shakespeare's London* (Oxford: 1927).

Yeatman, J.P., *The Gentle Shakespere*, 4th edn (Birmingham: 1906).

Index

Married women are indexed under their maiden name, with their married name in brackets